Basic Usage,
Vocabulary,
and Composition

D1417849

THIRD EDITION

Basic Usage, Vocabulary, and Composition

Lessons on Usage, Reading Selections, Writing Assignments

HULON WILLIS
Late of Bakersfield College

CHARLES M. COBB
Los Angeles Pierce College

HOLT, RINEHART AND WINSTON
New York   Chicago   San Francisco   Atlanta   Dallas
Montreal   Toronto

Library of Congress Cataloging in Publication Data

Willis, Hulon.
  Basic usage, vocabulary, and composition.

  1. English language—Rhetoric.   2. English language
—Grammar—1950–   3. College readers.   I. Cobb,
Charles M., joint author.   II. Title.
PE1408.W6126   1979   428′.2   78-10363
ISBN: 0-03-044401-2

PREFACE

Basic Usage, Vocabulary, and Composition is an omnibus text in that it provides materials in three of the most important areas of freshman English instruction: usage, vocabulary, and composition. Part 1 covers all ordinary aspects of conventional usage that are troublesome to college students. The lessons are presented on a practical rather than on a theoretical basis so that a review of school grammar is avoided. To handle the lessons, students need only a very elementary knowledge of traditional parts of speech. Added to this edition are four lessons explaining the basic subject-predicate combination of sentences with some of the more common sentence patterns. Part 2 consists of fifteen reading selections most of which have been newly selected for this edition. These updated readings have been chosen for both their general interest and their provision for vocabulary building. Each selection is accompanied by a vocabulary test, with the words involved appearing in boldface in the text. Also, most selections have short sentence-writing exercises based on words that have some similarity or that are often confused, such as *annual-biannual* and *anecdote-antidote*.

Part 3 consists of nine writing assignments, with close guidance given the students both in detailed instructions as to how to execute the writing assignment and in a model theme that students can imitate. In this new edition, a general introduction to college writing has been added and the assignment on job applications and résumés has been expanded and improved. Class time can be used profitably in discussing the models, but also the whole book is designed so that students can be, if the instructor chooses, left mostly on their own. Naturally, instructors will vary in their use of these writing assignments.

The book also contains a large number of supplemental bits entitled "Tips on Usage" and "Mini-Exercises." These features serve several purposes. First, they provide a little variety and can often be the basis of five or ten minutes of useful discussion. Second, students will often remember such isolated bits of knowledge better than they can retain material from a

v

full lesson. Also, some of these little fillers can serve partially as review. It is hoped that students and instructors alike will find the Tips and Mini-Exercises enjoyable and useful.

Because one of the purposes of this text is to help build the students' vocabularies, words have often been used in the text and in example sentences that are common but that might not be familiar to the students. For example, in the first paragraph of Lesson One, the words *erroneously, equated,* and *personnel* are used. Often the context will divulge the meanings of such words, but sometimes students may need to use their dictionaries. A few minutes of class time can often be used profitably in discussing some of these words. Also, the students will appreciate not being written down to.

Inside the front cover is a standard correction chart. Inside the back cover is a list of common words that give students the most trouble in spelling. This list is derived from many years' experience in a large remedial spelling program.

The Instructor's Manual—complimentary to instructors—is an important part of this text. It provides keys to exercises on usage and the mini-exercises for which keys are possible and also a key to the vocabulary tests. Such keys save instructors much time and are especially useful when the instructor has an assistant to help with the paper work. The Manual also provides an additional exercise, with a key, for each lesson on usage; these can be used as in-class or out-of-class exercises and can also be used for cumulative tests. In addition, there are cumulative tests, with keys, on both usage and vocabulary. These can be used in various ways. The additional spelling tests in the Manual need a word of explanation. Long experience indicates that dictated sentences rather than word lists provide the best method of spelling testing and also the best instructional device. Many aspects of spelling—such as the *d* on *supposed to*—cannot be tested with word lists. Another small point is that the long list of contemporary slang terms in Lesson Thirty-one has the meanings listed in the Manual. If instructors do not receive a copy of the Instructor's Manual with their examination copy of this text, they should write to the English Editor, College Department, Holt, Rinehart and Winston, 383 Madison Avenue, New York, N.Y. 10017, and ask for a copy.

Thanks are due to Richard S. Beal for his help in reviewing this book and to the following reviewers: Professors Chris Baker, Lamar University; James Childs, Middlesex Community College; Homer Duerr, Butte College; Becky Eterno, Boston University; Paul Miller, Marin Junior College; Nancy Rayl, Cyprus Junior College; and Ruth Reed, Detroit College of Business.

H.W   C.M.C.
Bakersfield, California   Agoura, California
1975   1979

CONTENTS

Part 2 • READING SELECTIONS   209

FROM "SELF-RELIANCE"   **297**
Ralph Waldo Emerson

THE DRIVER EDUCATION MYTH   **303**
Edward A. Tenney

Part 3 • WRITING ASSIGNMENTS   309

APPENDIX   363

Basic Usage, Vocabulary, and Composition

Part one LESSONS ON USAGE

Introduction

By the time students get to college, their professors expect them to be able to write well. Their writing may not be highly effective, but it should be correct. But the truth is that many college students are unable to write correctly and coherently. It is a fact that many college graduates prejudice themselves in applying for a job—or even on the job—by making errors in their writing.

The following thirty-two lessons in this book are designed to help you learn to avoid the common mistakes made in college writing. These are lessons in **usage**. Correct usage is that used by the educated members of a society; incorrect or substandard usage usually appears in the writing of those who are not well educated.

You do not need to know much formal grammar to study the following lessons and to do the exercises. A rudimentary understanding of the parts of speech and an understanding of the subject-predicate division of a sentence is all you need. These lessons are all practical and do not involve you in the theory of grammar.

1

1 THE BASIC SENTENCE

When we speak, we often use fragmentary statements, phrases, single words, and bits and pieces of sentences. We use these forms in the rapid give-and-take of ordinary conversation, especially in response to questions.

"Right here."
"Because it's there."
"In out of the rain."

When we write, however, we must use **complete sentences** to make our meaning clear. In addition, to punctuate accurately and to avoid errors like run-together and fragmentary sentences, we need to understand the construction of the English sentence. It is the basic unit of coherent communication and always has two parts, the **subject** and the **predicate**.

The Subject

The subject of the sentence is what the sentence is about. It is the thing, person, or idea that performs the action in the sentence. It may be thought of as the actor. An easy way to find the subject is to ask *who* or *what* about the action or state in the sentence.

Examples:

The warriors fight fiercely.

Who fights? *The warriors,* which is the subject˙

The battle was lost anyway.

What was lost? *The battle*, which is the subject.

The fighting was glorious.

What was? *The fighting* was, and that is the subject.

The **subject** precedes the verb in most English sentences. The **complete subject** consists of the thing, person, or idea that performs the action together with the words used to modify or describe that thing, person, or idea. The **simple subject** consists of the thing, person, or idea that performs the action in the sentences, but the simple subject does *not* include the other words used to modify or describe it.

Example:

The Greek and Trojan warriors in their glittering
armor fought fiercely on the windy plains of Troy.

The **complete subject** would be *The Greek and Trojan warriors in their glittering armor*. The **simple subject** would be the simplest answer to the question, Who fought? *Warriors* is the simple subject.

The Predicate

The **predicate** of a sentence is the verb and all of the words that go with it. If the subject names the actor in a sentence, then the predicate gives the action or state of the subject. Examples:

The warriors fought fiercely.

What did the warriors do? *Fought fiercely*, which is the predicate.

The fighting was glorious.

What was the state of the fighting? It *was glorious*, which is the predicate.

The Greek and Trojan warriors in their glittering armor fought
fiercely on the windy plains of Troy.

What did the warriors do? They *fought fiercely on the windy plains of Troy*, which is the predicate.

A Tip on Finding Predicates

The main word in the predicate is always the **verb**. The verb in a sentence is easily located as it is the only word that can change tense from the past to the present to the future and still have the sentence make sense. If you can change the time and it still makes sense, you have located the verb. Example:

The hunter runs from the lion.

What word can be changed to make the sentence take place in the past or future and still have the sentence make sense? The word *runs* can be changed to *ran* or to *will run* and is the verb. The complete predicate would be *runs from the lion*.

A MINI-EXERCISE In the blanks provided write the verb of each sentence in a different tense from that of the verb in the original.

Different tense

1. Hector used a spear.

   _____

2. Ajax the Great uses a short sword.

   _____

3. Paris will be an excellent archer.

   _____

4. Winning a war is difficult.

   _____

5. Odysseus was cunning and won the war.

   _____

   (second verb)

A Tip on Finding Complete Sentences

A useful method for telling whether a sentence is a complete sentence or not is to remember that a complete sentence must have a response that is either an *action*, an *answer*, or an *agreement* (or disagreement). Of course, the action is not always performed; the answer is not always given; the agreement (or disagreement) may not be stated. Examples:

Come here. (requires an action)
How are you today? (requires an answer)
I think that the rain is wonderful. (requires agreement)

Exercise 1

THE BASIC SENTENCE

DIRECTIONS *In the sentences below make a slash (/) between the complete subject and the complete predicate. In the blanks provided write the verb or verbs for each sentence.*

1. Heinrich Schliemann was the son of a poor German pastor.

   _____

2. As a child he read the story of the Trojan War.

   _____

3. He moved to Holland and became a rich merchant.

   _____

4. He traveled to Russia and to the United States.

   _____

5. At the age of thirty-four he learned Greek in six weeks.

   _____

6. By the age of forty-four he retired.

   _____

7. He then devoted himself to the study of archaeology.

   _____

8. He roamed the Near East in Turkey and nearby countries.

   _____

9. Nearing the age of fifty, he did two remarkable things.

   _____

10. He married an eighteen-year-old Greek girl.

    _____

11. He found the remains of the ancient city of Troy.

    _____

12. He spent the next twenty years excavating the site.

_____

13. To the amazement of scholars, he discovered a vast treasure. (careful)

_____

14. He claimed it was the treasure of Priam, king of Troy.

_____

15. He really had found the treasure of an earlier king.

_____

16. Nevertheless, the city he found was the Troy of legend.

_____

17. The story Homer told had a historical basis.

_____

18. Perhaps Achilles and Hector actually fought on the plains of Troy.

_____

19. Schliemann died, rich and famous, full of honors.

_____

20. How many other legends might have a basis in fact? (careful)

_____

2 CLAUSES

A clause is a group of related words that contains both a *subject* and a *predicate*. In written English there are two kinds of clauses, **independent** and **dependent**. To write correct sentences and to punctuate accurately, one must understand what clauses are and how they function.

Independent Clauses

A clause is called *independent* when it can stand independently as a sentence. *Independent clause*, then, is simply another name for the simple sentence.

Dependent Clauses

Although **dependent clauses** also contain both a subject and a predicate, they can not function as independent units. A dependent clause acts within the sentence as either a **noun**, an **adjective**, or an **adverb**.

The Noun Clause

Noun clauses are usually introduced by the words *that, what, who, which, whoever, whom, whomever,* and *whose.*

Examples:

> SIMPLE SENTENCE: I believe something.
> NOUN CLAUSE ADDED: I believe **that the world is flat.**

Notice that the clause **that the world is flat** does not meet the requirements for an independent clause or simple sentence.

9

SIMPLE SENTENCE: Someone is ignorant.

NOUN CLAUSE ADDED: **Whoever believes the world is flat** is ignorant.

A good test for the noun clause is to see if the group of words containing both a subject and a predicate and beginning with one of the words listed above (called relative pronouns) can be replaced with *someone* or *something*.

A MINI-EXERCISE *Underline the noun clauses in the following sentences.*
1. I hope that there is life on Mars.
2. Whatever lives there might be friendly.
3. We will send whoever wants to go on the next rocket.
4. The truth will be whatever the traveler reports.

Adjective Clauses

Adjective clauses are usually introduced by the words *who, whom, whose, which,* and *that*. These clauses act as **adjectives** within the sentence by modifying a noun or pronoun.

Examples:

SIMPLE SENTENCE: Anyone can succeed on this mission.

ADJECTIVE CLAUSE ADDED: Anyone **who really tries** can succeed on this mission.

SIMPLE SENTENCE: The space traveler will be famous.

ADJECTIVE CLAUSE ADDED: (slight sentence change): The space traveler **who gets there first** will be famous.

SIMPLE SENTENCE: NASA prefers astronauts.

ADJECTIVE CLAUSES ADDED: NASA, **which is in charge**, prefers astronauts **whose health is excellent**.

Adjective clauses usually directly follow the nouns they modify.

A MINI-EXERCISE *Underline the adjective clauses in the following sentences.*
1. The atmosphere that is indicated on instruments is very thin.
2. The unmanned space probe that landed on Mars is really a sophisticated robot.
3. The person who will be sent might well be a woman.
4. The Mars traveler could be a Russian, whose word for *astronaut* is *cosmonaut*.

Adverb Clauses

Adverb clauses are usually introduced by words like these:

after	before	since	unless
although	even if	so (that)	until
as	even though	than	when
as if	if	that	where
as though	like	though	whereas
because	once	so that	while

Adverb clauses act as **adverbs** within the sentence, or they may show a relationship between the adverb and the whole idea of the sentence. Examples:

SIMPLE SENTENCE: Science fiction writers assume interplanetary travel.

ADVERB CLAUSE ADDED: **When they write stories**, science fiction writers often assume interplanetary travel.

SIMPLE SENTENCE: Space heroes talk.

ADVERB CLAUSE ADDED: Space heroes talk **as if they had been raised in the Old West**.

A MINI-EXERCISE *Underline the adverb clauses in the following sentences.*

1. Many people were excited when the space program began.
2. No one landed on the moon until many years later.
3. As soon as the moon was reached, people turned their attention to Mars.
4. If we ever get to Mars, we will go on to Venus.

Exercise 2

CLAUSES

DIRECTIONS   *Read the following sentences carefully. If the sentence contains a* dependent clause, *underline that clause.*

_____ 1. Edgar Rice Burroughs, who wrote *Tarzan,* also wrote space operas.

_____ 2. His stories took place on Mars, which he called *Barsoom.*

_____ 3. The animals on Barsoom acted as if they were eternally hungry.

_____ 4. Whomever they encountered, they ate.

_____ 5. They scurried wherever they went on six or more legs.

_____ 6. All of the women on Barsoom were beautiful by earthly standards.

_____ 7. That these women laid eggs was merely incidental.

_____ 8. John Carter, who was the hero, had been a Confederate captain.

_____ 9. Whenever he went into a trance, he woke up on Mars.

_____10. The fact that he had earthly muscles made him very powerful on Mars.

_____11. Anyone who really tries can enjoy Burroughs's stories.

_____12. John Carter fought as if he were Superman.

_____13. That he was an effective fighter worked to his benefit.

_____14. John Carter eventually became the Warlord of Mars, the supreme ruler.

_____15. There he became a mighty warrior.

ADDITIONAL EXERCISE   If the clause you underlined is a noun clause, write *N* in the blank; if it is an adjective clause, write *ADJ*; if it is an adverb clause, write *ADV*; if there is no dependent clause, leave the blank blank.

3 PHRASES

A phrase is a group of words that does not contain both a subject and a verb. The phrase functions as a unit within the sentence, usually as a noun or as a modifier. Writers need to be able to recognize phrases in order to avoid errors in sentence structure and to punctuate correctly.

Prepositional Phrases

A **prepositional phrase** consists of a **preposition** and its object, usually a noun, and any modifiers that might be added. Prepositions are those words that show a space or a time relationship. Examples:

about	before	during	near	through
above	behind	for	of	till
across	beside	from	on	to
after	between	in	out	under
against	by	into	over	up

Preposition has been defined as "anything a rabbit can do to a hill." (A rabbit can go *over* the hill, *under* the hill, *beside* the hill, *to* the hill, and so on.) Here are some examples with the prepositional phrases in **boldface type**.

My sister travels **to San Diego on her Honda 550-K.**
She rides **down the freeway along the ocean.**
Before breakfast she may have traveled fifty miles.
One tankful **of regular gas** will take her 200 miles.
A list **of comfortable rest stops** is always **in her luggage.**

Verbal Phrases

There are several classes of **verbal phrases**, but to use this book you will not need to know all of their names. You will need to be able to recognize them, though, to eliminate a variety of sentence and punctuation errors from your writing.

A verbal phrase consists of the ordinary form of the verb preceded by *to* (*to start, to learn, to take*) or a verb form ending in *-ing* or *-ed* or *-en* (*starting, started; learning, learned; taking, taken*), together with other related words. The verbal phrase functions as a unit within the sentence but must *never* be considered a complete sentence. Following are some examples with the verbal phrases in **boldface**.

> **Riding a motorcycle** can be an exhilarating experience.
> Many people enjoy **speeding down the highway**.
> **To ride safely** takes great skill.
> **Riding more swiftly than the speed limit** can prove hazardous.
> **Never having been excited by the thrill**, many people are afraid of motorcycling.
> Others, **probably started by their enjoyment of bicycles**, do not find it frightening.
> A good way **to learn about safety** is **to take a class**.

Noun Phrases

A **noun phrase** consists of a noun and all of the words used to modify it. In many sentences the noun phrase is identical with the complete subject. The ability to recognize a noun phrase will help you to avoid a great many subject-verb agreement errors. Below are some sentences with the noun phrases in **boldface**.

> **Selecting a mate** is very important.
> **After the wedding** is too late to make the choice.
> **Your getting married in a hurry** may not be too wise.
> Some people like **to shop around**.

Exercise 3

PHRASES

DIRECTIONS *Show that you can recognize phrases by underlining the phrases in the following sentences.*

In the first group underline the prepositional phrases.
1. At one time, the only way people traveled was on foot.
2. Later they rode on the backs of animals.
3. After many centuries, people developed the wheel.
4. With the development of the wheel came carts, wagons, and chariots.
5. The invention of the steam engine enabled us to build railroads.

In the next group underline only the verbal phrases.
6. Burning wood and billowing smoke, early trains looked like metal monsters.
7. To take a train ride took great courage.
8. The internal combustion engine, being small and light, permitted the development of automobiles.
9. To chug along in an early automobile also took courage.
10. Filling stations being relatively scarce, fuel stops were often miles apart.

In the next group underline only the noun phrases.
11. The internal combustion engine gave us one more mode of travel.
12. A group of excited people visualized a flying machine.
13. Orville and Wilbur Wright developed the first primitive airplane.
14. Their creative technological achievement led to the supersonic jets that now scream through the skies.
15. A number of problems has arrived with the superplanes.

4 KINDS OF SENTENCES

read

Sentences have been classified in many ways: by their structure, by their meaning, by their form, and by a variety of other ways. Understanding the most common method of classifying sentences will be a tremendous aid in punctuating correctly and developing effective writing skills. To make the best use of this book, you need not be able to make a detailed analysis of sentences, but you do need to know the three main types: the **simple sentence**, the **compound sentence**, and the **complex sentence**.

The Simple Sentence

The **simple** sentence consists of one independent clause with one subject and one predicate. It has no dependent clause, although phrases may be included. Examples:

> Three hundred and forty-five million people speak English.
> Six hundred and twenty-eight million people speak Mandarin Chinese.

Notice that each of the preceding sentences has one subject and one predicate.

> Two hundred million women and one hundred and forty-five million men speak English.

Notice that although there is a compound subject (two parts, *women* and *men*), the preceding sentence is still classed as a simple sentence. There is no *dependent clause*.

> A total of three hundred million people speak and write English.

Notice that although there is a compound (two parts *speak* and *write*) verb in the predicate of the preceding sentence, it is still classed as a simple sentence. There is no *dependent clause*.

Compound Sentence

The **compound** sentence consists of two or more simple sentences connected with a **semicolon** or a **comma and a conjunction**, Examples:

> Six hundred and twenty-eight million people speak Mandarin Chinese, **and** forty-six million speak Cantonese Chinese.
> Over seven hundred and forty-three million people speak some form of Chinese; it is the most widely spoken language in the world.

A Tip on Coordination

Whenever you connect two sentences, be sure that the ideas in both are closely related. The most common conjunctions used to connect two or more simple sentences (called coordinating conjunctions) and using a comma are *and, but, or, for, nor, so,* and *yet.*

The Complex Sentence

The **complex** sentence consists of an independent clause and one or more dependent clauses. Examples with the *independent* clause in boldface follow:

> Although three hundred and forty-five million people speak English, **a total of seven hundred and forty-three million speak some dialect or other of Chinese.**
> **These figures are not totally accurate** because many people speak more than one language.

Dependent clause

There are many possible combinations of independent and dependent clauses. You can create a *compound-complex* sentence with two or more independent clauses and one or more dependent clauses. The limit to the possibilities is the limit of the complexity of the idea you are presenting to the reader.

Exercise 4   *Friday*

SIMPLE, COMPOUND, AND COMPLEX SENTENCES

DIRECTIONS *Classify each of the following sentences as either simple, compound, or complex. In the blanks provided write* S *if the sentence is a simple sentence,* Cp *if it is compound, or* Cx *if it is complex.*

__S__ 1. Language is one trait all human beings share.

__S__ 2. All groups of people on the face of the earth, from sophisticated to primitive, use language.

__Cp__ 3. There are nearly 5,000 different dialects, but merely 10 percent have a written form.

__Cx__ 4. Although most people speak only their native tongue, many know more than one language.

__Cp__ 5. The Swiss, for example, use three languages; they speak French, German, and Italian.

__S__ 6. French and German have often been considered the languages of diplomacy and science.

__S__ 7. Recently, though, English has become used and more widely accepted in both categories.

__Cx__ 8. Even though no one knows for sure, linguists guess about the origins of language.

__Cx__ 9. Some say it started with shouts of alarm whereas others believe it began with chants during dances.

__Cp__ 10. Language may have started with shouts, or it may have started with chants.

__Cx__ 11. There are some linguists who believe speech began with the copying of animal sounds.

__S__ 12. In spite of many theories, no one can be certain of the origin of language.

__Cp__ 13. We do know, however, that there was a "mother language" for all Western tongues; it has been called *Indo-European*.

__Cp&Cx__ 14. Indo-European has been theorized; it has been analyzed; it has been understood, although no one has ever heard it spoken.

__S__ 15. We have come a long way from shouts and chants.

5 RUN-TOGETHER SENTENCES AND COMMA SPLICES

Sentences end with periods, question marks, or exclamation points. Independent clauses (which are, in fact, sentences) may be joined by a coordinating conjunction, usually with a comma before the conjunction, or they may be joined with semicolons.

Run-Together Sentences

A sentence is supposed to begin with a capital letter and end with a period or other mark of end punctuation. When a second sentence is begun with no capital letter and no punctuation at all is placed between it and the previous sentence, the error known as **run-together sentences** is committed. Here are two examples:

WRONG: Reciprocal trade agreements make for flexibility in world commerce this is why almost all nations use them.

WRONG: A supernova was spotted it had the brilliance of a billion suns.

In these examples, either semicolons should be placed after *commerce* and *spotted* or else periods should be placed there and capital letters used to begin the second sentences. Usually run-together sentences occur because of carelessness or failure to reread. When a writer really doesn't know any better, he lacks what is known as **sentence sense**, the lack of which is a serious handicap to any writer.

Comma Splices

A much more common error is the **comma splice**, which occurs when only a comma and no coordinating conjunction (*and, but, yet, or, nor, for,* and *so*) come between two independent clauses. (Remember that an independent clause is really a full sentence in itself.) Here are a couple of typical comma splices:

> WRONG: In Economics 3A, students meet for a fourth hour each week in small groups, this gives them a chance to learn from each other.
>
> WRONG: The instructor continued to discuss the theory of natural selection, nobody told him the class period had ended.

The commas after *groups* and *selection* should be either semicolons or periods. Students who use comma splices of this sort are deficient in sentence sense, which usually means their writing is bad in many other ways, too. Such students deficient in sentence sense should study sentence structure until they have a feel for sentences—that is, can just instinctively recognize whether a construction is a complete sentence or not.

Another common kind of comma splice occurs when only a comma instead of a semicolon (or period) is used between independent clauses connected by a **conjunctive adverb**: *however, therefore, moreover, hence, thus, nevertheless, consequently, furthermore, then, afterwards*, and a few others. These connectives are not coordinating conjunctions, and when used to connect independent clauses, they may NOT be used with just a comma. Examples:

> WRONG: Senator Foreman was absent when his pork-barrel bill came up for a vote, however, his colleagues saw that it passed safely.
>
> WRONG: English teachers are likely to have personal prejudices about little matters of usage, thus students often feel that they have been given conflicting rules.

The commas after *vote* and *usage* should be either semicolons or periods.

Most of the conjunctive adverbs can be shifted to the interior of the second clause. If such a shift can be made (and it is often stylistically desirable), then a comma cannot correctly be used between the two clauses. Example:

> WRONG: The Watch and Ward Society banned *Three on a Honeymoon* in Boston, moreover, they announced that the movie based on the book would also be banned.
>
> RIGHT: The Watch and Ward Society banned *Three on a Honeymoon* in Boston; they announced, moreover, that the movie based on the book would also be banned.

Because *moreover* can be shifted, a comma between the clauses would positively be wrong.

   Comma splices are serious errors because the incorrectly used comma usually causes an experienced reader to stumble. However, we must mention that very short and closely related independent clauses are sometimes used with only commas separating them. Example:

   ACCEPTABLE TO MANY: The wind howled, the rain began, the thunder
                              cracked.

Good advice to students, however, is to avoid comma splices altogether.

A TIP ON USAGE   In the meaning of *nearly*, the word *almost* creates better style than the word *most*. Example:

   PREFERRED: **Almost** all of the holy relics were desecrated.

Assingment Tommorow

Exercise 5-A

RUN-TOGETHER SENTENCES
AND COMMA SPLICES

DIRECTIONS *Determine which of the following sentences have comma
splices or are run together. In the blanks provided, enter the proper
punctuation by rewriting the last part of the first sentence and the
first part of the last sentence, like this:* . . . *were doomed. However, we
were able* . . .

1. A college education helps one get a good job not everyone, however,
   needs to go to college.

   _____ *helps one get a good job; not you* _____

2. We decided to shift to a zone defense, this gave us better coverage
   on Abdul-Jabbar.

   _____ *helps me get a good job, everyone,* _____

3. I got an NDEA loan of $1,000, so I was able to stay in college.

   _____

4. I had never before received an *A* in English seldom had I even made
   a *B*.

   _____

5. We hurried to the stadium at 5:00 A.M., thus we were first in line.

   _____

6. Professor Anson did not lose his credentials because of smoking pot,
   because now that crime is only a misdemeanor.

   _____

7. Mr. Brixton did not mind being in debt, for he thought inflation would
   continue for years.   *correcting*

   _____

8. They weren't aliens, they were American citizens.

   _____

9. Between us we had $24.00, that was enough to buy Manhattan.

_____

10. The Federal Reserve Board raised the discount rate to 8 percent, this was clearly the time to save rather than expand.

_____

11. Not having prior knowledge of the merger, I did not buy any Litton stock.

_____

12. My history professor assigned a punitive term paper, moreover, he promised failure to those turning their papers in late.

_____

13. I spoke, not as a professor, but as a friendly, well-meaning mentor.

_____

14. The Dow-Jones average rose six points, it was the fifth straight day of gains.

_____

15. The rain came down in torrents; this ruined the rhubarb crop.

_____

16. Abdul-Jabbar scored thirty-six points, nevertheless, his team lost the game and a chance at the play-offs.

_____

17. The theater was full of Robert Redford fans, half of whom had seen the movie before.

_____

18. Congressman Clancy leaked the story to the press; he hoped in that way to attract public favor.

_____

19. The *ad hoc* committee found the senator guiltless, however, his career was damaged anyway.

_____

20. We continued to pay protection money, for the police had been bribed.

conjunctions

_____

Exercise 5–B   Assingment

RUN-TOGETHER SENTENCES
AND COMMA SPLICES

DIRECTIONS   *Determine which of the following sentences have comma splices or are run together. In the blanks provided, enter the proper punctuation by rewriting the last part of the first sentence and the first part of the last sentence like this: . . .*were doomed. However, we were able . . .

1. The current trend in movies is toward disaster and horror films, which seem to attract large audiences.

_____

2. Stories of demonic possession are popular, we like to be frightened.

_____

3. We don't mind being frightened, but we prefer it to happen in the safety of a theater.

_____

4. An ever-present problem is inflation, it has been with us for the last ten years.

_____

5. Today a man's suit costs $100, however in 1912 it would have cost $15.

_____

6. It would be nice to go back to 1912 and buy a suit but that would be impossible.

_____

7. In many science-fiction stories the hero travels in time, however, it has never happened in real life.

_____

8. He's not heavy, he's my brother.

_____

9. It is said that the study of algebra teaches one to think, because algebra is a logical discipline.

---

10. A great many people are not satisfied with their lot in life, they would rather be someone else.

---

11. If you could be anyone at all, who would you pick?

---

12. Would you select someone who had power or would you select someone who had great wealth?

---

13. Many people would opt for wealth, nevertheless, wealth brings many problems.

---

14. Surely rich people have problems but poor people also have problems.

---

15. As long as I have problems, I would prefer to solve them in comfort.

---

16. Mr. Fister is gradually going bald so he is going to have hair tatooed on his pate.

---

17. Anyone can have hair it takes a mature person to be bald.

---

18. Acrylic paints are better than oils, they last longer and dry faster.

---

19. If Leonardo da Vinci had used acrylics, *The Last Supper* would not have faded.

---

20. There is one more benefit in using acrylics, they do not stink.

---

6 SENTENCE FRAGMENTS

Most writing, especially that done in college, is supposed to consist of complete sentences, with each sentence beginning with a capital letter and ending with a mark of end punctuation, usually a period. There are times when a nonsentence is acceptable in writing, but very seldom in college writing. Therefore, you should avoid the very serious error known as the **sentence fragment**. People who write fragments are usually deficient in **sentence sense** and need to study sentence structure until they can know for certain whether a construction is a complete sentence or not.

Most fragments in student writing are of two types. The most common of these is the **detached clause** or **detached phrase**. To avoid this kind of fragment, you do not need to know enough grammar to identify various types of clauses and phrases. However, you do need to have sentence sense enough to recognize that a construction is not a complete sentence. Most people develop sentence sense quite early, but some have a difficult time differentiating complete sentences (independent clauses) from nonsentences.

The detached clause or phrase is a construction that should be attached to the previous sentence but that instead is begun with a capital letter and ended with a period. Here are examples with the detached clauses and phrases (which are sentence fragments and are unacceptable) being italicized. A correct version follows each incorrect construction.

WRONG: We couldn't buy any liquor. *Because we were not yet twenty-one.*

RIGHT: We couldn't buy any liquor, because we were not yet twenty-one.

WRONG: I thought *Sanctuary* was a good book. *Not just a cheap, sensational novel.*

RIGHT: I thought *Sanctuary* was a good novel, not just cheap and sensational.

WRONG: I had a very hard time in the third grade. *Having just moved into the town.*

RIGHT: I had a very hard time in the third grade, having just moved into a new town.

WRONG: My father voted for Senator Welker two times. *Though he later regretted it.*

RIGHT: My father voted for Senator Welker two times, though later he regretted doing so.

WRONG: I expect college to equip me for life. *To help me cope with the world better.*

RIGHT: I expect my college education to help me cope better with the world by equipping me for adult living.

In your writing be very careful not to give improper sentence status to a terminal constituent that needs to be attached to the preceding sentence.

Just about as bad as the sentence fragment is the phrase or dependent clause separated from a sentence by a semicolon rather than a comma. Examples:

WRONG: I decided to run for student-body office; because I want eventually to get into politics.

RIGHT: I decided to run for student-body office, because I want eventually to get into politics.

WRONG: I just stayed home; not having any money.

RIGHT: I just stayed home, not having any money.

The semicolons are wrong in these examples because the sentence parts following them are not independent clauses.

The second kind of unacceptable fragment is the use of a verb form as a sentence verb when the verb form cannot serve as a sentence verb. Example:

NONSENTENCE: The cops *not having arrived yet.*

SENTENCE: The cops *had not arrived yet.*

Had arrived can serve as a sentence verb, but *having arrived* cannot. People with sentence sense instinctively recognize which verb forms can serve as sentence verbs and which cannot. But actually, fragments due to the use of verb forms that will not make sentences are rare compared to the fragments due to detached phrases and clauses.

A final note: A sentence starting with a coordinating conjunction (*and, but, for,* and so on) is not a fragment. Examples:

RIGHT: Grammar is interesting to study. And a knowledge of it can help one write better.

RIGHT: We drove at excessive speeds. But we were too late.

Many students report that they have been taught not to begin a sentence with *and* or *but.* Such teaching is incorrect.

Exercise 6–A
SENTENCE FRAGMENTS

DIRECTIONS *In the blanks provided write an S to identify a complete sentence and an F to identify a fragment. When for one number there are two or more constructions beginning with a capital letter and ending with a period, enter an S or F for each, like this:* S; F; S.

1. _____A freight train of 100 cars going eighty miles an hour.

2. _____My minister agreed to give a series of lectures on Africa. Having just returned from Uganda.

3. _____Our team upset the conference champions. Winning twenty-one games.

4. _____I often get sleepy in class. Especially just after lunch.

5. _____Some insects have an extraordinarily complex social structure. For example, some species of ants keep slaves and fight wars.

6. _____To some people science is a mystery. To others it is a way of life. Though most scientists also like the humanities.

7. _____When hunting, one should wear a red jacket and hat. Making it easy to be identified as a hunter. Which might prevent a serious accident.

8. _____The bookstore manager learning that some of the books would be shipped late.

9. _____We now know how hurricanes originate. How they affect ecology. Really fascinating to learn such things.

10. _____Many modern movies treat sex explicitly. Which makes them draw large audiences.

11. _____The governor taking a sauna bath.

12. _____Susan had a GPA of 3.72. High enough to guarantee a scholarship.

13. _____The wind blowing briskly, causing the pine trees to moan softly.

14. _____We accepted the job. A task that required intelligence, moral fitness, and devotion to the welfare of others.

15. _____The qualifications required—enthusiasm, tact, and aggressiveness—all of which Kenney had in abundance.

16. _____George, needing the money badly, but did not have any way to earn it.

17. _____George, explaining the emergency to his uncle, borrowed the money.

18. _____George bought the science kit. But this did not bring him satisfaction.

19. _____The president ordered the terms of the treaty to be leaked to the press. Which pleased the reporters.

20. _____Let's get back to the causes of the quarrel. How it affected the election.

21. _____The date being placed at about 5000 B.C.

22. _____No one knowing the exact date.

23. _____The task, however, not taking more than two hours.

24. _____It's good we established diplomatic relations with Red China. Because she is the greatest threat to peace.

25. _____Air pollution must be stopped. For if it isn't, all life is in danger.

26. _____I want to live. To be free. To experience life.

27. _____Professor McCall did not like to discuss Marxism. Because students had misunderstood him.

28. _____The committee having been dissolved by executive fiat.

29. _____We were the last to leave. The others having got bored.

30. _____We thought John could succeed. He could.

Exercise 6–B
SENTENCE FRAGMENTS

DIRECTIONS *In the blanks provided write an S to identify a complete sentence and an F to identify a fragment. When for one number there are two or more constructions beginning with a capital letter and ending with a period, enter an S or F for each, like this*: S; F; S.

1. _____Notwithstanding the very great need for people to trace their cultural heritage.

2. _____In the Southwest there is a rich Mexican culture. Going clear back to the ancient Aztecs.

3. _____In the area surrounding Pennsylvania, and also to the north of that state. There is a strong German and Dutch influence.

4. _____The French influence is obvious in Louisiana. Stemming from the fact that the French settled that locale.

5. _____Across the country there are cultures coming from all over the world. Most have been partially absorbed into the American way of life.

6. _____This diversity is unique. We have developed a complex society. Owing to the variety of people who came here.

7. _____Tacos are interesting food. Little corn pancakes. Stuffed with meat, sauce, cheese, and lettuce.

8. _____The average person enjoying food and trying many new dishes.

9. _____We accept as part of our diet many once foreign foods. Including pizza, crepes, blintzes, and borscht.

10. _____Which makes us happy and fat.

11. _____Most chefs seem to be portly. Eating while they cook may be the cause.

12. _____Festooned with streamers, decorated with banners, and lighted with colored lamps. The new restaurant opened.

13. _____It featured good old American food: hotdogs, hamburgers, and apple pie. All tasty and inexpensive.

14. _____Obesity being one of our greatest health problems. We should cut down on calories.

15. _____The Elton John concert being canceled, causing many fans to demand their money back.

16. _____The promoter agreed. A job that required much effort, much time, and a great loss of money.

17. _____If people would get more exercise. If they would dance and not sit. Because dancing is very healthy.

18. _____The sound of music has reached 80 decibels. But the noise doesn't seem to bother the listeners.

19. _____Imagine a Mozart concerto playing at 80 decibels. An electronic harpsichord being played through a six-foot speaker.

20. _____Perhaps we could develop new instruments. An electric drum being a good example.

Lesson

7 COMMAS
In a Series and in Compound Sentences

Commas are used more than any other mark of punctuation, and probably 90 percent of all errors in punctuation involve misused or omitted commas.

The simplest use of commas is the separation of sentence elements in a series. Such elements can be single words or any kind of phrase or clause. You need not be able to analyse the grammar of these elements in a series but simply need to recognize that you have three or more similar elements in a row.

The Rule *Use commas to separate three or more similar sentence elements in a series.* Many writers omit the comma before *and* (or any other conjunction) between the last two items in a series. However, for complete clarity we recommend using a comma before the *and*. Examples:

The fans threw bottles, flashlights, and girdles at the umpire.
The candidate promised to lower taxes, increase unemployment pay, provide more money for schools, and rehabilitate all welfare recipients.
At the Fourth of July picnic the politicians made speeches, the young couples made eyes, and the children made trouble.
Neither the author of the book, the publisher's lawyer, nor the acquiring editor would admit guilt.
The host served beer, Scotch, bourbon, rum, and Coca-Cola.
The twins, Joseph, and Mary agreed to make an additional foursome.

Note that in the last two examples the reader would be momentarily confused if a comma were not used before *and*. Using the comma tells the reader that the rum and the Coca-Cola were served separately and that the twins are not named Joseph and Mary.

A comma is also usually used to separate the clauses in a compound sentence (one with two or more independent clauses).

37

The Rule   *Use a comma between independent clauses joined by a coordinating conjunction, unless the clauses are quite short.* The coordinating conjunctions are *and, but, yet, or, nor*, and *for*. Also, the conjunctive adverb *so* is often used as a coordinating conjunction.

Examples:

Edgar Allan Poe is popularly thought to have been highly neurotic and preoccupied with morbid thoughts, but actually he was a dedicated genius who worked hard to achieve greatness in literature.

The Commandant of the IX Corps made a secret deal with the supply sergeant, and as a result prices increased sharply in the PX.
The pay for shucking corn was raised to $4.00 per hour, yet not a single applicant for the job appeared.
The Board Chairman spoke and the "yes men" nodded.

In the last example the clauses are so short that a comma is not needed before *and*; but a comma in the position would not be wrong.
Regardless of the length of the clauses, always use a comma to separate independent clauses joined by *for*. Otherwise the *for* might be taken for a preposition and cause momentary confusion. Examples:

WRONG: We planned a party for Mary had reached her eighteenth birthday.
WRONG: I ordered a Mercedes-Benz for my wife wanted safe, reliable transportation.

Such sentences require a comma before the *for*, for otherwise the reader stumbles. Note the immediately preceding sentence as an example.

A TIP ON USAGE   In dates, use commas to separate the name of the day from the date of the month and the date of the month from the year.

RIGHT: On Tuesday, February 3, 1888, the Great Blizzard struck the plains.

In addresses, use commas to separate the name of a person or establishment from the street address, the street address from the city, and the city from the state. Opinion is divided about the use of a comma after the state.

RIGHT: We were directed to the Veterans Administration, 413 Hill Street, Los Angeles, California to take additional medical examinations.
A comma after *California* would be correct, too.

Exercise 7

COMMAS IN A SERIES AND IN COMPOUND SENTENCES

DIRECTIONS *Enter commas where needed in the following sentences.*

1. The ski lift operator was told to get more chairs to overhaul the motors and to check all of the cables.
2. Skiing can be delightful for there is a sensation akin to flying when racing down a mountain.
3. The book was dull and, moreover, incorrect in many details.
4. We have decided to sell our old house to purchase a new condominium and to move clear out of the state.
5. The new space shuttle was named *The Enterprise* for that name was reminiscent of the television starship.
6. The car skidded across the northbound lane sideswiped a truck and came to rest in a bank of snow.
7. The host served Scotch and soda rum and Coca-Cola vodka and tonic and bourbon.
8. A bank president must support community projects belong to civic organizations and donate generously to charity.
9. Drilling offshore oil wells must be stopped except in the case of a national emergency for the oil companies obviously cannot prevent pollution of the beaches.
10. I accepted the test materials read the directions and promptly passed out.
11. The senatorial candidate favored the construction of the neutron bomb and apparently a majority of his constituents agreed with him.
12. The birds were singing the sun was shining and my spirits were at an all-time high.
13. Members of Congress must give of their time to all sorts of people: job-seekers wives of prisoners of war influence peddlers curiosity-seekers reformers and do-gooders honest constituents and of course other Members of Congress.
14. The inclusion of an antistrike clause in the agricultural workers' contract was necessary for the crops could not wait as, say, automobile production can wait.
15. A movie projector two phonographs an overhead projector and six reels of film were missing from the audiovisual rooms.

16. The rainfall was heavy but floods were unlikely.
17. For breakfast we had ham and eggs toast apple jelly and a choice of coffee tea or milk.
18. The Internal Revenue Service took him to court the Justice Department investigated his relations with Cosa Nostra and the State Department voided his passport.
19. In order to have four more to play bridge, we invited the twins James and Mary.
20. We paid $20.00 each for our tickets yet we were still in a part of the stadium where we could hardly see.

A MINI-EXERCISE   In the following sentences enter commas where needed.

1. The great Blizzard ended on Wednesday February 27 1888 after having trapped 200 tipplers in Brown's Bar 449 Seventh Avenue Fargo North Dakota.
2 The culprit was tracked to the Maxon Building 223 Tenth Street Bloomington Indiana.
3 On Friday June 9 1974 we moved to 109 Sunset Boulevard North Platte Nebraska.
4. The Tivoli Theater at 33 North Street Miami Florida opened its doors on August 9 1936.
5. His apartment, located at 113 Central Park West New York New York was actually vacant from November 10 1974 to January 8 1975.

Lesson

8 COMMAS
To Set Off
Introductory
Expressions

An introductory expression in a sentence is one that comes before the sentence subject. It might be a single word, such as *lately*, or it might be a phrase or a clause like these.

> To get the most out of life, ...
> With nothing on his mind, ...
> As kangaroos are naturally high jumpers, ...

And so on.

The Rule   *Use a comma to set off an introductory expression if (1) the expression is long or (2) if there is a distinct shift in meaning after the expression or (3) if a comma is necessary to avoid ambiguity or confusion.*

The more careful writers are, the more likely they are to use commas to set off introductory expressions unless these are rather short and have little meaning shift.

1. Here are two examples of long introductory expressions that should be set off by commas:

> While the rest of the team went to the track for extra practice, Shodlock sneaked off to see his girl friend, saying, "A miss is as good as a mile."
> Without the least evidence of being upset or alarmed, Jones went about his daily tasks with assurance.

Length alone calls for commas to set off such introductory constituents.

2. Here are two examples of short introductory expressions that need to be set off because of the distinct shift in meaning in the rest of the sentence.

> Failing that, we must resort to force.
> Uncertain, George turned to me for an answer.

3. Here are three examples of the need for a comma to set off an introductory expression when the absence of the comma would cause ambiguity:

> WRONG: As we were about to leave the restaurant manager hastened to apologize to us.
> WRONG: Above the buzzards circled ominously.
> WRONG: As I mentioned the rules may occasionally be broken.

Commas are needed in these sentences to prevent the reader from momentarily thinking the constructions are *about to leave the restaurant, above the buzzards*, and *as I mentioned the rules*.

4. Introductory exclamations and words of assent, negation, or doubt are also set off. Examples:

> Why, we were old friends in optometry school.
> Yes, we feel that he is due compensatory damages.
> Well, perhaps he intended no disrespect.

5. When there is little danger of ambiguity and little meaning shift after it, an introductory expression need not be set off. Examples:

> RIGHT: In any event we will not surrender.
> RIGHT: Of course Gloria will manage to marry for money.

But commas after *any event* and *of course* would not be wrong.

Finally, it is generally good practice to set off introductory adverbial clauses and verbal phrases. Adverbial clauses are those starting with such subordinating conjunctions as *when, if, although, since, after*, and so on. Introductory verbal phrases are almost always either infinitives (*in order to eliminate competition, to be sure of your safety*, and so on) or the present participle (*ing* form) of a verb (*not realizing the danger, having little or no confidence in Randy*, and so on).

A TIP ON USAGE A comma is placed after the connective *that is*. Examples:

> RIGHT: Tommy is yellow—that is, he's a coward.
> RIGHT: He's not guilty; that is, he was insane when he committed the crime.
> RIGHT: I'll give up. That is, I'll marry you.
> RIGHT: I'll marry you, that is, if you'll have me.

If the construction following *that is* is a sentence (or independent clause), then a period or semicolon or dash should come before *that is*. If the construction following *that is* is not a full sentence, then a comma before *that is* is appropriate.

Exercise 8

COMMAS TO SET OFF INTRODUCTORY EXPRESSIONS

DIRECTIONS *Insert commas where needed in the following sentences. Decide which sentences would be correct either with or without a comma.*

1. From the beginning of the Christian era Christians have misunderstood, or else not heeded, the words of Christ.
2. As the boat turned about a dozen dolphins began to follow it.
3. Not being a strong student I entered graduate school with a little uneasiness.
4. Because the dog had started to run a way to catch him had to be devised.
5. As I expected the maid had been stealing the whiskey.
6. If two Irishmen were lost on a desert island they would start three political parties.
7. On the other hand two Welshmen would start a glee club.
8. Of course two or more Americans would immediately form a committee.
9. As I had already determined to fail the exam would mean the end of my college career and the beginning of my career as a worker.
10. Naturally the factory owners were glad the demonstration was peaceful.
11. As I was saying the Pledge of Allegiance seems to be Unitarian in origin, for it speaks of "under God, indivisible."
12. Whenever I get dispirited and generally at odds with the world I try to take a sea voyage.
13. To give an estimate about sixty students showed up for the rally to eliminate fighting on the basketball court.
14. Why the American Lit professor did not even assign *Huckleberry Finn*.
15. In spite of his judgment that arrangement precipitated a clash between Moslems and Christians.
16. To tell the truth about 50 percent of the term papers had been copied *verbatim* from *The Atlantic*.

17. Although dangerous alligators will usually retreat from human beings.
18. In order to provide the best possible conditions the chamber music concert was held in the Little Theatre.
19. When I started my car was in excellent condition, but when I returned it was a wreck.
20. As I investigated the stolen car turned up in my garage.

A MINI-EXERCISE Write intelligent sentences, using these three forms correctly.

1. a woman like:_____

   _____

   _____

   _____

2. a womanlike: _____

   _____

   _____

   _____

3. womanly: _____

   _____

   _____

   _____

9 COMMAS
To Set Off Parenthetic Expressions

A parenthetic expression is an interrupter than comes within a sentence and makes some kind of explanation or comment or provides transition from the previous sentence. We do not use the term *parenthetic expression* to apply to adjective clauses or appositive phrases, which will be considered in Lesson Ten.

The Rule   *Use commas on both sides of a parenthetical expression, or interrupter, to set it off from the rest of the sentence.*

1. Internal words in direct address are parenthetic and should be set off:

> Let me tell you, sir, that your insinuations are insulting.
> That's an ingenious device, young fellow, that will make you rich.
> If you come tomorrow, Jane, be sure to notify your Aunt Nellie.

When such words of direct address come at the beginning or end of a sentence, they are separated by commas but are not necessarily called parenthetic.

2. Words and phrases of transition are usually set off by commas when they parenthetically come within sentences. Examples:

> Wheat germ, for example, is a valuable food once just discarded.
> Murphy, at any rate, will stay with the team.
> The judge's decision, moreover, broke a hundred-year-old precedent.
> His income for the year, however, was less than his secretary's.
> Senator Stoner, of course, is a Democrat in name only.

The phrase *of course* is now often used without being set off, but if it is intended to have special emphasis, it should be set off.

3. Phrases or clauses of personal opinion are set off by commas when they take parenthetic form. Examples:

Your estimate, I'm sure, is accurate enough for our studies.
My Uncle Jurgen, according to reports, left me only a notebook full of good advice.
Two hundred dollars, from all estimates, will be sufficient for our needs.

Note how the above constructions differ from ones like this.

I think $200 will be sufficient for our needs.

4. When phrases are clearly intended to comment or give additional information within a sentence, they are parenthetic and need to be set off by commas. Examples:

Music, to be enjoyed, must be felt by one's sense of cadence.
Fred, not knowing what he was doing, alienated his best friend.
Cottage cheese, when not creamed, has a high percentage of protein.

5. When a word or phrase is placed into a sentence as a kind of afterthought, it is parenthetical and should be set off by commas. Example:

All of us daydream, and scheme, during our leisure moments.

Finally, be very careful not to omit one of the commas needed to set off a parenthetic expression. Examples:

WRONG: All admen, and salesmen too consider the public their enemy.
WRONG: A day at the beach, for example can restore one's zest for life.

Commas are needed after *too* and *example*. Such errors are due mostly to carelessness.

A TIP ON USAGE Do not put a comma directly after *and* or *but* unless a second comma is used to set off a parenthetic expression.

WRONG: I voted for Herman Welker, but, I later regretted it.

The comma after *but* is erroneously used.

RIGHT: Our team started brilliantly, but, as is often the case, they turned cold in the second half.

The comma after *but* is right, for *as is often the case* is a parenthetic expression set off on both sides. The point is that if a comma comes directly after *but*, a second comma will come soon to set off a parenthetic expression.

Exercise 9–A

COMMAS TO SET OFF
PARENTHETIC EXPRESSIONS

DIRECTIONS   *In the following sentences, enter commas where needed.*

1. We were wondering, Professor Gordon, whether you would include Andrew Marvell in your literature course.
2. The Ways and Means Committee for example has a firm hand on the nation's pocketbook.
3. The cost of living however rose .6 percent in August alone.
4. The superintendent's salary on the other hand was raised 10 percent.
5. The board however refused to enter negotiations for a raise in teachers' salaries.
6. One of the lakes Lake Erie had already "died."
7. He had the best intentions I'm sure but his plan caused an unnecessary rise in the tax rate.
8. The Millville School District if what the superintendent says is true will fulfill the court order to the letter.
9. Coffee if it is not to upset your stomach should be drunk in small quantities.
10. My conclusion therefore is that the state should bear more of the cost of operating community colleges.
11. The governor nevertheless has refused to increase state aid and has reduced local property taxes.
12. Now now Uncle Jasper remember your condition.
13. The annual rate of growth for a decade according to the Board of Trade's figures will be 7 percent.
14. We all worked and very hard to meet our quota for the month.
15. Bobby and Sue Carol as well refused to plan a summer vacation.
16. The feasibility of television was I think established as early as 1908 according to the Encyclopaedia Britannica.
17. The proper course I believe is to fine heavily all found guilty of defacing public buildings.
18. Mr. Gant as is his habit slipped out after midnight for a rendezvous.
19. We will all rest and maybe even study after we get the garden fully planted.
20. The curriculum in some cases at any rate does not seem to be prepared for average students.

A MINI-EXERCISE   Write three intelligent sentences of at least fifteen words each: one with an introductory phrase that needs to be set off, one with a parenthetic expression that needs to be set off, and one with a terminal (end-of-sentence) element that needs to be set off—all with commas.

1. _____

_____

_____

_____

2. _____

_____

_____

_____

3. _____

_____

_____

_____

Exercise 9–B

COMMAS TO SET OFF
PARENTHETIC EXPRESSIONS

DIRECTIONS *In the following sentences, enter commas where needed.*

1. I was about to ask when you interrupted if *The Silmarillion* is as good as *The Hobbit*.
2. Excessive surfing my dear young man develops knobby knees.
3. Every new president according to some political scientists needs at least a year to learn the job.
4. Honda motorcycles however continue to lead the market in the sale of street bikes.
5. Making stained glass windows if what the newspapers say is accurate is a rapidly growing hobby.
6. Say Fred do you ever watch late late movies?
7. It was Lincoln my mother said said a man's legs should be long enough to reach from his hips to the ground.
8. I would like to ask you Dr. Proctor if there will ever be a cure for baldness.
9. A college education some say is a lifelong asset.
10. A great many graduates on the other hand are still looking for employment.
11. Gazing intently at fluorescent lights according to rumor causes color blindness.
12. Nevertheless many factories continue to use these lights.
13. Human beings are not fallen angels but are risen apes at least according to Robert Ardrey.
14. The general decline in SAT scores for the most part can be the result of too much television.
15. The young lovers with a great amount of stealth met by moonlight.
16. A sudden rainstorm unhappily quenched their ardor.
17. That same rainstorm from another point of view was needed to ease the drought.
18. Any natural event don't you see can be a blessing.
19. Voltaire's *Satirical Dictionary* a slim volume is filled with wit and irony.
20. Many of his entries however sound strange to the modern reader.

Lesson
10 COMMAS
To Set Off Nonessential Elements

There are three kinds of constructions that can function either as **essential** or as **nonessential** elements within a sentence.[1] The *essential* element is one that is needed to identify clearly the noun it modifies. The *nonessential* element merely gives additional information about an already clearly identified noun. These three elements are (1) adjective clauses that are introduced by *who, whom, whose, which*, and *that* (called relative pronouns);[2] (2) appositives and appositive phrases that are repeaters; and (3) adjectival phrases (which may be verb phrases by form). Example:

A student *who cheats* only hurts himself.

The adjective clause *who cheats* is necessary to identify which student is meant and, therefore, is essential. On the other hand

Fred, *who cheats often,* is just harming himself,

is an example of an adjective clause that just gives further information about an already clearly identified noun. It is nonessential.

The Rule *Use a comma or commas to set off a nonessential (1) adjective clause, (2) appositive or appositive phrase, or (3) adjectival phrase. Do not set off an essential element.*

---

[1]These elements are also called **restrictive** and **nonrestrictive**. Also some authorities call adverb clauses essential and nonessential, but other authorities find adverb clauses quite different in behavior from adjective clauses.
[2]*Whom, which*, and *that* can sometimes be omitted from an adjective clause, but in that case the clause is always essential and never gives any trouble in punctuation.

1. **Adjective clauses** are always nonessential when they modify a proper noun, for the name identifies itself. Examples:

> We appealed to Professor Hurley, *who is known for his fairness.*
> The Great Teton Mountains, *which are the most magnificent in the fifty states*, are in a national park.

The italicized adjective clauses give additional information about nouns identified by name; thus they are nonessential and must be set off by commas.

Sometimes common nouns modified by adjective clauses are also fully identified. Examples:

> The first-ranked candidate, *who only recently joined the Democratic party*, had the backing of the administration.
> The soiled book, *which was priced cheap*, was in fact a rare first edition.

Because *candidate* and *book* are identified by first-ranked and *soiled*, the italicized adjective clauses are nonessential and must be set off by commas.

But sometimes common nouns modified by adjective clauses need the clauses to identify them, and then the clauses are essential. Examples:

> A book *that gives its reader a good idea* is worth many times its purchase price.
> One animal *that is not near extinction* is the coyote.

Both *book* and *animal* are unidentified without the italicized adjective clauses, and thus the clauses are essential and must not be set off by commas.

Thus if an adjective clause can be removed from its sentence and still leave a fully meaningful sentence, the clause is nonessential and must be set off by commas. But if the removal of such a clause would leave an indefinite sentence with an unidentified noun, the clause is essential and must not be set off by commas.

Sometimes adjective clauses that begin with *which* modify not a single noun but a whole idea in a sentence or large part of a sentence. Such clauses are always nonessential and must be set off by commas. Examples:

> Rodney loves to drag-race on downtown streets, *which is not only illegal but dangerous.*
> Bruce voted for every losing candidate, *which is to say that he had not studied the issues.*

These *which* clauses modify whole ideas, not single nouns, and thus they are nonessential.

One very good tip to remember is that an adjective clause introduced by *that* is always essential and thus is never set off by commas. Therefore you can test clauses that are introduced by *who, whom,* and *which* to see whether *that* can properly substitute for one of those words. If it can, the clause is essential and must not be set off; if *that* will not work, the clause is nonessential and must be set off by commas. Examples:

Roy is a husband *who never forgets his wife's birthday.*
Roy is a husband *that never forgets his wife's birthday.*

That will substitute properly for who; thus the clause is essential and must not be set off.

RIGHT: Roy *who never forgets his wife's birthday* is a mnemonic genius.
WRONG: Roy *that never forgets his wife's birthday* is a mnemonic genius.

That will not properly substitute for who; therefore, in the first sentence the *who* clause is nonessential and should be set off by commas. Also note that the *which* clause that modifies a whole idea can never have *that* substituted for it:

RIGHT: Making an *A* in organic chemistry, *which is hard to do*, will get you a scholarship.
WRONG: Making an *A* in organic chemistry, *that is hard to do*, will get you a scholarship.

Because *that* will not substitute for *which*, the *which* clause is nonessential. The *that* test is very useful.

2. **Appositives** are repeaters in that they rename nouns in different terms. Usually they are noun phrases that rename nouns already fully identified. If so, they are nonessential and must be set off by commas (or sometimes by dashes). Examples:

Anticholinergics, *drugs that reduce muscle spasm*, were used by ancient physicians.
Vivisection, *an indispensable aid to medical science*, is strongly condemned by many reformers.

Anticholinergics and *vivisection* are nouns identified by name, and thus the italicized appositives give additional, rather than essential, information and are, therefore, nonessential constituents that need to be set off by commas.

Sometimes appositives are verb phrases. Examples:

Bobo's fondest wish—*to be rich*—was always denied him.
My favorite pastime—*hiking in the Sierra*—is hazardous in winter.

Wish and *pastime* are fully identified; thus, the italicized verb-phrase appositives are nonessential and need to be set off. They could be set off by commas, but dashes are usually best to set off verb-phrase appositives.

Most essential appositives are ones that mention a title after a word such as *novel* or a person's name after a word such as *novelist* or *politician*. Such appositives are essential because they are needed to identify such nouns as *novel, novelist, politician,* and so on. Examples:

The movie *Star Wars* created great enthusiasm.
The short story *"Two Soldiers"* is one of William Faulkner's finest.
The author *Georges Simenon* wrote more than 400 detective novels.
The playwright *Tennessee Williams* has not won a Nobel Prize.

The italicized appositives are needed to identify the nouns *movies, short story, author,* and *playwright*; therefore, they are essential and must not be set off by commas. Setting off such essential appositives is a very common error. However, if a preceding sentence had made an identification of a noun such as *movie,* then in the next sentence the title might be a nonessential appositive. Example:

RIGHT: A movie starring two robots won an Academy Award yesterday. The movie, *Star Wars,* has created great enthusiasm.

3. **Adjectival phrases** are those of any form that modify nouns. They are very much like the adjective clauses and appositive phrases just illustrated. When such a phrase is needed to identify the noun it modifies, it is essential and is not set off by commas. Examples:

The girl *wearing the tight sweater* is attracting a lot of attention.
The convict *executed last Sunday* had only circumstantial evidence
presented against him.
The sailor *happiest to go to sea* is the one with a nagging wife.

The italicized adjectival phrases are needed to identify the nouns *girl, convict,* and *sailor,* therefore, they are essential and must not be set off by commas.

When an adjectival phrase just gives additional information about a noun that is already fully identified, it is nonessential and is set off by commas. Examples:

> Professor Benston, *grinning from ear to ear,* reported that every student had made an *A.*
>
> The Watson's watchdog, *excited by a cat,* woke the whole neighborhood with its barking.
>
> The new salesclerks, *eager to make a good impression on their boss,* spoke pleasantly to every customer.

The nouns *Benston, watchdog,* and *salesclerks* are fully identified; therefore, the italicized adjectival phrases are nonessential and must be set off by commas.

Exercise 10

COMMAS TO SET OFF
NONESSENTIAL ELEMENTS

DIRECTIONS *Some of the italicized adjective clauses, appositives, and adjectival phrases in the following sentences are essential, and some are nonessential. Enter commas where needed. Be prepared to explain why commas are or are not needed.*

1. The candidate *who receives the most votes* will be declared the absolute victor.
2. However, in 1874 Samuel J. Tilden *who received the majority of popular votes* was not elected president.
3. Existentialism is a philosophy *that declares that the world is absurd but that man is free to act in it.*
4. Granger *a Heisman Trophy winner in college football* was a disappointment in his first professional year.
5. Scientific determinism *which maintains that man has no free will* grew up in the eighteenth century.
6. Predestination *which ends in the same conclusion as determinism* is a theological rather than a scientific postulate.
7. Fatalism *which is like determinism and predestination* is an Oriental concept.
8. The philosophy *that I subscribe to* is eclectic.
9. We all went to bed early *which surprised my mother.*
10. Phrenology *the study of the relationship between bumps on the head and personality* is a fraud bordering on superstition.
11. Astrology *a study of the stars and planets for the purpose of forecasting events* is also a fraud.
12. William Brady *who rose to fame from the ghetto* maintains that freedom from the ghetto must come from within a person.
13. The reason *given most often for failure* is social oppression.
14. The South *which really failed to free blacks after the Civil War* is paying the penalty for the awful sin of slavery.
15. Northerners *who opposed slavery in the pre-Civil War era* were called abolitionists.
16. Ralph Waldo Emerson *who is famous for his transcendental essays* was a strong abolitionist.
17. The article *"How to Win at Blackjack"* greatly interested me.

18. William Faulkner's **The Reivers** *called "a reminiscence"* is about a 1905 auto trip from Mississippi to Memphis.
19. An adjective clause *that begins with* **that** is always essential.
20. The study of grammar *often confused with the study of usage* is a respectable college course of study.
21. A mother *the greatest individual in the world* is usually fiercely protective.
22. The game of football attracts about 60 million spectators a year *which is less drawing power than auto racing has*.
23. Eugenics *the science of selective breeding* could greatly increase the quality of human beings.
24. The students *who protested offshore drilling* were found to be the most intelligent on campus.
25. The game of jai alai *which is thought to have originated in Spain* is played only in Miami in this country.
26. Sinclair Lewis's novel *Arrowsmith* is about the medical profession.
27. Professor McCall *who is one of the most popular teachers on campus* was at one time a dean.
28. Mervin Brawshaw *a doctor at Mono General Hospital* would prefer to be a teacher.
29. Cattle *that contract hoof-and-mouth disease* must be shot and buried.
30. **Romeo and Juliet** *based on a medieval tale* is one of Shakespeare's most popular plays.

Lesson

11 AVOIDING UNNECESSARY COMMAS

Do not add useless or obstructive commas to any sentence. Adding a comma where one should not be is in many people's opinion a worse error than omitting a needed one. (Of course there are cases, as with introductory elements or short compound sentences, where the use of a comma or its omission are both acceptable.) It is generally wise not to use a comma unless you have a specific, known reason for using it.

1. Do NOT separate a subject from its verb with a single comma:

WRONG: The eighteen-year-old in California, is now an adult.
WRONG: That scientists will ever find a final truth, seems doubtful.
WRONG: A man who spoils his children, just makes life hard for them later.

However, two commas separating a parenthetic element that comes before a verb are entirely correct:

RIGHT: The eighteen-year-old in California, though not allowed to buy alcohol, is now an adult.

Note that there are two voice pauses before the verb *is*.

2. Do NOT separate a verb from its complement (direct object, predicate noun, and so on) with a single comma:

WRONG: Senator Tushure's solution to the impasse with Russia was, to eliminate our bases in the Near East.
WRONG: My present opinion is, that trade with Red China should be increased.

This error usually occurs when the verb is a form of *to be* and the complement is an infinitive phrase or noun clause, as in the examples.

59

3. Do NOT set off an essential appositive with commas:

WRONG: The belief, that a depression is inevitable, seems to be widespread.

WRONG: Somerset Maugham's novel, *Of Human Bondage*, has been a best seller for sixty years.

The erroneous punctuation of the second example would mean that Maugham wrote only one novel. If he had written only one novel, the commas would be required. Similarly, in

My brother, Clive, intends to apply to med school.

the commas mean that I have only one brother. If the commas are removed, the meaning is that I have more than one brother and am specifying the one who is applying to med school.

4. Similarly, do NOT set off an essential adjective clause or adjectival phrase:

WRONG: It's true that nurses, who work night shifts, find it hard to sleep in the daytime.

The erroneously used commas here give the meaning that all nurses work night shifts.

WRONG: The first book, written by William Faulkner, was *The Marble Faun*.

With commas erroneously setting off the essential adjectival phrase, the meaning, literally, is that the first book ever written was written by William Faulkner and was entitled *The Marble Faun*. Note that in these examples the use of commas changes the meaning of the sentence.

5. Do NOT separate with a comma noncoordinate adjectival modifiers of a noun. Noncoordinate adjectival modifiers are those that cannot be joined with *and* and still sound natural. Examples:

WRONG: I would like to own a new, brick house.

WRONG: I found an old, Vulgate Bible in our attic.

Note that *new and brick house* and *old and Vulgate Bible* do not fit standard writing patterns.

6. Usually, two sentence predicates in a series should NOT be separated by a comma:

POOR STYLE: We laid out our music and snacks, and began to study.

POOR STYLE: We watched the televised hearings, but didn't enjoy them.

Exercise 11

AVOIDING UNNECESSARY COMMAS

DIRECTIONS *In the following sentences strike out commas wrongly used. Do not strike out commas correctly used. Be able to explain why the unnecessary commas are wrongly used.*

1. The most important attribute of a ball player, is quick reflex actions.
2. The reason given to us was, that the police force had no extra patrolmen.
3. That I might make an *A* in English, never entered my mind.
4. The assumption, that man has free will, is only that—an assumption.
5. Teachers, who are dedicated, may not be the most popular, but they are the most respected.
6. The kind of house, that I have always wanted, is a red, brick one.
7. The sweater, worn by Raquel Welch in *Myra Breckinridge*, was auctioned off for $200.
8. I turned the corner, and ran smack into a patrol car.
9. We were advised, that we should bring a clean, heavy woolen blanket.
10. The movie that I liked best, was *Star Wars*.
11. To tell the truth, the only reason why I bought the set of books was, that the salesgirl was so pretty.
12. The poem, which I quoted, was "If" by Rudyard Kipling.
13. The first of the poems, which was quite long, was assigned for Wednesday.
14. Tickets were priced at $3.50, and $2.50.
15. The causes of Parkinson's disease, are mostly unknown.
16. That we could actually win the game, never entered the coach's head.
17. The belief, that like produces like, is at the basis of much superstition.
18. He is a very dignified, old man.
19. His first book, which sold only twenty-five copies, was *The Marble Faun*.
20. The custodian, of the Humanities Building, keeps all the windows spotless.

A MINI-EXERCISE   In the blanks provided, write the correct forms of the pronouns below the blanks.

1. _____ books are _____.
   (*Them or Those?*)   (*they*)

2. I do not like _____ kind of program.
                     (*that or those?*)

3. The dog hurt _____ while eating _____
                        (*it*)   (*it*)

   supper.

4. _____ going out for football pleased my father.
      (*Me or My?*)

5. When _____ through with _____ bar-
              (*you*)   (*them or those?*)

   bells, return them to _____ owner.
                                    (*they*)

6. _____ the one who said _____ conceited?
         (*Who*)   (*you*)

7. _____ counselor said _____ cutting
         (*Who*)   (*we*)

   class was indefensible?

8. _____ interfering with _____ helping
            (*You*)   (*they*)

   _____.
         (*they*)

9. John and _____ were excused because of
                     (*I, me, myself?*)

   _____ having high scores.
            (*we*)

10. _____ paper received a higher grade than
               (*Who*)

   _____?
         (*you*)

Lesson
12 SEMICOLONS

A semicolon is used only between those sentence parts that are coordinate, equal in rank, or have the same form. It is not used between parts that are unlike each other, such as a dependent and an independent clause.

1. A semicolon is used to separate independent clauses (which are really sentences) in a compound sentence that has no connective word between the clauses. A writer uses a semicolon in this position when the two independent clauses are so closely related that the writer wants them in the same sentence. Examples:

> RIGHT: An espousal of leftist causes ruined the political career of Herman Dougfield; he was even defeated recently in his race for state senator.
>
> RIGHT: Even the closest stars appear only as points of light through the most powerful telescopes; astronomers must use spectroscopes to deduce information about their surfaces.

Periods in place of semicolons in such sentences (making two sentences) would not be wrong but might produce an inferior style.

2. A semicolon is used to separate independent clauses joined by a connective word **other than** *and, but, yet, or, nor, for,* and *so* (coordinating conjunctions). Usually such a connective is a so-called conjunctive adverb: *therefore, however, nevertheless, consequently, furthermore, then, afterwards,* and so on. Examples:

> RIGHT: In California there are over one million more registered Democrats than Republicans; nevertheless, the state often elects Republican officials.
>
> RIGHT: Candidate Cook felt that integrity was more important than political victory; therefore, he refused to stoop to slander in his campaigning.

Usually a conjunctive adverb can be shifted to the interior of the second clause. That is one test you can use to see whether a semicolon is needed.

Now a word of caution: The use of a comma instead of a semicolon in the two positions just illustrated produces the notorious and unacceptable comma splice, which is explained in Lesson Five.

3. Semicolons rather than commas are used to separate items in a series when such items are long or have internal punctuation of their own. Semicolons are correctly used in such sentences because the items are coordinate, or similar to each other. Examples:

RIGHT: We sent appeals to three foundations: the Coe Fund for Academic Freedom, 925 Melrose, Dekalb, Illinois; the McCall Foundation for Anthropological Studies, 483 Main Street, Umatilla, Oregon; and the Libermann Associates Foundation, 806 Beverley Lane, Philadelphia.

RIGHT: Professor Reifsnyder's researches disclosed that students with IQ's over 140 have a dropout rate greater than those with IQ's of 120 to 125; that students with IQ's of 110 to 120 make better grades in the humanities than in science; and that grades assigned in science classes correspond more closely with student IQ's than grades assigned in humanities classes.

Because the list separated by semicolons in the first example has commas of its own, the use of just commas to separate those items would be confusing. In the second example the items in the series are so long they should be separated by semicolons.

A TIP ON USAGE Many students incorrectly put a semicolon after the connective *such as*. No mark of punctuation should be put after *such as*, but a comma should be put *before* it. Examples:

RIGHT: I have several ailments, such as hangnails, hangovers, and hang-ups with women.

RIGHT: We were supposed to bring small gifts, such as flowers, candy, or half-pints of whiskey.

A MINI-EXERCISE Explain the difference in meaning between the two following phrases.

1. seventy-odd Americans
2. seventy odd Americans

Exercise 12

THE USE OF SEMICOLONS

DIRECTIONS *In the following sentences enter semicolons where they are called for. Some sentences may require not semicolons but commas; enter them, too. Explain why each semicolon is needed.*

1. Governor Shammon seems eager to place teachers in a lower rank than union members;he even submitted a bill prohibiting any further fringe benefits for teachers.
2. Eighteen-year-olds in our state cannot legally buy alcoholic beverages; however, they have no trouble whatsoever buying them illegally.
3. All this junk should be sorted into three piles: cloth, leather, and plastic;appliances;and furniture and tools, electrical cords and plugs, and miscellaneous pieces of metal.
4. Wherever George wants to be that's where Georgine will be, too.
5. Our library should place shelves of popular, good books near the entrance;and exit;this would encourage people to read books they otherwise would ignore.
6. After dating Charlotte for six months;I concluded that she had every intention of stripping me of every dollar;I had;that her feeling for men in general was one of dislike;with a desire for exploitation;and that even if we should get to the point of marching down the church aisle;she would desert me for someone else.
7. First we made a very detailed study of the structure of the First National Bank;later;we were able to remove cement blocks and walk right into the vault.
8. Whatever the cause turns out to be the cure is sure to be expensive.
9. I simply gave up;that seemed the best course.
10. The Senate refused to override the president's veto of the Veterans Appropriation Bill;therefore;the disabled veterans were denied an increase in compensation for the third straight year.

A MINI-EXERCISE Write three meaningful sentences, using the following three forms correctly.

1. the teacher's desire _____

_____

_____

2. the teachers' desire _____

_____

_____

3. the teachers desire _____

_____

_____

A MINI-EXERCISE   Write meaningful sentences, using these three forms correctly.

1. sometimes: _____

_____

_____

_____

2. sometime: _____

_____

_____

_____

3. some time: _____

_____

_____

13 VERB PROBLEMS

Principal Parts of Verbs

One source of errors in English usage is the misuse of verb forms. English verbs have five **principal parts**: (1) the plural present or stem (*go, talk, eat*); (2) the singular present (*goes, talks, eats*); (3) the past (*went, talked, ate*); (4) the present participle (*going, talking, eating*); and (5) the past participle (*gone, talked, eaten*). The two present forms give no trouble except in subject-verb agreement, which will be taken up in Lesson Fourteen. The present participle is completely regular and never gives any trouble. But the past and past participle forms are sometimes confused because many are irregular. Such confusion is the source of some of the grossest errors in usage.

The problem exists because there are regular and irregular verbs in English. Regular verbs end in *ed* in both the past and the past participle. Examples:

Past	Past Participle
talked	talked
roped	roped
played	played

As the two forms are the same, regular verbs give no trouble.

Sometimes irregular verbs are identical in the past and past participle forms, and sometimes they are different, as the list below indicates:

Past	Past Participle
gave	given
began	begun
swam	swum
dealt	dealt
brought	brought
led	led

Most errors in misused verb forms fall into two classes: (1) the misuse of an irregular past form for the past participle form (such as *I had began* instead of *I had begun*) and (2) the improper conversion of an irregular form into a supposed regular form (such as *I knowed it* instead of *I knew it*).

Actually, few high school graduates make many errors in verb forms, but most people are bothered occasionally. The remedy is either to memorize the principal forms of the common irregular verbs or to refer to a grammar book like this one or to look the forms up in a dictionary.

The next step, then, is to distinguish between the past and past participle forms. The *past form* is always used by itself (*I gave*). The *past participle* is always used with a helping verb or auxiliary (*I have given*).

Following are the principal parts (with the exception of the singular and present participle forms, which give no trouble) of the most common irregular verbs:

Present	Past	Past Participle
bear	bore	have borne
begin	began	have begun
bite	bit	have bitten
blow	blew	have blown
break	broke	have broken
bring	brought	have brought
burst	burst	have burst
catch	caught	have caught
choose	chose	have chosen
come	came	have come
deal	dealt	have dealt
dive	dived (dove)	have dived
do	did	have done
draw	drew	have drawn
drink	drank	have drunk
drive	drove	have driven
eat	ate	have eaten
fall	fell	have fallen
flee	fled	have fled
fly	flew	have flown
forbid	forbade	have forbidden
forget	forgot	have forgotten
freeze	froze	have frozen
give	gave	have given
go	went	have gone
grow	grew	have grown
know	knew	have known
lay	laid	have laid
lead	led	have led

Present	Past	Past Participle
lie	lay	have lain
lose	lost	have lost
raise	raised	have raised
ride	rode	have ridden
ring	rang	have rung
rise	rose	have risen
run	ran	have run
see	saw	have seen
send	sent	have sent
set	set	have set
shake	shook	have shaken
sing	sang	have sung
sink	sank	have sunk
sit	sat	have sat
speak	spoke	have spoken
spring	sprang, sprung	have sprung
steal	stole	have stolen
swear	swore	have sworn
swim	swam	have swum
swing	swung	have swung
take	took	have taken
tear	tore	have torn
throw	threw	have thrown
wear	wore	have worn
wring	wrung	have wrung
write	wrote	have written

Two Troublesome Pairs of Verbs

Two pairs of verbs—*lie* and *lay* and *sit* and *set*—cause a good deal of trouble because they are somewhat similar in meaning but function differently in sentences. Here are the principal parts of these verbs:

Present	Past	Past Participle
lie	lay	have lain
lay	laid	have laid
sit	sat	have sat
set	set	have set

The distinction between the verbs in each pair is that *lie* and *sit* are **intransitive** verbs; that is, they do not take direct objects. The subject of *lie* or *sit* does some thing but does not do it to any *thing*. *Lay* and *set*, on the other hand, are **transitive** verbs and take direct objects. The subject of *lay* or *set* does something to something else.

Here are examples of the use of the intransitive verb *lie*:

RIGHT: I **lie** in bed often because I like to **lie** in bed. (present tense and infinitive; no direct objects)

RIGHT: John **lies** down every afternoon because he likes **lying** down. (present tense and present participle; no direct objects)

RIGHT: Last week I **lay** in bed three days. (past tense; no direct object)

RIGHT: I have **lain** in this position all day. (past participle; no direct object)

Lie, lay, lain simply mean that a person or thing takes a reclining position.

Here are examples of the transitive verb *lay*, with the direct objects italicized:

RIGHT: I will **lay** the *book* down after he **lays** his *gun* down. (future and present tense; direct objects *book* and *gun*)

RIGHT: I was **laying** the *book* down as he **laid** the *gun* down. (present participle and past tense; object *book* and *gun*)

Here are examples of the use of the intransitive verb *sit*:

RIGHT: John **sits** in his chair while I am **sitting** on a stool. (present tense and present participle; no direct objects)

RIGHT: While John **sat** there I was lying down. (past tense; no direct object)

RIGHT: John has **sat** there for hours. (past participle; no direct object)

Sit, sat, sat simply mean that a person or thing takes a sitting position.

Here are examples of the use of the transitive verb *set*, with the direct objects italicized:

RIGHT: Mary **set** the *pitcher* down as I was **setting** the table. (present tense and present participle; direct objects *pitcher* and *table*)

RIGHT: Yesterday I **set** *John* on his ears. (past tense; direct object *John*)

RIGHT: I have **set** the *world* on fire many times. (past participle; direct object *world*)

Nobody ever misuses *sit* for *set*, only *set* for *sit*.

Note that things as well as persons can *lie* or *sit*, but usually only persons *lay* or *set* other things.

Exercise 13–A

VERB PROBLEMS

DIRECTIONS *In the blanks in the following sentences, write the correct form of the verb that appears in parentheses below the blank.*

1. After she had _____ in bed all day, she
   (to lie)

   _____ the bell for her maid.
   (to ring)

2. The class _____ on time, before all the students had
   (to begin)

   _____ down.
   (set or sat?)

3. I _____ my wet clothes out before I _____
   (to wring)   (to swim)

   to the barge.

4. Mrs. Smith has _____ fourteen children, all of whom
   (to bear)

   had _____ college by last year.
   (to begin)

5. I thought I had _____ it away, but the jar still
   (to throw)

   _____ on the shelf.
   (set or sat?)

6. Won't you _____ down before I _____
   (lie or lay?)   (sit or set?)

   the kettle on the fire?

7. He had _____ ten limbs before he had
   (to break)

   _____ ten feet.
   (to climb)

8. She _____ in the rocker after he had
   (set or sat?)

   _____ down for a nap.
   (to lie)

9. I had _____the books on the table before I
(*lain or laid?*)

_____ down for a nap.
(*to lie*)

10. I _____ him to _____ there all day.
(*to forbid*)   (*lie or lay?*)

11. The car was _____ apart after it had
(*to shake*)

_____ over the rocks.
(*to run*)

12. I _____ into the pool after John had
(*to dive*)

_____ in six times.
(*to dive*)

13. I _____ my books aside and _____ down
(*set or sat?*)   (*to lie*)

for a nap.

14. The hen _____ on the eggs till they were almost
(*set or sat?*)

_____.
(*to break*)

15. The barometer had _____ six points before we had
(*to fall*)

_____ ten miles.
(*to drive*)

16. I _____ his keys on the piano and then
(*lay or laid?*)

_____ into a daydream.
(*to sink*)

17. The moon has _____ on time every night that I have
(*to rise*)

_____ in bed.
(*lain or laid?*)

18. After the pipe had _____ I _____ my
(*to burst*)   (*lay or laid?*)

tools aside.

19. I have _____ to the cabin more often than I have
(*to drive*)

_____ there.
(*to swim*)

20. I could have _____ him if I had not _____
(*to beat*)   (*to swing*)

so hard.

Exercise 13–B

VERB PROBLEMS

DIRECTIONS *In the blanks in the following sentences write the correct form of the verb that appears in parentheses below the blank.*

1. The watchdog _____ the crook who
(*to bite*)

_____ my stereo set.
(*to steal*)

2. It was _____ at a discount store that
(*to buy*)

_____ a free tape with each set.
(*to give*)

3. As the moon _____ early that night, I should
(*to rise*)

_____ him entering the yard.
(*to see*)

4. The noise he made would _____ the dead, and he
(*to raise*)

_____ a terrible oath.
(*to swear*)

5. The sneaky fellow _____ the set down and
(*to lay*)

_____ into the bushes.
(*to run*)

6. I would _____ to the sheriff if I _____
(*to write*)   (*to lose*)

it.

7. The elk _____ up from the thicket and
(*to spring*)

_____ in my direction.
(*to come*)

8. I _____ my camera as he _____ up.
(*to raise*)   (*to rise*)

9. But the crimson hat I _____ startled him, and he
   (to wear)

   _____ and _____.
   (to stumble)   _(to fall)_

10. He _____ to his knees and just _____
    (to sink)   _(to lie)_

    there.

11. I _____ the camera down to help.
    (lay or laid?)

12. Before I reached him, though, he _____ bolder and
    (to grow)

    _____ into the forest.
    (to flee)

13. A fly _____ by and _____ in my soup.
    (to fly)   _(to fall)_

14. The fly just _____ there till I _____ it
    (lay or laid?)   _(to take)_

    out.

15. I reached in, but I had _____ that the soup
    (to forget)

    _____.
    (to freeze)

16. The bells _____ out as I _____ along.
    (to ring)   _(to ride)_

17. If I had _____, I would _____ a song.
    (to think)   _(to sing)_

18. Last week Fred _____ in bed until he was well enough
    (lay or laid?)

    to _____ up.
    (sit or set?)

19. He had _____ his leg and _____ a
    (to break)   _(to tear)_

    ligament.

20. The doctor _____ to him and _____ him
    (to speak)   _(to bring)_

    the medicine he _____ to ease the pain.
    (to choose)

Lesson
14 SUBJECT-VERB AGREEMENT

An error generally considered quite serious is **faulty agreement in number between subject and verb.** One of the first rules of grammar everybody learns is that a verb is supposed to agree in number with its subject. In grammar **number** is the term meaning the number of units involved. English grammar has two numbers: (1) the singular (one) and (2) the plural (more than one). (Some languages have a *number* for one, another for two, and another for more than two.) English nouns and pronouns have one form for the singular—*book, it, this, horse,* and so on—and another for the plural—*books, they, these, horses,* and so on. Some nouns use the same form for both singular and plural: many *sheep,* one *sheep;* school of *fish,* one *fish.* Most verb forms in English can be used with both singular and plural subjects: a horse *should eat,* all horses *should eat;* he *talked,* we *talked.* But one verb form (third person, singular, present tense) is used only with singular subjects. Examples:

Plural form	**Singular form**
We talk	He talks
They run	She runs
These fluctuate	That fluctuates

Nonstandard speakers make many errors in subject-verb agreement.

WRONG: They was coming.
WRONG: Some people is just crazy.

But most high school graduates make such errors only in certain trouble spots in the language. Following are explanations of these troublesome areas of English grammar.

Intervening Prepositional Phrases

A prepositional phrase coming between a subject and its verb does not affect the verb form. Quite often the object of an intervening propositional phrase is a plural noun when the true subject is a singular noun. The singular subject governs the verb. Examples, with the subject and verb in boldface and the prepositional phrase italicized, follow:

RIGHT: A **list** *of honor students* **was** posted in the library.
RIGHT: A **tray** *of cold cuts* **was** left for the boys.

The plural nouns *students* and *cuts* are objects of prepositions and do not affect the verbs, which must be singular to agree with the singular subjects *list* and *tray*.

Two prepositions that often lead writers into using plural verbs improperly are *together with* and *as well as*. The objects of these prepositions do not affect the verb. Examples, with the subject and verb in boldface and the prepositional phrase italicized, follow:

RIGHT: The **professor** *together with six of the demonstrating students* **has** been called to court.
RIGHT: The **mayor** *as well as the councilmen* **refuses** to endorse the bill.

The plural nouns *students* and *councilmen* are objects of prepositions and do not affect the verbs, which must be singular to agree with *professor* and *mayor*.

Words like *crowd, number*, and *group* may take plural verbs when an intervening prepositional phrase makes them seem plural. Example:

RIGHT: A **number** of spectators **were** injured.

In such a sentence *number* is thought of as plural and thus may take a plural verb. But a singular verb is also correct with such nouns.

Indefinite Pronouns as Subjects

The indefinite pronouns *one, each, either* and *neither* are always singular and thus as subjects require singular verbs. The indefinite pronoun *one* is likely to be incorrectly used with a plural verb only when there is an intervening prepositional phrase. The other three mentioned are often misused with plural verbs even when there is no intervening prepositional phrase. Examples:

RIGHT: **One** of the students **was** (not *were*) given a citation for bravery.
RIGHT: **Neither is** (not *are*) acceptable.
RIGHT: **Each** of the books **is** (not *are*) a classic of American literature.

The indefinite pronouns *none* and *any* are correctly used with either a singular or a plural verb, and thus no errors occur with them. Other indefinite pronouns never give any trouble.

Compound Subjects

A compound subject consists of two or more subjects joined by *and*, and it is of course plural and requires a plural verb. Singular nouns in a compound subject seldom lead any writer into an error. Example:

> One **bottle** and one **corkscrew were** missing.

Almost no one would erroneously use *was* in such a sentence.

But when the parts of a compound subject are verb phrases, some writers will mistakenly use a singular verb. Examples:

> **Watching TV** and **playing records take** (not *takes*) up most of my sister's time.
> **Eating candy** and **drinking soft drinks lead** (not *leads*) to tooth decay.

The *and* in a compound subject signals the need for a plural verb.

Correlative Constructions

A correlative is a two-part conjunction. The correlative *both* . . . *and* forms a compound subject, which takes a plural verb. But the correlatives *either* (*neither*) . . . *or* (*nor*) and *not only* . . . *but also* do not form true compound subjects. When these constructions are used in subjects, the verb agrees in number with the part of the subject nearest the verb; the part farthest from the verb has no effect on the verb. Examples, with the both parts of the subject and the verb in boldface:

> RIGHT: Either the **judge** or the jury **members were** wrong.
> RIGHT: Either the jury **members** or the **judge was** wrong.
> RIGHT: Not only the **president** but also the various **deans were** at the meeting.
> RIGHT: Not only the various **deans** but also the **president** was at the meeting.

Reversing the parts of the subject changes the verb form.

Inverted Word Order

There are two types of sentences commonly used in English where the normal pattern of **subject + predicate** is reversed. In the first type the writers place the subject of the sentence *after* the verb for added emphasis. The verb must always agree in number with the subject following it. Examples, with the verbs and subjects in boldface:

> RIGHT: On the front lawn **were** two battered **lawn mowers**.
> RIGHT: Behind the billboard **was** a motorcycle **cop**.
> RIGHT: Over yonder **are** my most deadly **enemies**.

The second type of inverted word order occurs in sentences introduced with *there*. The true subject follows the verb, and the verb agrees in number with that subject. Examples, with the verbs and subjects in boldface:

> RIGHT: There **was** only a **dollar** between me and starvation.
> RIGHT: There **exists** one last **hope** for the human race.
> RIGHT: There **were** three **redheads** in the chorus line.

Relative Pronouns

When they function in adjective clauses, *who, which*, and *that* are called relative pronouns. When one of them is the subject of its clause, its verb agrees in number with the antecedent of the pronoun (the noun the pronoun refers to). Thus these relative pronouns are both singular and plural. Examples, with the antecedent, relative pronoun, and verb in boldface:

> RIGHT: The **theory that was** provisionally adopted was Hoyle's.
> RIGHT: The **theories that were** at first discarded were later proved correct.
> RIGHT: Some **men** of distinction **who like** Lord Calvert are the Southern senators.
> RIGHT: Joseph is one of those **men who think** they know everything.

Note in the last sentence that *men* and not *one* is the antecedent of *who*.

Exercise 14–A

SUBJECT-VERB AGREEMENT

DIRECTIONS *In the blanks in the following sentences write the correct form of the verb that appears in the parentheses below the blank.*

1. Neither of the skunks _____ denatured.
   (*to be*)

2. Each of Dickens's characters _____ carefully delineated.
   (*to be*)

3. On the back of the truck _____ six farm workers.
   (*to be*)

4. Every one of Faulkner's novels _____ some violence
   (*to have*)

   in it.

5. A syllabus and a booklet _____ required in Chemistry
   (*to be*)

   3A.

6. Not only a dog but also two cats _____ at home in his
   (*to be*)

   garage.

7. Not only two doves but also a bobwhite _____ in the
   (*to be*)

   aviary.

8. Either a dollar or two box tops _____ required for
   (*to be*)

   admission.

9. Either two box tops or a dollar _____ required for
   (*to be*)

   admission.

10. The North Star as well as Arcturus _____ chosen for
    (*to be*)

    study.

11. Venus and one other planet _____ to be selected for
    (to be)
    possible exploration.

12. One of you _____ to be appointed chairperson.
    (to be)

13. Both a poem and a short story _____ been written by
    (to have)
    the young author.

14. I am the one who _____ ahead of the rest.
    (to stay)

15. I am one of those people who _____ ahead of the rest.
    (to stay)

16. Neither of the men _____ sure about his duties.
    (to be)

17. Running counter to Heisenberg's theory _____the
    (to be)
    discoveries of Einstein.

18. Alan Cranston together with two other senators _____
    (to be)
    to attend the conference.

19. Jim as well as the twins _____ sure to receive a
    (to be)
    scholarship.

20. Neither the animals nor their keeper _____ prepared
    (to be)
    for the storm.

21. He was one of those keepers who _____ eager to take
    (to be)
    good care of beasts.

22. There _____ a half-dozen ways an animal can be
    (to be)
    disturbed.

23. Several bolts of lightning _____ flashing in the sky.
    (to be)

24. A pair of aardvarks _____ been pacing back and forth.
    (to have)

25. Neither of the animals, however, _____ unduly excited.
    (to be)

Exercise 14–B

SUBJECT-VERB AGREEMENT

DIRECTIONS *In the blanks in the following sentences write the correct form of the verb that appears in the parentheses below the blank.*

1. There _____ new theories about the brain.
   (*to exist*)

2. Each of them _____ insights into how we think.
   (*to offer*)

3. One of them _____ developed by Roger Sperry.
   (*to be*)

4. Both the left half and the right half of the brain _____
   (*to serve*)

   different functions.

5. Both halves of the brain _____ to function.
   (*to have*)

6. Otherwise, neither _____ truly efficient.
   (*to be*)

7. Sperry is one of those scientists who _____ sophisti-
   (*to perform*)

   cated experiments.

8. He has shown that the left half of the brain of human beings

   _____ mainly logical.
   (*to be*)

9. There in the distance _____ the wizards.
   (*to stand*)

10. Each of them _____ peculiar powers.
    (*to have*)

11. Neither of them _____ real magic.
    (*to do*)

12. A list of their tricks _____ a page.
    (*to fill*)

13. The tall one is one of those who _____ rain making
    (*to think*)

    is possible.

14. Neither of his methods _____.
    (*to work*)

15. Not only two wizards but also a witch _____ there.
    (*to stand*)

16. Not only the witch but also both wizards _____ frauds.
    (*to be*)

17. Every one of their spells _____.
    (*to fail*)

18. The witch as well as the wizards _____ unsuccessful.
    (*to be*)

19. There _____ a million reasons why witchcraft doesn't
    (*to be*)

    work.

20. One of a great many reasons _____ that you can't fool
    (*to be*)

    Mother Nature.

A MINI-EXERCISE List as many negative prefixes as you can think
of, such as the *a* in *amoral*. A few positive words to work with are
favorable, legal, conclusive, proper, and *enchanted.* Supply others
yourself.

Lesson
15 SHIFTS IN NUMBER, PERSON, AND TENSE

A shift within a sentence or between two sentences is an error of inconsistency. Such errors, of which there are a number of different kinds, are common in careless writing. We will limit our discussion to the most common three kinds of shifts, those in **number, person,** and **tense**.

Shifts in Number

Often a writer will begin a construction, using a singular noun or pronoun, and then will shift to the plural when consistency calls for a continuation of the singular. Here is a typical example, with the words in question in boldface:

WRONG: If a **student** cheats, **they** are very likely to be caught.

Because the sentence starts out discussing students in the singular, for consistency it should use *he* or *she* (singular) instead of *they* (plural) to complete the discussion.

There are two causes for this very common error—or perhaps it should just be called a serious weakness in style rather than an error, because it is so common. The first is that our language allows us to talk about people in general in either the singular or the plural. For example, the following two sentences mean exactly the same thing:

A football **player** is supposed to learn good sportsmanship.
Football **players** are supposed to learn good sportsmanship.

The fact that one sentence uses the singular and the other the plural makes no difference in meaning. However, this characteristic of our language often leads writers into shifts in number, such as *a football player . . . they.*

The second cause of the error is that our language does not have (as many other languages do) a singular personal pronoun to refer to both

male and female human beings—only *he* and *she*. Thus when writers
start with a singular noun such as *student*, they sometimes feel uneasy
about using either *he* or *she* or *he or she* as a continuation. So writers
resort to *they*, which is both masculine and feminine. But in spite of
Women's Lib, it is customary in English to use the masculine pronoun
he when the sex reference is indefinite. Thus we traditionally write *a
person . . . he, a student . . . he, a musician . . . he, one . . . he*, and so on
when the reference can be either to males or females. Consistency calls
for such usage.[1]

Here are a couple more examples of shifts in number, with revisions:

> POOR STYLE: **A parent** should be kind to **their** children, but **they**
> should not spoil them.
>
> GOOD STYLE: **A parent** should be kind to **his** children, but **he** should
> not spoil them.

It would be just as logical to use *him* to refer to *children* as *they* to refer
to *parent*. Of course, the sentence could be written with *parents . . . they*.

> POOR STYLE: **A swinger** can get a lot of dates, but **they** often can't
> get the same girl to date **them** twice.
>
> GOOD STYLE: **A swinger** can get a lot of dates, but **he** often can't get
> the same girl to date **him** twice.

Also for best style you should use *everyone . . . his* rather than the inferior
everyone . . . their.

Shifts in Person

There are three persons in grammar: (1) the **first person** (*I, me, we, us*);
(2) the **second person** (*you*); and the **third person** (*he, him, she, her,
it, they*, and any noun or indefinite pronoun). The only common shift in
person—and it is quite common—is from the third person to the second,
as in this sentence:

> WRONG: **A student** should never cheat, for even if **you** don't get
> caught **you** will still harm **yourself**.

As the sentence starts out with the third-person *student*, for consistency
it should continue with the third-person pronouns *he* (*doesn't*), *he*, and
himself.

---

[1]Another way of saying this is that for the sake of simplicity only, we sometimes use the
masculine generic pronouns; they should always be understood to mean either sex.

The cause of this error, or serious weakness in style, is that in English we can talk about people in general in either the third person or in the so-called indefinite second person. For example, the following two sentences mean exactly the same thing when no individual is spoken to directly:

> **One** should not cheat, for **he** is sure to harm himself.
> **You** should not cheat, for **you** are sure to harm yourself.

This characteristic of our language leads many writers into carelessly shifting from the third person to the second, as in this sentence:

> POOR STYLE: **One** should not cheat, for **you** are sure to hurt yourself.

Many teachers ask their students not to use the indefinite second person (*you*) in their writing in order to guide them away from the faulty shift. Yet professional writers in such magazines as *The Atlantic* and *Harper's* commonly use the indefinite second person.

Here are a couple more examples of faulty shifts in person, with revisions:

> POOR STYLE: When **someone** cheats, **he** may get a better grade, but usually **you** are caught and lose **your** grade.
> GOOD STYLE: When **someone** cheats, **he** may get a better grade, but usually **he** is caught and loses **his** grade.
> POOR STYLE: **A student** should study conscientiously, but don't lose out in **your** social life.
> GOOD STYLE: **A student** should study conscientiously, but **he** shouldn't lose out in **his** social life.

Shifts in Tense

There are many tenses in English, but here we will discuss only the present and the past. It is a characteristic of English that we can talk about the past—that is, in recounting history or in summarizing fiction—in either the past tense or the so-called historical present tense. For example, the following two sentences have the same meaning:

> The war **went** badly for England, but in 1710 Queen Anne **appointed** a new Cabinet and things **improved**.
> The war **is** going badly for England, but in 1710 Queen Anne **appoints** a new Cabinet and things **improve**.

Many writers use the historical present tense, as in the second sentence, to summarize history or fiction. But all writers should be careful not to shift from the past to the present or from the present to the past. For example, this sentence is faulty:

> The war **is** going badly for England, but in 1710 Queen Anne **appoints** a new Cabinet and things **improved**.

The shift from the present in the first two verbs to the past in the third is inconsistent.

A TIP ON USAGE Use a comma to separate coordinate adjectives modifying a noun. Adjectives are coordinate when *and* between them would sound right. Example:

> RIGHT: A beautiful, sophisticated woman is always in demand.

Note that *and* between *beautiful* and *sophisticated* would sound correct. Do not use a comma between noncoordinate adjective, between which *and* does not sound right. Example:

> WRONG: A bent, old man was strolling in the park.

Note that *and* between *bent* and *old* would sound very awkward.

A MINI-EXERCISE On the basis of the following sentence, how many wives would you say Don Anderson has? Why?

> Don Anderson's wife Carol was runner-up in the Miss America contest.

And on the basis of this sentence, how much publishing would you say Henry Brady has done? Why?

> Henry Brady's article, "The Last of the Winnebagoes," contains inflammatory rhetoric.

Exercise 15

SHIFTS IN NUMBER, PERSON, AND TENSE

DIRECTIONS *In the following sentences encircle any words that rep-resent faulty shifts. Be prepared to say what kind of shift is involved and how it can be corrected.*

1. A teacher should not be a baby-sitter; instead, they should educate their students.
2. A football player should pay more attention to their team's welfare than to their own performance.
3. One can find many educational TV programs, but usually you will just seek entertainment.
4. At the beginning of the novel, Gronski is in love, but by the end he was a misogynist.
5. A newspaper reporter should always be ready to go to the scene to get the news, but sometimes they just rely on hearsay.
6. At first a player gets angry at being hit so hard, but you soon get used to it.
7. The War of Jenkins' Ear displeases King George, but he vowed to win it.
8. A college student should spend two hours of study for every hour in class, but sometimes you can get by with less.
9. A phrenologist claims to be able to analyze a person's personality by examining the bumps on their head, but they are really frauds.
10. A parent is eager to reform children, that is, everybody's but theirs.
11. Philip Carey is clubfooted and suffers psychologically because of his ailment. But he eventually triumphed over his mental pain.
12. If a student crams for an exam, he may pass it, but you really get little permanent learning from such study.
13. An unabridged dictionary is very useful, but they are too heavy to carry around.
14. One should not hurry through a novel; instead, give yourself time to enjoy it.
15. A good football game is exciting, but they are hard on the players.
16. One should take their health problems seriously.
17. The Renaissance is a time of great intellectual achievement. Many of the world's greatest artists and philosophers flourished then.

18. A dietitian feeds everybody's children well but their own.
19. A person should not disturb their neighbors, for if you do you are sure to create enmity.
20. I want each of you to put on their hat.
21. There are politicians who don't know what he is going to do next.
22. A person who takes life too seriously may often be unhappy; you should always maintain a sense of humor.
23. An alcoholic may have flabby muscles, for they tend to sit around all day.
24. Jody looks forward to getting his pony, but he was saddened when Nellie had to be sacrificed.
25. A mechanic keeps everybody's car in good condition but their own.

A MINI-EXERCISE   Write meaningful sentences, using the following two forms correctly. Do not write questions.

1. who think: _____

_____

_____

2. who thinks: _____

_____

_____

Lesson

16 PRONOUN CASE FORMS

Most nouns change form to show possession (Lesson Twenty-four); the form that a word takes to indicate its use in a sentence is called the **case form**. Most nouns and pronouns change form only in the *possessive case* and, thus, are never troublesome. There are, however, six pronouns that have different forms for each of the three cases used in English: the **subjective case** (used as subject of a verb), the **objective case** (used as the object of a verb or preposition), and the **possessive case** (used to show ownership of something).

Formal writing and educated conversation require the choice of the case form that shows the function of the pronoun in the sentence. Here are the case forms of pronouns.

Subjective Case	Objective Case	Possessive Case
I	me	my, mine
you	you	your, yours
he	him	his
she	her	her, hers
it	it	its
we	us	our, ours
they	them	their, theirs
who	whom	whose

Note: *You* and *it* change only in the possessive case; and *this, that, these, those*, and *which* do not change at all and cause few possible errors.

Subjective and Objective Case Forms

Educated people react negatively to the confusion of *I-me, he-him, we-us*, and so on. About the only likelihood of error here among high school graduates is the confusion of cases in compound structures. Few if any native speakers would ever say

89

He spoke to **I**.
Me failed chemistry.
The letter was for **he**.

But people with little education often say

WRONG: Tom and **me** failed chemistry.
WRONG: You and **us** should get together.

And even a few well-educated people are sometimes heard to say

WRONG: Between you and **I**, Cherie is a witch.
WRONG: The message was for my father and **I**.

Thus confusion of case forms generally arises only when there is a compound structure.

When you are unsure about the case form of a pronoun in a compound structure, you can test by omitting one of the nouns or pronouns. If you omit the constructions in parentheses in the following examples, the correct form should be immediately clear:

The package was for (my sister and) _____.
                                      (*I or me?*)

Just between (you and) _____, I'm scared.
                            (*I or me?*)

He passed the message on to (Sara and) _____.
                                              (*she or her?*)

Another test is to understand that a compound subject may be written as two simple sentences

Fred drove to the valley. She drove, too.

(Fred and) _____ drove to the valley.
                (*she or her?*)

Tod may enroll in English 1. He may enroll, also.

(Tod and) _____ may enroll in English 1.
              (*he or him?*)

Use of this simple test should prevent you from making case errors of this sort. But note particularly that the objective form follows *between, to,* and *for*:

between you and **me**
for you and **me**
for their father and **her**
to John and **me**

Case Forms After the Verb *to Be*

In informal usage it is acceptable to use the objective pronoun form after the verb *to be*:

It's **me**.
Was that **her**?
Could it have been **him**?

But in formal or semiformal writing or conversation, it is still common to use the subjective form in such constructions:

It's **I**.
Was that **she**?
Could it have been **he**?
The guilty ones were **we**.

For semiformal writing you should learn to use the subjective case form after a form of the verb *to be*.

Who and *Whom*

There is a steady trend for most speakers and many writers to ignore the difference between *who* and *whom*. More and more, *who* (and *whoever*) is replacing *whom* (and *whomever*) in all constructions. Formal writing, though, still distinguishes between the *subjective* form, *who*, and the *objective* form, *whom*. There are some devices that will enable the writer to be precise in the use of *who* and *whom*.

1. Always use *whom* directly after a preposition.

To **whom** were you speaking?
For **whom** was it intended?
I don't care to **whom** you give it.

2. In a question, convert the question into a statement and substitute *he* or *him*. If *he* is correct, use *who*; if *him* is correct, use *whom*.

(*Who or whom?*) were you talking to?
SHIFT: You were talking to *him*. Therefore, use *whom*: *Whom* were you talking to?
(*Who or whom?*) did you say was coming?
SHIFT: You did say *he* is coming. Therefore, use *who*: *Who* did you say is coming?

3. You can also use this device to select the proper form in other sentences. If *he* fits, use *who*; if *him* fits, use *whom*.

Mr. Arthur, _____ the council voted to reprimand,
           (who or whom?)

decided to resign.
(The council voted to reprimand *him*. So use *whom*.)

Professor Thomas, _____ I believe is the popular
                 (who or whom?)

choice for the award, feels that I should receive the honor.
(*He* is the popular choice. So use *who*)

This test is, of course, useful mostly in writing, for in ordinary talk one usually doesn't have time to think the matter through. In any case, when in doubt use *who*, for that form is becoming dominant.

Pronoun Forms in Comparative Constructions

Comparative constructions are those using the words *than, as,* and *as . . . as.* Both subjective and objective pronoun forms may follow these words, and meaning is determined by which form is used. Example:

Professor Lockford praised Susan more highly than

_____ .
(I or me?)

You can test for the correct form by filling out the sentence with a clause that is ordinarily understood:

Professor Lockford praised Susan more highly than (he praised) **me.**
Professor Lockford praised Susan more highly than **I** (praised Susan).

As you can see, in such a sentence the pronoun form chosen determines the meaning.
Here are some other examples of the way to use this test:

Professor Elliott is more likely to favor the proposal than

_____ (is likely to favor it).
(he or him?)

Dennis defeated Reggie by a bigger score than (he defeated)

_____ .
(I or me?)

Professor Howard gave Ed more individual help than (he gave)

_____.
      (I or me?)

Muriel is as good a student as _____ (am a good
                                      (I or me?)

student).

This test is both simple and reliable.

A final note: In the *we men-us men* construction, use the pronoun that you would use if the noun *men* (or whatever) were omitted. Examples:

RIGHT: **We** (men) like Tareytons.
RIGHT: Give some high grades to **us** (girls).

The test is simple.

A TIP ON USAGE   Never use *at* after *where*. Just use *where* alone.

UNEDUCATED: Where is the methyl alcohol **at**?

A TIP ON USAGE   Do not use an *is when* or *is where* sentence unless the subject of the sentence specifies a time or place (which is seldom).

POOR STYLE: One type of watch is when quartz crystals vibrate to make the hands move.
IMPROVED STYLE: In one type of watch, quartz crystals vibrate to make the hands move.
POOR STYLE: Duplicate bridge is where every couple plays the same hands.
IMPROVED STYLE: In duplicate bridge every couple plays the same hands.

Exercise 16

PRONOUN CASE FORMS

DIRECTIONS *In the blanks provided, write the proper case form in each of the following sentences.*

1. _____ girls have always loved grammar.
   (us or we?)

2. Between you and _____, Professor Lipmann's popu-
   (I or me?)
   larity is undeserved.

3. If I had known it was _____, I would have answered
   (they or them?)
   the call.

4. Manski is the player _____ I think will make all-
   (who or whom?)
   American.

5. Winning the raffle gave Fred and _____ an extra fifty
   (I or me?)
   dollars each.

6. I wonder if Judy was as angry as _____.
   (I or me?)

7. The door-to-door salesman _____ I had been expecting
   (who or whom?)
   was sick.

8. Everyone except Fyodor and _____ learned to speak
   (I or me?)
   Russian.

9. We were to give the package to _____ arrived
   (whoever or whomever?)
   first.

10. I didn't know _____ the professor meant when he said
    (who or whom?)

    someone was cheating.

11. The dinner prepared by Jane and _____ was for
    (I or me?)

    _____ was not afraid to eat it.
    (whoever or whomever?)

12. Nobody but _____ adults was allowed to attend.
    (us or we?)

13. Was it _____ _____ the policeman
    (they or them?)   *(who or whom?)*

    questioned?

14. It must have been _____ _____ the de-
    (he or him?)   *(who or whom?)*

    tective arrested.

15. _____ do you think will win the game?
    (Who or Whom?)

16. John is a better dancer than _____.
    (I or me?)

17. Cheryl was more seriously injured than _____.
    (I or me?)

18. It was _____ two _____ the coach
    (we or us?)   *(who or whom?)*

    punished.

19. Billy didn't make as good a grade as _____.
    (I or me?)

20. The accident didn't injure John and _____ as much as
    (I or me?)

    _____.
    (she or her?)

21. The proceeds were divided between Tom and _____.
    (I or me?)

22. It was _____ _____ I think deserved
    (she or her?)   *(who or whom?)*

    the award.

23. It was Jack and _____ who led the chase.
    (I or me?)

24. The award was given to both Albert and _____.
    (I or me?)

25. Do you believe that the reprimand was intended for

    _____ sterling characters?
      (us or we?)

26. My Uncle Luigi and _____ shared an apartment.
      (I or me?)

27. Between Luigi and _____ there was some friction.
      (I or me?)

28. Luigi is a man _____ I learned to know well.
      (who or whom?)

29. The woman _____ we both loved went away.
      (who or whom?)

30. _____ found her and brought her back would
      (whoever or whomever?)

    get to keep the apartment.

A TIP ON USAGE In such sentences as 28 and 29 above, many writers simply omit the pronoun with no loss of understanding.

Luigi is a man I learned to know well.
The woman we both loved went away.

A TIP ON USAGE Avoid the past tense *bursted,* just as you avoid *bust* and *busted.* The principal parts of the verb are *burst, burst, burst.*

A MINI-EXERCISE On a separate sheet of paper write five meaningful sentences of at least fifteen words each, using each of these five forms correctly: *lain, laying, lay* (intransitive), *laid,* and *lay* (transitive). The intransitive *lay* will be in the past tense, and the transitive *lay* will be in the present tense.

Lesson
17 FAULTY PRONOUN REFERENCE

A pronoun is usually defined as a word standing for a noun or for a noun substitute, either of which is called the pronoun's **antecedent**. Example:

> Wolves make good parents, for they never abandon their young.

In this sentence the pronoun *they* clearly refers to *wolves*, which is its antecedent. (*Antecedent* is a word that means "going before.") Thus a pronoun has clear meaning only when it refers clearly to another word or word group. Careless writers often use pronouns unclearly, producing the errors known as **ambiguous reference, faulty broad reference,** and **vague reference**.

Ambiguous Reference

The word *ambiguous* means "having two or more possible meanings," and thus ambiguity means one kind of lack of clarity. Pronoun reference is ambiguous when the reader cannot tell which noun the pronoun refers to. For example, note the boldface pronouns in these two sentences:

> Mr. Hoxie and Mr. Grimes are about to split up their partnership. **He** claims **he** cheated **him** by juggling their books.

Neither *he* nor *him* is clear because the reader cannot tell which noun (*Mr. Hoxie* or *Mr. Grimes*) they refer to. Thus the reference is ambiguous. Here is another example:

> Although the motorcycle hit the abutment with considerable force, **it** was not damaged.

The *it* could refer to either *motorcycle* or *abutment*, and thus its reference is ambiguous. For clarity, each of the above sentences would have to be rewritten, as in this example:

The motorcycle, which was not damaged, had hit the abutment with
considerable force.

Remember that what is clear to you in your mind might not be clear on
paper to your reader. Always keep your reader in mind, and reread your
writing (for revision) as though you were the first reader of it, not the
writer.

Faulty Broad Reference

Broad reference occurs when a pronoun (usually *it, this, that,* or *which*)
refers to a whole idea rather than to a single noun, and clear broad
reference is not only acceptable but very common in the best writing.
Example:

> RIGHT: I suspected that some startling new college policy would be
> announced, and **that** is exactly what happened.

The *that* refers to the whole idea of the first clause and thus has broad
reference, but the reference is quite clear and acceptable.

But somtimes broad reference is not clear, and then it is faulty and
unacceptable. Example:

> WRONG: Professor Edwards said that Claire had charged that Lonny
> was cheating. **This** is true.

Does the *this* mean that Claire made the charge or that Lonny was indeed
cheating? The broad reference is faulty. For clarity, the sentence would
have to be rewritten, perhaps like this:

> RIGHT: Professor Edwards mentioned Claire's charge that Lonny
> was cheating, and we all knew the charge to be true.

Here is another example of faulty broad reference:

> WRONG: It is rumored that President Burns expects Dean Chadfire
> to resign. I don't believe **this**.

Again, it is not clear what the writer believes. Be especially careful of
your use of *this* as a broad-reference pronoun and avoid faulty broad
reference by avoiding ambiguity.

Vague Reference

Pronoun reference is vague when there is no apparent antecedent for the pronoun. The reader may be able to make out the intended meaning, but the writing is faulty because of the vagueness that accompanies the pronoun reference. The pronoun *this* is often used vaguely as well as ambiguously. Example:

> WRONG: Playing varsity sports is good for a person. President Eisenhower was a good athlete. There are many examples of **this**.

Examples of what? Of former athletes becoming president? Or perhaps just of former athletes becoming successful? The reference is too vague for the writing to have any value. So again, be careful of your use of *this* in broad reference.

Also, vague reference occurs when a pronoun is forced to refer to an adjective rather than a noun. Examples:

> WRONG: Lorrie is quite amorous, but she keeps **it** under control.
> WRONG: If our teen-ages are irresponsible, a good deal of **it** is due to their parents.

In the first sentence *it* is forced to refer to the adjective *amorous*, and in the second to the adjective *irresponsible*. What happens is that the reader's mind is forced to manufacture the nouns *amorousness* and *irresponsibility* in order to extract meaning. But though understandable, the original sentences are badly written because of the vague reference. For immediate clarity and good style, they need to be recast, perhaps like this:

> RIGHT: If our teen-agers are irresponsible, much of the blame is due to their parents.

Now the faulty reference has vanished.

Vague reference also occurs when a pronoun refers only to an implied noun, not to one actually in the sentence. Again, the meaning can often be ascertained, but the writing is bad because of the faulty reference. Examples:

> WRONG: I like Ireland because **they** are all so friendly.
> WRONG: When I went to a professional football game, I was surprised at how big **they** all are.

Neither *they* has an apparent antecedent, and thus each is vaguely used. In the first sentence *they* is supposed to refer to *the Irish* and in the second to *professional football players*, but without these nouns in the sentences, faulty reference occurs. Such sentences need to be rewritten, perhaps like this:

RIGHT: When I went to a professional football game, I was surprised at how big the players all are.

Just a little thought and carefulness will prevent your using faulty reference.

A TIP ON USAGE *Born* as a past participle is used only with a form of the verb *to be* (*is, was, were, has been*, and so on) as an auxiliary. Example:

RIGHT: Beethoven was **born** in Bonn in 1770.

Borne as a past participle is used with all auxiliaries that do not contain a form of the verb *to be*. Examples:

RIGHT: My mother has **borne** six children.
RIGHT: Kay has **borne** her adversity with dignity.
WRONG: Bob was **borne** on February 29.

A TIP ON USAGE A comma is always used after *for example*, and normally *for example* is preceded by a period or a semicolon or a dash, unless it comes within a sentence as a parenthetic element. Examples:
RIGHT: Joseph cannot do a blessed thing right. For example, he even poured oil in his car's radiator.
RIGHT: We'll take any form of payment—for example, Custer's credit card.
RIGHT: Many foods are misunderstood, Cream, for example, has little food value except calories.

A MINI-EXERCISE Write meaningful sentences using the following pairs of words correctly.

1. a. altogether: _____

_____

_____

b. all together: _____

_____

_____

2. a. hung: _____

_____

_____

b. hanged: _____

_____

_____

3. a. past: _____

_____

_____

b. passed: _____

_____

_____

Exercise 17–A

FAULTY PRONOUN
REFERENCE

DIRECTIONS   *Most of the following sentences have one or more instances
of faulty reference. Strike out the pronouns that are unclearly used,
and in the blanks provided write a clear version of each sentence or
suggest how the reference can be made clear.*

1. We were told that the committee chairperson had charged that Baxter
   was ineligible. This was not true.

   _____

   _____

2. Although the plane's landing gear banged against the car, it was not
   damaged.

   _____

   _____

3. The quarterback was very cautious, and it kept him from passing
   very often.

   _____

   _____

4. We ignored the posted warning that the road ahead was dangerous,
   which was very exciting.

   _____

   _____

5. The driver of the car took great care to shift into the lowest gear.
   This was difficult.

   _____

   _____

6. The police officer reported to the magistrate that the driver had been drinking. That took nerve.

_____

_____

7. Being professor of an endowed chair has many advantages. Professor Thomas is a good example of this.

_____

_____

8. Every student should be able to pass Professor Longueil's courses because he explains it all so clearly.

_____

_____

9. Even the president came to hear the Sierra Club's complaint, which was astounding.

_____

_____

10. Parents today don't seem to understand their children's desire to experiment. They really are just like they were in past ages.

_____

_____

Exercise 17–B

FAULTY PRONOUN
REFERENCE

DIRECTIONS *Most of the following sentences have one or more instances of faulty reference. Strike out the pronouns that are unclearly used, and in the blanks provided write a clear version of each sentence or suggest how the reference can be made clear.*

1. Although the wrestler outweighed the boxer, he clearly won the bout.

   _____

2. The fight promoter claimed that the wrestler stated the boxer had a horseshoe in his glove. This is true.

   _____

3. The boxer asked the wrestler for another bout, but he said that he refused.

   _____

4. The young woman was very healthy, and it kept her looking fit.

   _____

5. I am never happy in Washington, D.C. because they never invite me to parties.

   _____

   _____

6. If the dollar is devalued, most of it is due to inflation.

_____

7. Mikhail told Petrov that he was being sent to Siberia.

_____

8. When the linebacker tackled the quarterback, he was uninjured.

_____

9. My Aunt Tillie was very ugly, and it kept her from getting married.

_____

10. I agreed with the suggestion of my agent that I increase my insurance
    to one million dollars, which was wise.

_____

11. Alice and Phyllis are bilious, and she claims it is because of her bad
    blintzes.

_____

12. Even though the VW ran into the Cadillac at the traffic light, it was
    not even scratched.

_____

13. I hear that Victoria claimed that Albert had promised to build the
    Crystal Palace. Is this true?

_____

_____

14. Many poor students become famous people. Albert Einstein never graduated from high school. There are always exceptions to this.

   _____

   _____

15. I don't like college because they always give me too many exercises to do.

   _____

   _____

16. The salesman and the customer had a dispute. He claimed that he had damaged the merchandise.

   _____

   _____

17. My boss objected to my arriving late for work. This was unnecessary.

   _____

   _____

18. Perry was quite adventuresome, and it caused him to leave home frequently.

   _____

   _____

19. I spent my summer in Italy, and I really liked them.

   _____

   _____

20. We heard that the chief counselor was informed of our practical joke, which caused the president to intervene.

   _____

   _____

Lesson

18 COMPARATIVE CONSTRUCTIONS

A comparison shows a likeness or dissimilarity between two things and usually requires a comparative word or phrase such as *like, than, more than, less than* or the comparative form of an adjective (such as *noisier*) plus *than, as*, and *as . . . as*. Examples:

> Alexander was **greater than** Napoleon.
> Folk dancing is **more** fun **than** ballroom dancing.
> Hod-carrying pays **less than** brick-laying.

However, several kinds of errors are often made in the use of comparative constructions.

Pronoun Forms in Comparative Constructions

Both the subjective form of a pronoun (*I, he, they*, and so on) and the objective form (*me, him, them*, and so on) may follow such comparative words as *than* and *as*. The proper pronoun form should be used according to meaning. Consider this example:

> My father gave the solicitor more money than _____.

The correct form depends on the meaning. The pronoun *I* should be used if my father gave more money than I gave; the pronoun *me* should be used if my father gave more money to the solicitor than he gave to me.

   The correct form for such a sentence can be established by filling out the sentence with a clause that is normally understood. You can test by entering the understood clause in this way:

> My father gave the solicitor more money than (he gave) **me**.
> My father gave the solicitor more money than **I** (gave the solicitor).

Here are some other examples. You can easily select the proper pronoun form when the understood clause is expressed.

111

John is more intelligent than _____. (am intelligent).
(I or me?)

The bull hurt Tom less severely than (it hurt) _____
(I or me?)

The bull hurt Tom less severely than _____ (hurt
(I or me?)

Tom)

Susan is not as likely to fail as _____, (am likely to
(I or me?)

fail).

Godfrey is heavier than _____ (am heavy).
(I or me?)

The test is simple. Always use it when in doubt.

Incomplete Comparisons

Incomplete comparisons should be avoided in college writing. These are constructions in which only one part of the two-part comparison is mentioned. They are common in advertisements:

> El Ropo cigars smoke fresher.
> Bilgewater Cola tastes better.
> Irish Tape is stronger.

A reader may ask, "Fresher than what?" Perhaps such a construction is justifiable in advertising, but it should be avoided in semiformal writing.

Another construction of this sort is the use of *too* and *so* without a completing constituent. Examples:

> POOR STYLE: Horace is just too intelligent.
> POOR STYLE: Helen is so pretty.

Such constructions are acceptable in ordinary informal talk, but they should be avoided in writing. Instead, the construction should be completed:

> GOOD STYLE: Horace is just too intelligent for me to compete with
> him.
> GOOD STYLE: Helen is so pretty that she is swamped with requests
> for dates.

Omitted Comparative Words

Careless writers often omit an important part of a comparative construction, leaving a kind of false comparison. Example:

WRONG: John is more intelligent than any student in the class.

The logical objection to this construction is that, because John is in the class, the sentence says he is more intelligent than himself. The phrase *any other* should be used in such constructions:

RIGHT: John is more intelligent than **any other** student in the class.

Here is a variation of this kind of incorrect comparison:

WRONG: June is kinder than anyone in the class.

June cannot be kinder than herself. The completing word *else* is needed:

RIGHT: June is kinder than anyone **else** in the class.

Now the comparison is complete.

The comparative word *as* is also occasionally improperly omitted in a double comparison. Example:

WRONG: Professor Silver is as learned or perhaps more learned than Professor Stansbury.

As learned as and *more learned than* are the two comparisons. The second *as* is needed:

RIGHT: Professor Silver is as learned **as** or perhaps more learned than Professor Stansbury.

Now each of the two comparisons is complete.

Improper Comparisons

Sometimes a careless writer will create a false comparison by comparing two things that cannot be alike. Example:

WRONG: I wanted to find a tent like the American Indian.

Here a tent is being compared to an Indian. The writer really wanted to compare a tent to an Indian's **tent**. The sentence should have read:

RIGHT: I wanted to find a tent like the American Indian's.

Now the word *tent* is understood after the possessive *Indian's*, and the comparison is proper. Here is another example:

WRONG: My Ford's performance is better than a Chevrolet.

A Ford's performance cannot be compared to a car but only to another car's performance. The sentence should read:

RIGHT: My Ford's performance is better than a Chevrolet's.

Now, with the second *performance* understood after the possessive noun, the comparison is proper.

Here are other examples of such false comparisons:

WRONG: The dialogue on TV shows is generally more authentic than novels.
WRONG: A cat's claws are sharper than a dog.
WRONG: The effect of marihuana is more pleasant than alcohol.

These incorrect sentences may be corrected by converting the terminal nouns to possessives: *novels'* (*dialogue*), *dog's* (*claws*), and *alcohol's* (*effect*).

A TIP ON USAGE Singular verbs are used when phrases that name sums of money or periods of time or measurements are used as subjects. Examples:

RIGHT: Six dollars **is** a lot for such a small book.
RIGHT: Three years **is** a long time to be incarcerated.
RIGHT: Four yards of the material **is** all I need.

A TIP ON USAGE When referring to countable objects, use *number* and *fewer*; when referring to quantities not countable, use *amount* and *less*. Examples:

POOR STYLE: A large **amount** of students matriculated, but **less** than last year.
GOOD STYLE: A large **number** of students matriculated, but **fewer** than last year.

A MINI-EXERCISE In the blanks provided, write the correct forms of the pronouns given below the blanks. For example, the possible forms of *I* are *I, me, my, myself,* and *mine.*

1. The dean was annoyed at _____ interfering with the
   (I)

   school bell.

2. You should check out _____ books to get an answer to
   (them or those?)

   _____ kind of question.
   (that or those?)

3. It was _____ who stole _____ .
   (they)   *(you)*

4. You shouldn't interfere with _____ studying.
   (they)

5. He saw _____ coming and objected to
   (I)

   _____ coming in a catamaran.
   (I)

Exercise 18

COMPARATIVE
CONSTRUCTIONS

DIRECTIONS *In the blanks provided fill in the correct pronoun form,
or indicate what should be done to establish a proper comparative
construction.*

1. Susan is much prettier than _____.

(I or me?)

2. Fogarty runs faster than anyone on the team.

   _____

3. I wanted to write a novel like Thomas Hardy.

   _____

4. My French teacher has an accent like Jean-Pierre Aumont.

   _____

5. Muriel is more intelligent than anyone I know.

   _____

6. Have you ever met anyone more friendly than _____?

(she or her?)

7. Jerry is so free with his money.

   _____

8. He spends more money than any member of his family.

   _____

9. Nobody is more profligate than _____.

(he or him?)

10. Inflation bothered him less than _____.

(I or me?)

11. Her academic ability is like a Phi Beta Kappa.

    _____

12. I like Pepsi because it really tastes better.

_____

13. Remember, Durn detergent gets clothes cleaner!

_____

14. Craig is not as heavy as _____.
    (*I or me?*)

15. A Mercedes's suspension is better than a Porsche.

_____

16. Professor Ford is better informed than any professor at State.

_____

17. Fred told Mable that he likes Carrie better than _____.
    (*she or her?*)

18. John is as intelligent or perhaps even more intelligent than his teachers.

_____

19. I own a Volkswagen just like James.

_____

20. When Allen was on the team, he was harder working than

    _____.
    (*I or me?*)

A MINI-EXERCISE Write meaningful sentences, using the following pair of words correctly.

1. a. less:_____

   _____

   _____

   b. fewer: _____

   _____

   _____

Lesson
19 MISUSED MODIFIER FORMS

A **modifier** is a word or word group that restricts, adds to, or describes another word or word group. Modifiers can be improperly used in various ways. In this lesson we will deal only with errors that result when the wrong form of a modifier is used.

Adjective and Adverb Forms

Adjectives usually modify nouns; adverbs usually modify verbs. Although there are many exceptions, in English an adverb is usually formed by adding *ly* to an adjective. Examples:

> Richard is **careless.** (adjective modifying *Richard*)
> Richard talks **carelessly.** (adverb modifying *talks*)

Confusion of these two forms results in an error known as a **misused modifier.**

No native speaker of English ever uses an adverb to modify a noun. For example, such sentences as these would sound peculiar even to an illiterate:

> WRONG: He is a **quietly** man.
> WRONG: I have a **happily** dog.

But occasionally even a high school graduate will erroneously use an adjective to modify a verb. Here are typical examples:

> WRONG: He talks **careless** about his wife.
> WRONG: He is breathing **normal** again.
> WRONG: She mixes **easy** in a group.
> WRONG: When she returned, she seemed to talk **different**.
> WRONG: He performed his tasks **satisfactory**.
> WRONG: You don't come as **frequent** as you used to.
> WRONG: The faucet is leaking **bad** again.
> WRONG: The train ran **smooth**.

119

Note how much more natural each sentence sounds if the *ly* is added to make an adverb. Adverbs are needed because each of the boldface modifiers is modifying a verb in its sentence.

Adjectives with Linking Verbs

Linking verbs are those that link the subject of a sentence with either a noun that is the same as the subject *(Luis became mayor)* or an adjective that modifies the subject *(Luis became angry.* Such an adjective is called a predicate adjective. An error occurs if an adverb is used in place of a predicate adjective.

The chief linking verbs are *to be, to become, to grow, to seem, to appear, to remain, to act, to stay, to look, to sound, to smell, to feel,* and *to taste.* Some of these may also be used as action verbs, in which case they are modfied by adverbs. Note the difference in meaning between these two sentences:

> Brian looked **hateful**.
> Brian looked **hatefully**.

In the first, *looked* is a linking verb, and *hateful* is a predicate adjective modifying *Brian*. Brian himself appeared hateful to others. In the second, *looked* is an action verb, and *hatefully* is an adverb modifying *looked*. Brian looked at some thing in a hateful way; that is, he was not hateful-looking to others but looked at something as though he hated it.

Occasionally, a person will use an adverb with a linking verb, thus committing the error known as a **misused modifier**. Example:

> WRONG: Rufus felt **boldly** enough to ask Lily for a date.

If the *ly* is dropped from *boldly,* a proper predicate adjective will result.

Bad and *Badly*

But probably over 50 percent of the errors that occur with linking verbs are due to the misuse of *badly* for *bad* after the linking verb *feel.* This is such a common error that it deserves a separate section of its own. The thing to remember is that you always *feel bad.* The following boldface adverbs are misused:

> WRONG: Don't feel **badly** if you fail the first time.
> WRONG: I haven't felt so **badly** about anything since my dog died.

In these sentences the predicate adjective *bad* should be used. Saying *I feel badly* is equivalent to saying *I feel gladly*. The meaning of *feels badly* is that one's sense of touch is so faulty that he can't tell much about an object by feeling it.

When an action verb is involved, however, the proper form to use is the adverb *badly,* as in these examples:

> RIGHT: I drive **badly** when my mother is along.
> RIGHT: Joe was beaten **badly**.

It is only with linking verbs—usually *feel*—that the adjective *bad* is used.

Good and *Well*

The misuse of the adjective *good* for the adverb *well* is also so common that this pair of modifiers deserves a separate section. The main principle to learn is that *good* is an adjective and is never an adverb. Consequently, *good* should not be used to modify a verb. Many people misuse *good* in sentences like the following:

> WRONG: I did **good** in organic chemistry.
> WRONG: After taking Nasaldrin, I can breathe **good** again.
> WRONG: Everything is going **good** for the family business.
> WRONG: My Citroen runs **good** on regular gas.
> WRONG: Acting pays **good** if you can get a job.

In all of these sentences the adjective *good* should be replaced by the adverb *well,* which would modify the verbs *did, breathe,* and so on.

Almost all errors involving *good* and *well* occur in sentences like the above. Otherwise, *good* and *well* take care of themselves and give little trouble.

Double Negatives

Most high school graduates have learned to avoid ordinary double negatives, such as these:

> WRONG: Lucy did**n't** know **nothing** about skiing.
> WRONG: I have**n't** got **no** money.
> WRONG: The accident did**n't** hurt **no one**.

Although common in the speech of the uneducated, such constructions are rare in college writing. Another kind of erroneous double negative, however, is rather commonly used by some college students. This is the double negative involving the words *scarcely* and *hardly*. These two words are already negative; thus if another negative is put with them, a double negative occurs, as in these examples:

WRONG: I have **scarcely no** paper left.
WRONG: I could**n't hardly** see in the fog.

The proper forms are these:

RIGHT: I have **scarcely any** paper left.
RIGHT: I **could hardly** see in the fog.

The *couldn't hardly* error is most common. Be sure to avoid it.

Sure and *Surely; Real* and *Really; Near* and *Nearly*

In college writing you should avoid using the adjective form *sure* when the adverb form *surely* is called for. Examples:

POOR STYLE: We **sure** tried our best.
POOR STYLE: I **sure** sould like to drop calculus.

In informal usage, *sure* is acceptable in such constructions, but in college writing the adverb form *surely* or *certainly* should be used. Example:

GOOD STYLE: I **certainly** would like to drop calculus.

Similarly, *real* should not be used for *really* in college writing. Examples:

POOR STYLE: I feel **real** good today.
POOR STYLE: Our team was **real** sharp last night.

Actually, in college writing it is better to use a word such as *especially* or *quite* rather than *really*. Example:

GOOD STYLE: I feel **especially** good today.

Also avoid using *near* for *nearly*. Examples:

WRONG: I didn't do **near** as well as you on the test.
WRONG: You didn't make **near** as many errors as I did.

The adverb form (modifying the adverb *well* and the adjectival determiner *many*) should be used in such construction. Example:

RIGHT: I didn't do **nearly** as well as you on the test.

Exercise 19

MISUSED MODIFIER FORMS

DIRECTIONS *In the following sentences cross out misused modifiers, and in the blanks provided write the correct form. Some sentences may be correct.*

1. Terry plays quarterback as good as Haden.

   _____

2. The game hadn't hardly started before it set in to rain.

   _____

3. This was sure a mild winter.

   _____

4. Mrs. Kipper is a real generous housemother.

   _____

5. Jane behaves more pleasant than Joan.

   _____

6. When you are a parent, you will think different about children.

   _____

7. I felt badly about not having done good on my final exams.

   _____

8. The coach talked friendly at first, but then he spoke abusive to the linesmen.

   _____

9. Whether you win is not near as important as how you play.

   _____

10. The old Sunbeam mixer runs smoother than the new one.

    _____

11. You can see the distant mountains good with these binoculars.

    _____

12. Oriental music sounds oddly to Westerners.

_____

13. Professor Lester felt uneasily about having to substitute for Professor Gordon.

_____

14. The guide stepped cautiously into the clearing.

_____

15. The proctor stared angrily at me as I tried to see my neighbor's paper.

_____

16. I felt safely enough to volunteer for the night patrol.

_____

17. Chamberlain always played well during the first half.

_____

18. My father was real disturbed at my failure to play good against El Camino.

_____

19. There is scarcely no way to defend against Kermit Washington.

_____

20. It sure is odd how Henry never studies but always does good on tests.

_____

21. Does you car run well enough to enter the drags?

_____

22. The band members thought they had performed as good as could be expected.

_____

23. Only an *A* student feels badly about making a *B*.

_____

24. Professor Elliott hasn't hardly an equal at the school.

_____

25. After losing the game by such a large score, we all felt miserably.

_____

Lesson

20 MISPLACED MODIFIERS

Modifiers are single words, phrases, or clauses that are used to qualify or restrict the meaning of other words. Adjectives and adverbs are the most commonly used modifiers. Coherent writing and effective style require that modifying words, phrases, or clauses must be placed in a sentence where they clearly indicate what other element they modify. A **misplaced modifier** will either make readers pause or stumble or will confuse them about your meaning. Consider this example:

OBSCURED MEANING: Whitman felt that nature offered solace and comfort **instead of organized places of worship**.

The boldface modifier seems to modify the verb *offered*, and makes the sentence mean that nature did not offer places of worship. Placing the modifier correctly shows what the writer really meant to tell.

CLEAR MEANING: Whitman felt that nature, **instead of organized places of worship**, offered solace and comfort.

Now the phrase is properly placed so that it is in apposition (which is like modification) to *nature*, and the reader can proceed smoothly. Consider another example of how a misplaced modifier can confuse the reader.

POOR STYLE: Half of all women over twenty-five years of age have not finished high school **in this country**.

The alert reader is made to speculate whether some of the women have finished high school in other countries, for *in this country* seems to modify *finished*. Now note how proper placement of the modifier clarifies the sentence:

CLEAR STYLE: Half of all women **in this country** over twenty-five years of age have not finished high school.

125

Now the phrase is seen to modify *women* properly. Also the phrase could be placed after *age*, for two prepositional phrases modify *women*.

In dealing with modification in a sentence you need only determine *what goes with what*; you do not need to be able to analyze the grammar. For example, in the poor-style sentence above you need only ask, "What does *in this country* go with?" And the answer is obviously *women*.

Here are some more examples of misplaced modifiers:

POOR STYLE: This course can be completed by anyone who has had beginning chemistry **in six weeks.**

What does *in six weeks* go with? For the sentence to be meaningful, the phrase must go with *completed*:

CLEAR STYLE: This course can be completed **in six weeks** by anyone who has had beginning chemistry.

Now the pattern of modification is crystal clear. Another example:

POOR STYLE: People worry from the time they get up until they go to bed **about many things.**

What does *about many things* go with? Obviously, it goes with *worry*:

CLEAR STYLE: People worry **about many things** from the time they get up until they go to bed.

Now the proper modification is unmistakable. Another example:

POOR STYLE: "Song of Myself" was Whitman's first attempt to rebuke the Puritan tradition, **in which his belief in the wholesomeness of the body is evidenced.**

What does the boldface clause go with? For any sensible meaning, it can go only with "Song of Myself" and thus should be placed next to that title:

CLEAR STYLE: "Song of Myself," **in which his belief in the wholesomeness of the body is evidenced**, was Whitman's first attempt to rebuke the Puritan tradition.

Now readers need not pause or stumble as they read the sentence.

To avoid misplaced modifiers in your writing, you need to reread your paper carefully two or three times. *Good writing cannot be achieved without proofreading and revision.* Remember that easy reading is the result of hard writing!

Exercise 20

MISPLACED MODIFIERS

One two

DIRECTIONS *Most of the following sentences are unclear or absurd because of misplaced modifiers. Rewrite each faulty sentence so that the modifiers in it are clearly placed.*

1. The news came to me about my sister's wedding in a letter.

   _____

2. In bed at night it occurred to me that I was not a good sport suddenly.

   In bed at Night it Suddenly occured to
   Me that

3. I had trouble knowing what I was going to do about it at first.

   _____

4. ~~But~~ I decided that I was going to emulate the coach the next day.

   _____

5. The coach pointed out what I should do quickly.

   _____

6. Half of the naturalized citizens cannot understand the Constitution in this country.

   _____

   _____

127

7. This simple operation can be learned by anyone who has had high school algebra in eight hours.

_____

_____

8. A mother wants to know what her daughter's plans are for her own satisfaction.

_____

_____

9. *The Sound and the Fury* was the second novel William Faulkner published in 1929, in which the decay of an aristocratic Southern family is portrayed.

_____

_____

10. We must confess our wrongdoings to the priest.

_____

_____

11. You can easily prepare to be a diesel engineer for GM in a technical school.

Da gm tecgnical school _____

_____

12. I was afraid to propose to Julie while her mother was present at first.

I was afraid at first _____

_____

13. I was not able to understand just what he intended to do clearly.

_____

_____

14. Bacon pointed out the fallacies that the mind has excellently.

_____

_____

15. There is for sale a fine piano by an elderly lady with carved legs.

   _____

   _____

16. Going to the movies often makes my mother cry.

   _____

   _____

17. The magnificent Rembrandt caught the eye of every artist on the south wall.

   _____

   _____

18. I bought a new hat at a small neighborhood store that cost over $20.00.

   _____

   _____

19. My other hat only cost $15.00.

   _____

   _____

20. In the future a good hat will nearly cost $50.00.

   _____

   _____

A TIP ON USAGE   Avoid the redundant *and etc.*, for *etc.* already contains the meaning of *and*. Nowadays, however, most writers prefer *and so on* or *and so forth* to *etc.*

Lesson

21 DANGLING MODIFIERS

Another type of misplaced modifier is so common and so confusing that it deserves special treatment. It is the **dangling modifier**. A dangling modifier is a verbal phrase—such as *bellowing at the top of his voice*—that is used to begin a sentence, but is not followed directly by the subject of the sentence.

> WRONG: **Driving with furious speed,** the race would surely be won by Campbell.

The sentence is written so that the race seems to be doing the driving, hence the opening phrase dangles. True, the name Campbell is in the sentence, but it is not placed properly for clear modification. To correct and clarify, shift the position of the subject of the sentence.

> RIGHT: **Driving with furious speed.** Campbell pulled far ahead of the other racers.

Campbell is doing the driving and therefore is properly named directly after the introductory verb phrase; also *Campbell* is the subject of the sentence. Some sentences are also opened with introductory prepositional phrases that refer to a person or thing with some sort of common noun, such as *teacher* or *player*, or with a possessive pronoun, such as *his*. In such a sentence the person who is the teacher or player or whatever should be named directly after the phrase and be the subject of the sentence. In another example the introductory prepositional phrase is clearly unattached to the obvious noun and may be said to dangle.

> WRONG: **As an ecdysiast,** we were all wild about Shirley.

Here it seems as though we (plural) are the ecdysiast (singular). The phrase dangles because the real ecdysiast is not named directly after the phrase. To correct, recast the sentence, putting the thing modified in the position of the subject.

RIGHT: **As an ecdysiast,** Shirley was a spectacular success.

Shirley is the ecdysiast and thus is named directly after the phrase. Here are two more examples of dangling modifiers:

WRONG: **As a teacher who is interested in creativity,** we ask your assistance in bringing this conference to the attention of your students.

The *we* is not the teacher; instead, *you* should be named as the teacher:

RIGHT: As a teacher interested in creativity, you will want to inform your students about this conference.

Now the phrase doesn't dangle. Another example:

WRONG: **Having expressed his opinion that the proposal would not work,** a quick vote was taken by the chair person.

Because the vote did not express its opinion, the phrase dangles. The noun *chairperson* should come directly after the phrase:

RIGHT: Having expressed his opinion that the proposal would not work, the chairperson took a quick vote.

Now the pattern of modificiation is clear.
Occasionally, a dangling modifier comes at the end of a sentence. Example:

WRONG: A possible solution was to try studying, **not having done that before**.

The terminal verb phrase has no word to modify and thus it dangles. The sentence needs to be recast:

RIGHT: A possible solution was to try studying, because I had not done that before.

With the verb phrase converted into a clause with the subject *I*, the dangler has vanished.

Exercise 21

DANGLING MODIFIERS

DIRECTIONS *Each of the following sentences contains a dangling modifier. In the blanks provided write a corrected version of each sentence.*

1. By shifting one of the running backs to end, the game was won by
   a small margin.

   The game was won by a small margin,
   by the coach shifting one of the running backs to the end.

2. By ignoring him, the dog quieted down and went away.

   The dog quieted down, by us ignoring
   him.

3. Knowing that we would cheat if we could, a second proctor was
   brought in.

   a second proctor was brought in _by our teacher_ _knowing_
   that if we could, we would cheat

4. Not seeing the following patrol car, the car speeded up.

   The car, not seeing the patrol
   car, speeded up.

5. When depressed, a church is a good place to go.

   a church is a good place to go
   when you are depressed.

6. By applying a tourniquet, the blood stopped flowing.

   The blood stopped flowing from
   the gash, by applying a tourniquet

7. Many marriages take place when three months pregnant.

Many Marriages take place when the bride is three Months pregnant.

8. While answering the first alarm, arsonists set another house afire.

arsonists set another house afire While fireman were answering the first alarm.

9. Being shy by nature, dates often were uncomfortable affairs.

Dates often were uncomfortable affairs for her, being shy by Nature

10. Coming after a severe illness, I was unable to take advantage of the good opportunity.

after a severe illness, I was unable to take advantage of the good up and coming opportunity

11. Although authorized by the chief of police, the demonstrators tried to give the impression that the authorities were against them.

_____

_____

12. Besides being quite educational, children also enjoy "The Saturday Morning Doodlers."

_____

_____

13. The reefers are usually put out when satisfied.

_____

_____

14. By conducting open meetings, the citizens can better judge the effectiveness of the county supervisors.

_____

_____

15. The party was especially exciting, not having been to a country club before.

_____

_____

A TIP ON USAGE   So many people of moderate education now use the construction *everyone . . . their* that it cannot be considered an out-and-out error. However, for choice English use *his, he,* and *him* to refer to *everyone, everybody, nobody,* and so on, and also use *he, him,* and *his* to refer to such singular nouns as *person, student, teacher,* and so on. Such usage is not an offense against women. English just does not have a singular personal pronoun that can refer to both males and females; hence we use *he, him,* and *his* to refer to indefinite or mixed sexes. Examples:

GOOD STYLE: Everyone placed **his** order.
GOOD STYLE: Nobody should forget **his** manners.
GOOD STYLE: If a person persists, **he** will succeed.
GOOD STYLE: When a student is down, no one will help **him**.

The use of *their* in the first two sentences and of *they* and *them* in the last two would create coarse style.

Lesson
22 FAULTY PARALLELISM

Effective parallelism is one of the most powerful devices a good writer can use. **Faulty parallelism** can destroy the smooth flow of ideas, disrupt the balance of the sentence, and confuse the reader. In writing, parallelism means using similar grammatical constructions for similar ideas. Look back at the second sentence above. Notice the parallel structure for the parallel ideas:

> Faulty parallelism can (1) *destroy* . . .
>   (2) *disrupt* . . .
>   (3) and *confuse* . . .

Here are some other examples of effective parallelism:

> **English** and **history** are required subjects. (two nouns in parallel structure)
> The colonel **ranted, raved**, and **pounded** his desk. (three verbs)
> That's a story **that I have heard before, that I expect to hear again,** but **that I wish I had never heard the first time.** (three adjective clauses)
> **Expecting his aunt to drop in** but not **relishing the idea of talking to her,** Henry became increasingly nervous. (two participial phrases)

Many other kinds of ideas can also be put in parallel structure, which means that the ideas joined by a coordinating conjunction are alike in grammatical structure.

Faulty parallelism, a serious error, occurs when the elements joined by a coordinating conjunction are not alike in structure. Here is an example:

> WRONG: **With the cards running right** and **my parents were sure to be asleep already,** I decided to play blackjack late into the night.

137

Here a prepositional phrase and an independent clause are erroneously joined by *and*, producing a disjointed, jarring sentence. Proper parallelism will produce a smooth sentence:

> RIGHT: With **the cards running right** and **my parents sure to be asleep already**, I decided to play blackjack late into the night.

Now *with* has two similar objects (they are called nonfinite predications), and the parallelism is correct.

Here are three more examples of faulty parallelism, with revised sentences:

> WRONG: Several committee members **were at the secret meeting** but not **agreeing to change their votes.**
>
> RIGHT: Several committee members **were at the secret meeting** but **did not agree to change their votes.**
>
> WRONG: I believe **that the United Nations has been fairly effective** but **we can improve it.**
>
> RIGHT: I believe **that the United Nations has been fairly effective** but **that we can improve it.**
>
> WRONG: **To listen to classical music** and **reading great novels** are pastimes too few students enjoy.
>
> RIGHT: **Listening to classical music** and **reading great novels** are pastimes too few students enjoy.

You need not be able to analyze the grammar of a sentence in order to spot faulty parallelism. A simple method of determining whether the grammatical form of similar ideas is parallel is just to jot them down and look at them. Example:

> WRONG: Some favorite winter activities are **skiing, tobogganing, and to sit by the fire.**
>
> ANALYZED: Activities are (1) skiing,
>   (2) tobogganing, and
>   (3) to sit . . .

Clear, *to sit by the fire* has a different form from the other items in the series. The sentence must be revised.

> RIGHT: Some favorite winter activities are **skiing, tobogganing, and sitting by the fire.**

After some practice you will be able to revise in your head without the need to write the phrases.

Exercise 22

FAULTY PARALLELISM

DIRECTIONS *Each of the following sentences has an error in parallel-*
ism, with the elements in faulty parallelism printed in italics. In the
blanks provided write a corrected version of each sentence by placing
the elements in parallel structure.

1. *After debating the amendment for a week* yet *they did not come to an*
agreement, the committee members gave up in disgust.

   after debating the amendment for a week
   they did not yet come to an agreement, so the

2. Professor Billings had *neither a knowledge of human nature* and *he*
did not like people.

   professor billings neither had a knowledg of
   human nature nor, did he like people

3. Professor Billings knew *that we had cheated* and *we were pretending*
that we studied hard.

   professor billing knew that we had

4. Six players *were knocked out on the play* but *not being seriously*
injured.

5. *To read recommended books* and *watching educational TV* are helpful
in gaining a real education.

6. The coach suggested *two hours extra practice* and *that we should go to bed at nine o'clock.*

_____

_____

7. The coach thought the play was *strategic, effective,* and *could be used several times*

_____

_____

8. The registrar notified me *that I was on probation* and *I should repeat two courses.*

_____

_____

9. When we *hunt pheasants, guinea hens,* or *fish for steelheads,* we are helping to destroy wild species.

_____

_____

10. Political activists want *participation in policy making, to have political freedom,* and *giving minorities a chance at education.*

_____

_____

11. *Agriculture uses water not only for irrigation,* but *industry needs great amounts,* too.

_____

_____

12. The story opens with *a male student missing class* and *is so in love he doesn't notice.*

_____

_____

13. The books in my library are all paperbacks, *many costing only $1.00* and *some cost only $.50*.

   _____

   _____

14. The armed forces offer *financial security, opportunity for travel*, and *to learn of people from different cultures*.

   _____

   _____

15. Many children enjoy *reading, playing,* and *to watch television.*

   _____

   _____

Lesson
23 MIXED SENTENCE STRUCTURE

Errors in sentence structure are among the worst that can be made in writing. You have already studied about sentence fragments, comma splices, shifts, faulty reference, misplaced modifiers, dangling modifiers, and faulty parallelism—all of which may be called errors in sentence structure. Also **mixed sentence structure** is a very serious error. Usually, this error occurs when a careless writer starts a sentence with one kind of structure or word choice and then shifts to another, incompatible kind of structure or word choice. Example:

>   WRONG: My first reaction to being placed in a large class frightened me.

The writer shifted structure (or word choice) after the word *class* and produced a foolish and mixed sentence. It was not his reaction that frightened him but the large class. He could have continued with a compatible construction after *class*:

>   RIGHT: My first reaction to being placed in a large class was that I felt frightened.

Or he could have used a different initial construction to suit the last part of the sentence:

>   RIGHT: Being placed in a large class frightened me.

Thoughtlessness and carelessness, more than ignorance, are responsible for mixed sentences being very common in student writing. Careful proofreading for revision will help you avoid mixed sentences.

Here are some other examples of sentences that are hopelessly garbled:

>   WRONG: We need alleys that would have access to trash cans.

143

Is the alley going to collect the garbage? Corrected:

> RIGHT: We need alleys that would give garbage collectors access to trash cans.

Now the right people have access to the cans. Another example:

> WRONG: If this land that is being destroyed by rains, storms, and human beings themselves is not stopped, the people will not survive.

The subject-verb combination of the opening clause is *If this land . . . is not stopped*. How can you stop land? Corrected version:

> RIGHT: If the destruction of land by rains, storms, and human beings themselves is not stopped, the people will not survive.

Now destruction is to be stopped, a possibility. Another example:

> WRONG: Our parents know that when we need money how we will work for it.

The *that* and the *how* cannot both be used to introduce one dependent clause. Corrected versions:

> RIGHT: Our parents know that when we need money we will work for it.
> RIGHT: Our parents know how we will work for money when we need it.

Think about the structure of your sentences, and you will write better ones.

TWO TIPS ON USAGE Do NOT put a comma after *including*, but do put one **before** it. Example:

> RIGHT: We will explain to you the benefits of ownership, including the potential for rental income.

Use *farther* to refer to distance and *further* to refer to degree or quantity.

> RIGHT: Let's not drive any **farther**.
> RIGHT. Loren had nothing **further** to say.

Exercise 23   MIXED SENTENCE STRUCTURE

DIRECTIONS   *The following sentences are mixed in their structure. In the blanks provided write a corrected version of each.*

1. Too many traffic violations ignore the basic vehicle code.

   _____

   _____

2. Eating would be another cause of disease.

   _____

   _____

3. The Good Samaritan is doing good to others.

   _____

   _____

4. For professors to put their jobs in danger for students would take people of conscience.

   _____

   _____

5. The past was very different from what it is now.

   _____

   _____

6. An understanding of the role of a university is one of learning and scholarship.

   _____

   _____

7. Another advertising deception is soap.

_____

_____

8. Another way to study effectively is during your lunch hour.

_____

_____

9. The greatest argument between my parents and me is sex.

_____

_____

10. Another example of wasted tax money is in little-used parks.

_____

_____

11. Another way to kill time is a deck of cards.

_____

_____

12. Faulkner's *The Reivers* was written as a young boy staying in a house of prostitution.

_____

_____

13. My opinion about students insulting the flag should be punished severely.

_____

_____

14. My favorite TV advertisement is Dodge cars.

_____

_____

15. Unless our educational system, being marred by inflated grades, easy courses, and low requirements that make a degree worthless all have to be changed.

_____

_____

A MINI-EXERCISE   Explain the difference in meaning between each of the following pairs of sentences.

1. a. My sister Fern is a public health educator.
   b. My sister, Fern, is a public health educator.
2. a. This quotation is from the earliest printing of the play by John Skott in 1530.
   b. This quotation is from the earliest printing of the play, by John Skott in 1530.

Lesson

24 THE APOSTROPHE
Possessive Nouns

An apostrophe is used to show possession when a noun does the possessing; an apostrophe is NOT used with personal pronouns that already show possession (*whose, its, yours*, and so on).

The Test for Distinguishing the Possessive Construction

There are two ways of showing possession in English: (1) with the so-called **possessive construction**, in which case the person or thing doing the possessing comes in front of the thing possessed (as in *Jim's girl friend*); and (2) with the use of an *of* or *belonging to* phrase. Examples:

Bill's car *or* the car belonging to Bill
the dean's office *or* the office of the dean
several students' cars *or* cars belonging to several students

In our speaking and writing we use the possessive construction more often than the *of* or *belonging to* phrase, but to use the apostrophe correctly we must understand the use of the *of* or *belonging to* phrase.

Any possessive construction can be **transformed** into an *of* or *belonging to* phrase. For example:

Mr. Smith's dog *transforms into* dog belonging to Mr. Smith

If a construction can be transformed into an *of* or *belonging to* phrase, that is 100 percent proof that the original construction is possessive and requires an apostrophe if a noun does the possessing. If a construction cannot be transformed into an *of* or *belonging to* phrase, that is 100 percent proof the construction is not possessive and thus must not have an apostrophe.

For example,

> The Joneses are our neighbors.

will not meaningfully transform into

> WRONG: neighbors belonging to the Joneses and thus an apostrophe must not be used to spell *Joneses*.

The *of* or *belonging to* transformation also tells **where** to place the apostrophe. At the end of the transformation is the **possessing noun**. In the following examples the possessing nouns are italicized:

> the car's transmission = transmission of the *car*
> Betty's blue jeans = blue jeans belonging to *Betty*
> James's dog = dog belonging to *James*
> The Gillises' liquor = liquor belonging to the *Gillises*

You must learn to make such transformations if you want to use the apostrophe correctly.

Where to Place an Apostrophe

In placing an apostrophe correctly, you are not interested in whether the possessing noun is singular or plural; *you are interested only in whether it ends in s or not.* The rule is simple: (1) If the possessing noun (singular or plural) does NOT end in *s*, in the possesssive construction you add an *s* and place an apostrophe BEFORE it. (2) If the possessing noun (singular or plural) does end in *s*, in the possessive construction, regardless of the pronunciation, a correct spelling is simply to put an apostrophe after the *s*. Examples:

> Marys sin = sin belonging to *Mary*

The possessing noun does not end in *s*; therefore, the correct spelling is

> Mary's sin

But in

> Thomas (es) horse = horse belonging to *Thomas*,

the possessing noun ends in *s*; therefore, a correct spelling is

Thomas' horse.

Do not let the pronunciation fool you. **An *es* is never added to make a possessive, but only to make a plural.**

The Apostrophe with Proper Names

There are four possible forms of a name: (1) the singular (*Mr. Smith*); (2) the singular possessive (*Mr. Smith's boat*); (3) the plural (*the Smiths*); and (4) the plural possessive (*the Smiths' neighbors*). Normally, we use only the first two of these forms with first names, but we commonly use all four with last names. You should learn all four forms.

The last three forms of a name (and of a common noun, too) are all pronounced alike, but they are spelled differently because they have different meanings (in the possessive they will have different possessing nouns). Examples:

The Gradys are rich.

will not transform; therefore, the name is only plural and must not take an apostrophe. But

Mr. Gradys car = car belonging to *Mr. Grady*

The possessing noun does not end in *s*; therefore, the correct spelling is

Mr. Grady's car.

If the possessing noun or name ends in *s*, an apostrophe is necessary. Examples:

Mr. Willis (es) car = the car of Mr. Willis

The possessing noun ends in *s*; therefore, the correct spelling is

Mr. Willis' car.

Do not let the pronunciation fool you. This is the singular possesssive. But

The Willises live in Bakersfield.

will not transform; therefore, the name is only plural and must not take an apostrophe.

The Willises cats = the cats of the Willises

The possessing noun ends in *s*; therefore, the correct spelling is

The Willises' cats.

This is the plural possessive.

Also common nouns (*student, counselor, sophomore, books*, and so on) are handled in the possessive in exactly the same way as proper names.

We must make an additional point, though you can ignore it if you wish. The above explanations are all you need in order to handle possessive constructions correctly. But if a possessing noun ends in *s* and *is singular*, an alternate spelling is to add an *'s* to it in the possessive. Example:

Lois (es) cost = coat of *Lois*

The possessing noun ends in *s* and is singular; therefore, an alternate correct spelling is

Lois's coat

Many people prefer this form because it has the proper pronunciation. If a possessing noun ends in *s* and is plural, the *only* correct spelling in the possessive construction is an apostrophe after the *s*. For example,

the Joneses' garden

is the only correct spelling, because *Joneses* is plural.

Possessive Constructions at the End of Sentences

We need to explain one other possesssive construction. Quite frequently a noun at the end of a sentence will be possessive, with the thing owned just being understood. Example:

RIGHT: John's car is newer than Jane's.

Jane's car is understood; the transformation is

car belonging to *Jane*.

Since the possessing noun does not end in *s*, and *'s* is added to make the possessive. One point to remember is that there are only two reasons for adding an *s* to a noun: (1) to make the noun just plural (*two students*), in which case no apostrophe is used; and (2) to make a noun just possessive (*a student's book*), in which case an apostrophe is placed before the *s*. When in doubt, you can ask yourself whether a noun has an *s* added to make it plural or possessive. But remember that after an *s* or *es* is added to make a noun plural, an apostrophe may then be added to make it possessive also, but no other *s* may be added.

When a possessive pronoun is used, *no apostrophe may be added*. Example:

RIGHT: The phonograph is *hers*.

No apostrophe is ever added to *hers, yours, ours,* or *theirs*.

A MINI-EXERCISE   Write meaningful sentences using these two words correctly.

1. affect: _____

_____

_____

_____

2. effect: _____

_____

_____

_____

Exercise 24–A

THE *OF* OR *BELONGING TO* TRANSFORMATION

DIRECTIONS *Some of the following constructions are possessive and can be transformed into of or* belonging to *phrases. Some are not possessive and cannot be transformed. Write out the transformations of those that can be transformed, and tell where the apostrophe should be placed in the possessive construction.*

1. Rays bloodhound: _____

2. the boss (es) secretary: _____

3. two bosses of the company: _____

4. the Harrises neighbors: _____

5. Mr. Harris (es) goat: _____

6. Judas (es) bribe:_____

7. the crocuses in the yard _____

8. the Millers of Denver: _____

9. the Dabbses of Denton:_____

10. the Coreys daughter: _____

11. Mrs. Coreys health:_____

12. Doris (es) complaint: _____

13. two Dorises in our class: _____

14. one sophomores counselor:_____

15. two sophomores counselors: _____

16. my professors advice: _____

17. Dollys dolls: _____

18. two athletes at lunch: _____

19. a lawn mowers blades: _____

20. two lawn mowers owners: _____

Exercise 24–B

THE APOSTROPHE IN POSSESSIVE NOUNS

DIRECTIONS *In the blanks provided write the correct spelling of the word in parentheses beneath the blank.*

1. _____car
   (*James*)

2. the _____ toys
   (*children*)

3. _____ coat
   (*Thomas*)

4. _____ suit
   (*Mr. Thomas*)

5. the _____ mistake
   (*policeman*)

6. the _____roots
   (*tree*)

7. the _____ leaves
   (*trees*)

8. _____niece
   (*Betty*)

9. my _____office
   (*counselor*)

10. its _____ request
    (*owner*)

11. the _____ house
    (*Jones*)

12. Mr._____ house
    (*Jones*)

13. The _____ are waiting.
    (*Jones*)

14. the _____ temper
    (*boss*)

15. _____skirt
    (*Sally*)

16. one_____bicycle
    (*boy*)

17. three_____ bicycles
    (*boy*)

18. three_____ cubs
    (*lioness*)

19. the _____ house
    (*Gillis*)

20. the _____ house
    (*Smith*)

A MINI-EXERCISE   Write intelligent completions of the following first parts of sentences.

1. Bathing beauties are_____

_____

_____

2. Bathing beauties is _____

_____

_____

A MINI-EXERCISE   Discuss the difference in meaning, if any, between the following two sentences.

1. All students are not lazy.
2. Not all students are lazy.

Lesson
25 THE APOSTROPHE
Contractions;
Possessive Pronouns;
Indefinite Pronouns

Contractions

Using the apostrophe in contractions is mostly just a matter of not carelessly omitting the mark. The simple rule is that an apostrophe is placed where one or more letters are omitted from two or more merged words. Examples:

don't	can't	you've
doesn't	I'd	we'll
o'clock	I'll	he'd

We should mention that some instructors ask their students not to use contractions in their themes and term papers. Such a request is entirely justifiable, for contractions are not used in many kinds of formal writing. However, contractions do appear in such good magazines as *Harper's* and *The Atlantic* and in some high-level books. Therefore, other instructors have no objection to them.

Dates written in numerals are also often contracted:

John owns a '74 Mercedes-Benz.
The depth of the Great Depression was reached in '32.

In such contractions, the century meant must be absolutely clear.

The apostrophe is also used to show omitted letters in words that are not true contractions, as in reported dialogue. Example:

"Somethin' funny 'uz goin' on," the hillbilly said.

Possessive Pronouns

Apostrophes are used with pronouns *only* in contractions, *never* in personal possessive pronouns. It is a very low-level error to confuse these constructions:

its (*belonging to it*)	it's (*it is, it has*)
whose (*belonging to whom*)	who's *who is, who has*)
your (*belonging to you*)	you're (*you are*)
their (*belonging to them*)	they're (*they are*)

It is very easy to test for the meaning, and thus the correct spelling, of these pronoun forms.

Other personal possessive pronouns are these:

hers	ours
yours	theirs
his	mine

These words *never* take an apostrophe. Note that you would not use an apostrophe with *his* or *mine*, which are the same kind of words as the other four.

Indefinite Pronouns

The following words (among others that are not used in possessive constructions) are called indefinite pronouns. They behave just like nouns and really should be called noun substitutes:

one	anybody
no one	everybody
anyone	somebody
everyone	nobody
someone	another
other	one another
each other	

These words are often used in possessive constructions, and in such constructions they require apostrophes. The *of* or *belonging to* transformation works with them just as it does with nouns. Examples.

anyones girl friend = girl friend belonging to *anyone*

The possessing noun (indefinite pronoun) does not end in *s*; therefore, the correct spelling is

anyone's girl friend.
nobodys business = business of nobody

The possessing noun does not end in *s*; therefore, the correct spelling is

nobody's business.
each others good will = good will of *each other*

The possessing noun does not end in *s*; therefore, the correct spelling is

each other's good will.

Though some of the indefinite pronouns can be made plural, they very seldom are, except for *one* and *other*. Therefore, you can put it into your mind that any time you hear the *s* sound on one of these words, except *one* and *other*, the spelling will always be *'s*.

The phrases *no one else, somebody else*, and so on are also often used in posssessive constructions. The transformation works:

somebody elses car = car belonging to *somebody else*

The possessing noun does not end in *s*; therefore, the correct spelling is

somebody else's car.

You can put it into your mind that any time you hear the *s* sound on *else*, the spelling will be *'s*.

A MINI-EXERCISE Write six meaningful sentences using the following three pairs of words correctly.

1. a. I'll_____

_____

_____

b. aisle _____

_____

_____

_____

2. a. its _____

_____

_____

_____

b. it's _____

_____

_____

_____

3. a. who's _____

_____

_____

_____

b. whose _____

_____

_____

Exercise 25

THE APOSTROPHE IN CONTRACTIONS, POSSESSIVE PRONOUNS, AND INDEFINITE PRONOUNS

DIRECTIONS   *In the blanks provided write the correct contracted or possessive form of the word or words under the blank.*

1. ____*Don't*____ come.
   (Do not)

2. The book is ___*yours*___ .
   (you)

3. *You're sombody's* friend.
   (You) (somebody)

4. ____*It's*____ mine.
   (It)

5. Love _____ cats.
   (one another)

6. *whose It's* owner?
   (Who) (it)

7. ____*They're*____ coming.
   (They)

8. *That's sombody's* car.
   (That) (somebody else)

9. *It's their* house.
   (It) (they)

10. *who's* been here?
    (Who)

11. *Whose* beer is that?
    (Who)

12. _____ wife came.
    (Each one)

13. ___*you're*___ my friend.
    (You)

14. _____ brother is sick.
    (No one)

15. ___*your*___ friend is here.
    (You)

16. Is that car_____ ?
    (they)

17. _____ car runs.
    (No one else)

18. _____ .
    (It) (her)

19. Several _____ were here.
    (other)

20. _____ grade is high.
    (Nobody)

21. We received ___*ours*___ .
    (we)

22. Let_____ religion alone.
    (one)

23. _____ to blame?
    (Who)

24. _____ house is in the yard.
    (It)

25. _____ a house.
    (It)

26. We shared_____ joy.
    (each other)

27. _____ dog is rabid?
    (Who)

28. _____ you come?
    (Can not)

29. _____ it work?
    (Does not)

30. _____ got it.
    (I have)

A TIP ON USAGE   Many people do not hear the *s* on the plural nouns *scientists, Communists,* and *atheists* and thus write such badly erroneous phrases as *several scientist.* Always put the *s* on these nouns when they are plural, as in

a dozen scientists   a few atheists
many Communists   some German scientists

Similarly, many people leave the *s* off the singular form of the verb *consists,* thus making such an error as

It consist of several pages.

Always put the *s* on the singular, present tense form *consists,* as in

This exam consists of four eassay questions.

The same principle applies to the verbs *resists, insists, exists* and *persists.*

A MINI-EXERCISE   Write meaningful sentences, using these three forms correctly.

1. nobody: _____

_____

_____

_____

2. no body: _____

_____

_____

_____

3. nobody's: _____

_____

_____

_____

Lesson
26 THE APOSTROPHE
Other Possessive Constructions; Plural Spellings

Words Naming Periods of Time

Though, strictly speaking, a period of time or a sum of money cannot possess something else, English uses possessive constructions with nouns that name periods of time and sums of money; and the apostrophe is used in such constructions exactly as it is with other nouns. The *of* transformation works as follows:

one month's vacation = vacation of one *month*.

The "possessing" noun does not end in *s*; therefore the correct spelling is

one month's vacation.

That proves such a construction is possessive. Therefore, though in *two months vacation* the pronunciation is the same, the construction must be possessive, with this transformation:

vacation of two *months*.

Now the "possessing" noun ends in *s*; therefore, in the possessive the correct spelling is

two months' vacation.

There is also a nonpossessive construction in English that means the same thing:

a one-month vacation.

In such a construction the indefinite article *a* and a hyphen in *one-month* must be used. We more often use the possessive construction.

Here are other examples of words naming periods of time in the possessive construction:

an hour's delay	Monday's lesson
two hours' delay	tomorrow's newspaper
the year's end	February's weather

Words Naming Sums of Money

Also, words naming sums of money are used in the possessive construction. The transformation works:

one dollars worth = worth of one *dollar*.

The "possessing" noun does not end in *s*; therefore, the correct spelling is

one dollar's worth.

Though the pronunciation is the same, the word in the plural may also be possessive:

two dollars worth = worth of two *dollars*.

Now the "possessing" noun ends in *s*; therefore, the correct spelling is

two dollars' worth.

Here are other examples of words naming sums of money in the possessive construction:

a nickel's difference	a penny's purchasing power
two cents' worth	a quarter's relative value

Plural Spellings

An apostrophe is sometimes used in spelling some plurals. The plurals of lower-case (small) letters are always spelled with an apostrophe, for otherwise confusion would arise. Examples:

There are four *s's* in Mississippi.
You should form your *a's* more carefully.

Some people use apostrophes in spelling the plurals of capital letters, and some do not. Equally correct:

C's	Cs
four F's	four Fs

Also, some people use apostrophes in spelling the plurals of abbreviations in capital letters, and some do not. Equally correct:

six PhD's	six PhDs
two CPA's	two CPAs

Also some people use apostrophes in spelling the plurals of numerals, and some do not. Equally correct:

four 7's	four 7s
two 0's	two 0s

For the sake of complete clarity, we recommend the use of an apostrophe in spelling the plurals of capital letters, abbreviations, and numerals.

Many authorities on usage use an apostrophe in making the plurals of words used as words and not used for their meaning. Such words are also italicized. Examples.:

There are too many *if's* in your proposal.
But me no *but's*.
Sprinkle your writing with a few *therefore*s and *thus's*.

Words used as words may also be made plural correctly without the use of an apostrophe.

Finally, the ordinary plural of a noun used for its own meaning is *never* spelled with an apostrophe. Example:

WRONG: The cop's discovered several joint's.
RIGHT: The cops discovered several joints.

A TIP ON USAGE   Many people do not hear the *d* on *supposed to* and *used to* and thus make the errors **suppose to* and **use to*. Except in rare constructions that you will probably never use, any time one of these two words if followed by *to*, it requires the *d*. Examples:

RIGHT: You're not supposed to eat fish.
RIGHT: I'm used to hard tests.

Exercise 26

THE APOSTROPHE IN WORDS NAMING PERIODS OF TIME AND SUMS OF MONEY

DIRECTIONS *In the blanks provided write the correct spelling of the word in parentheses beneath the blank.*

1. one _____ difference
   (nickel)

2. three _____ difference
   (cents)

3. _____ newspaper
   (yesterday)

4. an _____ delay
   (hour)

5. three _____ delay
   (hours)

6. one _____ worth
   (dollar)

7. two _____ worth
   (dollars)

8. a _____ glory
   (moment)

9. the _____ end
   (year)

10. five _____ in the hole
    (dollar)

11. one _____ salary
    (month)

12. two _____ vacation
    (month)

13. your two _____ worth
    (cents)

14. _____ lesson
    (today)

15. _____ lesson is
    (Wednesday)

16. harder than _____ .
    (Tuesday)

A MINI-EXERCISE Write one meaningful sentence with the plural of a lowercase letter and of a capital letter. Write another intelligent sentence with the plural of an abbreviation and also the plural of a word used as a word.

1. _____

_____

_____

2. _____

_____

A MINI-EXERCISE: Write four intelligent sentences, using the following pairs of words correctly.

1. a. your: _____

_____

_____

  b. you're: _____

_____

_____

2. a. except: _____

_____

_____

  b. accept: _____

_____

_____

Lesson

27 CAPITALIZATION

Capitalization is probably the least important aspect of spelling, and, like all aspects of spelling, it is wholly conventional. Rules exist, but they are arbitary. Actually, practice in capitalization varies rather widely among good writers of English. All careful writers capitalize the first word of a sentence, the pronoun *I*, and proper names. But thereafter writers diverge in their practices. For example, both of the following spellings are frequently used, and thus either is correct:

Protestant	protestant
Catholic	catholic
the Romantic Age	the romantic age
The Nineteenth Century	the nineteenth century
Negro	negro
the Senator	the senator
the Great Depression	the great depression
the British Army	the British army
Civil Service	civil service
Communism	communism
School Board	school board
the Student Body	the student body
the Federal Government	the federal government

Many more examples could be listed, but this list will give you an idea of the latitude that is exercised in capitalization.

The following rules of capitalization are more or less standard. You can follow them with assurance, but on occasion you might purposefully break one of the rules without necessarily being incorrect.

Rule 1 *Capitalize the first and last words and all other words except articles, prepositions, and coordinating conjunctions in a* **title** *or* **chapter heading**:

TITLE OF A BOOK: *The Rise and Fall of the Third Reich*
TITLE OF AN ESSAY: "Sound and Sense in Poetry"
CHAPTER HEADING: The Status of Women in the Nineteenth Century

171

Rule 2   *Capitalize all proper names and adjectives formed from proper names:*

Asian	French
Caucasian	Swedish
Georgian	Oriental
English	Platonism

Rule 3   *Capitalize reference to the Deity, the names of divine books of all religions, and references to specific religions or religious sects:*

Baptist	Koran
Bible	our Lord
Book of Mormom	New Testament
Christ	Seventh Day Adventist
God	the Trinity
Jewish	the Upanishads
Apollo	Zeus

Rule 4   *Capitalize the titles of relative when used with the person's name and when the person is addressed directly, but do not capitalize such names when used with the pronoun* **my**:

Aunt Margaret
Grandfather Hughes
"Oh, Mother, can you come here?"
My mother is a schoolteacher.

Rule 5   *Capitalize the titles of officials when a specific individual is meant, whether or not the person's name is included:*

Mayor Karlin	the Lieutenant
Vice-President Smith	the Mayor
Colonel Wetzler	the Board Chairman
Dean Merson	the Dean

Rule 6   *Capitalize the days of the week and the months of the year but not the seasons:*

Tuesday	summer
February	autumn

Rule 7 *Capitalize the names of streets, avenues, parks, rivers, mountains, cities, states, provinces, nations, continents, oceans, lakes and specific geographical regions, but do not capitalize the names of directions:*

First Street	Africa
Central Park	the Midwest
the Red River	the South
the Congo	the Western Hemisphere
the North Pole	the Central Plains
Bear Mountain	Lake Tahoe
Alaska	the Far East (an area)
British Columbia	east (a direction)
the East Coast	south

Rule 8 *Capitalize the names of buildings:*

the Bijou Theater	the Capitol
the First Baptist Church	the Sill Building
the Humanities Building	the Empire State Building

Rule 9 *Capitalize the names of private organizations:*

Kiwanis	the American Legion
the Lions Club	the Renegade Knights

Rule 10 *Capitalize the names of governmental organizations:*

the Veterans Administration	the United States Navy
Congress	the Peace Corps
the Senate	the Cabinet

Rule 11 *Capitalize the names of historical documents, events, and periods or eras:*

the Constitution	the Battle of Midway
the Bill of Rights	the Diet of Worms
the Missouri Compromise	the Middle Ages
World War I	the Renaissance

Rule 12 *Capitalize the names of specific school courses:* •

Senior Problems	American Literature
History 3A	Advanced Organic Chemistry

Rule 13 *Capitalize brand names but not the name of the product:*

a Ford car	*Camay soap*
Goodyear tires	*Mum deodorant*

Rule 14 *Do NOT capitalize the names of foods, games, diseases, occupations, animals, plants, musical instruments, or general subject-matter areas (unless they are proper names, such as English):*

spaghetti	engineer	maple
golf	doctor	piano
cancer	robin	history

A TIP ON USAGE   Use a possessive pronoun *(my, his,* and so on), not an objective pronoun *(me, him,* and so on), before an *ing* form of a verb when reference is just to one aspect of a person and not the whole person. Example:

RIGHT: Professor Thiroux objected to **my** talking.

The Professor did not object to *me,* but to the *talking,* which was mine. More examples:

RIGHT: **His** (not *him*) coming and going disturbed me. (The *coming and going* is his. He as a whole did not disturb me, but only his coming and going.)

RIGHT: He saw **me** arriving, but he did not like **my** arriving in a jeep. (In the first clause he saw *me* as a whole, but in the second it is only my *arriving in a jeep* that he did not like.)

A MINI-EXERCISE   Write meaningful sentences, using these two forms correctly.

1. everyone: _____

_____

_____

_____

2. every one: _____

_____

_____

_____

Exercise 27

CAPITALIZATION

DIRECTIONS *Change the lowercase letters to capital letters when necessary in the following sentences.*

1. After talking to dean wattron, I decided to take organic chemistry 3A and a course in physics.
2. We went to the federal office building, which is on ninth avenue near the uptown theater.
3. along the east coast one sees an unusually large number of mercedes-benz automobiles.
4. Being in the peace corps is as satisfying as being in the united states army.
5. To cure my malaria dr. yaussy prescribed dolin tablets, which are made by the pfizer company.
6. I have biology 4B in the art building and english in the science building.
7. My father is a christian scientist, but my aunt, who lives in turkey, is a mohammedan.
8. My uncle tony will worship god only in the assembly of god church.
9. I favor platonic philosophy because it is nonmaterialistic.
10. The course called freshman composition is sometimes a course in issues of the day.
11. In the orient there are 900 million buddhists and 100 million taoists.
12. The national football league opens its season in the fall and plays until midwinter.
13. The cascade mountains in eastern washington are a part of the coast range.
14. Many lawyers think the bill of rights is the most important part of the constitution.
15. In the second world war the united service organizations were the soldier's second home.
16. The second chapter of *introduction to archaeology* is entitled "egyptian artifacts."
17. The poem entitled "to an athlete dying young," which opens with the line "the time you won your town the race," appears in a. e. housman's *a shropshire lad.*
18. The veterans of foreign wars is an organization that complements the american legion.

19. The midwest has a continental climate, being colder than the east in winter and hotter in summer.
20. Members of the house of representatives are called members of congress, and members of the upper chamber are called senators.
21. The treaty of utrecht ended the war of the spanish succession.
22. I like to wash in the pacific ocean with camay soap.
23. The rotary club meets every tuesday in the matador room of the folsom building.
24. Most people wanted the new state college to be located on white wolf grade.
25. my mother attended humboldt state college in arcata, california.
26. the seventh day adventists believe in a literal interpretation of the new testament.
27. I interviewed major general brooks, commandant of the fourth army corps.
28. The battle of midway was the turning point in the war against japan.
29. The grand teton national park is near the jackson hole country of wyoming.
30. During and after the civil war many southerners had to live in caves.

A MINI-EXERCISE   On a separate piece of paper write two intelligent sentences, using the forms *maybe* and *may be*.

A TIP ON USAGE   The proper expression is *take it for granted*. The boner *take it for granite* causes knowledgeable people to laugh in derision at its user.

Lesson

28 THE USE OF THE HYPHEN

Like the apostrophe, the hyphen is a mark used in spelling, NOT in punctuation. The hyphen should not be confused with the dash, which is longer and which is a mark of punctuation. Following are the rules for use of the hyphen:

Rule 1 *In dividing a word at the end of a line of script, typewriting, or print, divide between syllables and indicate division with a hyphen. If you are uncertain where to divide a word, check any good dictionary for the proper syllabication.*

Rule 2 *Hyphenate compound numbers and fractions:*

twenty-two	one-half
thirty-four	a half
one hundred and sixty-three	three-fourths
fifty-fifth	sixty-three and one-third

Rule 3 *Hyphenate compound nouns when hyphenation contributes to clarity:*

close-up	cross-country
tie-ups	Mr. So-and-so
son-in-law	passer-by
decision-maker	half-century

Rule 4 *Use a hyphen to separate a prefix when the first letter of the root and the last letter of the prefix are the same vowel:*

anti-industrial	re-echo
de-emphasize	semi-independent
pre-existent	ultra-articulate

Rule 5 *Use a hyphen to separate a prefix from a root that is normally capitalized:*

crypto-Communist   post-Reconstruction
mid-August   pre-Freudian
non-Christian   un-American

Rule 6 *Use a hyphen to separate a prefix when the lack of a hyphen might be ambiguous:*

co-op *and* coop   re-sort *and* resort
re-collect *and* recollect   re-cover *and* recover
re-count *and* recount   re-create *and* recreate

Rule 7 *Hyphenate two or more words that serve a single adjectival in front of a noun:*

cradle-to-grave needs
two-fisted gesture
double-parked automobile
all-too-human attributes
law-school faculty
civil-rights battle
an eight-year-old girl
dirty-gray water
all eighth- and ninth-grade pupils
all first-, second- and third-ranked candidates
air- or waterproof clothes

A TIP ON USAGE For choice English, use the phrase *different from* rather than *different than*. Examples:

PREFERRED STYLE: Your text is **different from** mine.
PREFERRED STYLE: Times are **different from** what they used to be.

Different than is not an error, but it is not good style. Note that you would say "This differs from mine," not the incorrect "This differs than mine."

Exercise 28

THE USE OF THE HYPHEN

DIRECTIONS *Choose the words in the following sentences that should be hyphenated, and rewrite them in the spaces provided.*

1. In the pre Christian era, an up to date philosophy usually implied magic.

   _____

2. Alaska, the forty ninth state, still has a frontier like atmosphere.

   _____

3. His I can't tolerate you attitude upset my preexisting plans.

   _____

4. Her peaches and cream complexion aroused an all but murderous jealousy in her junior high sister.

   _____

5. A manufactured in Syria label was found on twenty two items.

   _____

6. Her let me help attitude belied her unchristian philosophy.

   _____

7. A cross country race was organized by the Chase and Catch Society.

   _____

8. My mother in law's house has a come up to see me sometime look.

   _____

9. A nine or ten mile race is an all but impossible task for a horse.

   _____

10. The peace now petition was signed by thirty six tenth grade pupils.

   _____

11. A semiindependent Congo was Objukma's long held dream.

_____

12. Evel Knievel is the epitome of the do or die daredevil.

_____

13. Custom built furniture can be built by an out of work craftsman.

_____

14. The high school will deemphasize ninth and tenth grade sports.

_____

15. Resort the IBM cards so we can recreate a true to life situation.

_____

16. For the twenty seventh straight time, Frisbie scored a hard to hit birdie.

_____

17. Sixty six and one third yards were marked off against the boiling mad Cougars.

_____

18. An indistinctly marked off area was set aside for first and second grade pupils.

_____

19. The twelve thousand dollars a year teacher had a fifty thousand dollar education.

_____

20. By mid July the company had experienced a ten years' growth.

_____

Lesson

29 DASHES; PARENTHESES; COLONS

Dashes

The dash should not be used as a mark of punctuation to end a sentence; instead it has uses somewhat similar to those of commas. The chief difference between a dash and a comma is that the dash indicates a greater emphasis is to be placed on the parenthetical word or expression. On the typewriter, two hyphens (--) make a dash, even though there is a small space between the hyphens. The dash should not be confused with the hyphen, which is a mark used in spelling, not punctuation. On the typewriter, the hyphen is only half as long as the dash. Do not use a hyphen (-) as a dash (—); also do not use the underlining mark (_) as a dash.

1. Use dashes to set off a parenthetic expression (1) that is especially emphatic or (2) that has commas of its own or (3) that is a sentence construction by itself. Examples:

RIGHT: The world's most important person—me—is not sufficiently recognized.

RIGHT: Our minister—even our beloved, incorruptible minister—succumbed to the pressures of the Society for the Advancement of True and Sacred Democratic Principles.

RIGHT: The threatening mob—thrill-seekers, bums, criminals, extremists, dupes—was dispersed with tear gas.

RIGHT: My yearning for peace and quiet—I would not have said this a few years ago—now surpasses my yearning for money.

Note that there is no space either before or after a dash.

2. Use a dash to set off a terminal construction that has the tone of a delayed afterthought. Examples:

RIGHT: In the popular mind, astronomy and astrology are still often confused—like religion and occultism.

181

RIGHT. After extensive research, Professor Sackett reported that the lower a family's income, the larger percentage of it they spend on food—hardly a novel discovery.

Note that a comma instead of a dash would not give enough emphasis to produce the same effect in these sentences.

3. A dash may be used to introduce an explanation or explanatory series. Normally, a colon is used in this structural position; a dash represents a more informal usage. Examples:

RIGHT: One alternative to war is uncomplex—surrender.

RIGHT: The first moon colony was plagued with difficulties—mechanical breakdowns, sudden psychological aberrations, showers of meteorites, and interruption of radio communication with earth.

Parentheses

1. Use parentheses to set off an internal or terminal element that has a tone of isolation or that is intended as an aside rather than as an emphatic addition to the sentence. Examples:

RIGHT: In 1921 Trinity College (later to become Duke University) moved its campus to Durham, North Carolina.

RIGHT: Atomic fission was first demonstrated in 1938 (a year before World War II began).

Note that the period comes after the parenthesis mark; a period comes within the parenthesis mark only when a whole sentence is enclosed in parentheses.

2. Use parentheses to enclose numerals or letters used to number elements in a series. Example:

RIGHT: Use dashes to set off a parenthetic expression (1) that is especially emphatic or (2) that has several commas of its own or (3) that is a sentence construction by itself.

3. Use parentheses to enclose cross-references and other information inserted parenthetically in a sentence. Example:

RIGHT: Epicureanism is the system of moderate and refined hedomism (see AXIOLOGY) taught by Epicurus (342–270 B.C.)

There are, of course, some instances in which either commas or dashes are acceptable and in which either dashes or parentheses are acceptable. Writers must learn for themselves how to choose between them.

Colons

1. A colon is used after the saluation in a formal letter; a comma in this position means more informality. Examples:

Dear Professor Lockford: (formal)
Dear Professor Lockford, (indication of friendly acquaintance)

2. A colon is used after an introductory label. Examples:

colloquial: It's me.
formal: It's I.

3. A colon is used to introduce a series following a noun that establishes the series. Examples:

> Professor Whitehead made three important points: (1) that religion, like science, must be prepared to change and grow; (2) that the idea of the brotherhood of man rather than of the chosen people must underlie all sound religion; and (3) that a balance must be drawn between the need for a learned clergy and the need for each individual to find his own faith.
> Joyce was eclectic in her choice of college subjects: literature, anthropology, physics, comparative religions, ancient history, wine making, and typing.

Note the use of parentheses and semicolons in the first example.

4. A colon may be used to introduce a sentence that functions as an explanation of, rather than a continuation of, the preceding sentence. The sentence following the colon may begin with a small or capital letter, according to individual preference. Examples:

> Teaching is not a 9:00 to 3:00, nine-months-a-year job: all good teachers spend hours a day every day of the year preparing themselves for their work.
> Enlightened school boards and administrations should insist that all teachers take a sabbatical leave every seventh year: Teachers cannot stave off staleness unless they undergo massive intellectual refreshment every few years.

This is a sophisticated use of the colon that you can ignore if you want to.

5. A colon may be used to introduce a direct quotation, especially a formal or long one. Example:

> In protesting the Puritan emphasis on continual busy-ness, Thoreau said: "Why should we live with such hurry and waste of life? We are determined to be starved before we are hungry. We say that a stitch in time saves nine, and so they take a thousand stitches today to save nine tomorrow. As for *work*, we haven't any of any consequence."

In ordinary quotations, a comma is used instead of a colon.

Do not use a colon or any other mark of punctuation after the connective *such as*.

A TIP ON USAGE Usage varies in handling numerals and spelled-out numbers, but you will be safe if you spell out numbers from zero to twelve and use numerals (figures) from 13 up. Example:

> One count showed that Casey won the election by nine votes, but another showed that he lost by 39.

Never begin a sentence with a numeral. Example:

> RIGHT: Eight hundred and thirty-three Democrats registered.

Always use numerals for dates, street and room numbers, pages of a book, percentages and decimals, hours of the day when used with A.M. or P.M., numbers involving dollars and cents, and a series of numbers. Examples of correct usage:

> I went to room 432 at the Essex Hotel at 322 Westlake Street at 9:22 A.M. and paid $4.50 to interview 8 percent of the occupants. On page 9 I found that the daily results were 66, 7, 101, 2, 13, and 10 and that on Tuesday there was a remainder of .0432.

A MINI-EXERCISE Punctuate the following two sentences correctly.

1. Steve was not in however yet the caller persisted in his efforts to see him.
2. Antibodies to fight infection in the body exist in countless numbers however many people still contact diseases.

Exercise 29

DASHES AND PARENTHESES

DIRECTIONS *Enter dashes or parentheses where needed in the following sentences. If any commas are needed, enter them also.*

1. If you fail your math course I'm really serious I will cut off your allowance.
2. The items for sale a Coleman stove a lantern two sleeping bags and a tent were all in first-class condition.
3. Professor Sam McCall even good old Sam himself was booed by the students.
4. The best way to stop a quarrel I learned this at age eight is to pretend to agree with your adversary.
5. Several countries participate in the European Common Market Italy, Belgium France and Germany.
6. Eggs bacon cheese milk all of these foods are high in cholesterol.
7. I enlisted in the navy in 1940 that was also the year I dropped out of college and stayed in through World War II.
8. The Theory of Forms see also PLATONISM is a philosophy that maintains that only ideas have reality.
9. Only one course was open to us surrender.
10. All sorts of soft drinks Coca-Cola Pepsi-Cola Orange Crush Dr. Pepper and others were available.
11. Not a single creature not even a mouse was heard in the stillness of the house.
12. Several sects the Methodists the Baptists and the Presbyterians for instance boycotted the convention.
13. I ordered frogs' legs I much prefer them to steak at the French restaurant.
14. There was only one thing to do study till dawn.
15. The mediators I think I am safe in saying this were partisan.
16. One vehicle the motorcycle is responsible for most noise pollution.
17. He slowly stalked out of the room like an insulted Indian.
18. And who volunteered Professor Benston himself.
19. Judge Carswell later to be nominated for the Supreme Court had ruled against civil rights.
20. His birth and death dates 1660–1685 coincided with the reign of Charles II.

A MINI-EXERCISE Write two meaningful sentences, using colons correctly.

1. _____

   _____

   _____

   _____

2. _____

   _____

   _____

   _____

A MINI-EXERCISE On the basis of the following sentence, how many kinds of white-light coronagraphs do you suppose exist? Why?

The white-light coronagraph, designed by Robert MacQueen, is inexpensive to manufacture.

Lesson
30 QUOTATION MARKS AND UNDERLINING

Quotation Marks

The main use of quotation marks, of course, is to enclose direct quotations. However, there are several other conventional uses that every writer needs to know.

1. Use quotation marks to enclose direct quotations. Regardless of the length of a direct quotation, quotation marks are used only at the beginning and end unless there is an interruption or unless the quoted material consists of more than one paragraph, in which case quotation marks are not used at the end of a paragraph (except, of course, the last) but are used at the beginning of each new paragraph.

2. Use quotation marks to enclose titles of short or minor literary works: short stories, short poems, short plays, chapters from books, articles, essays, songs, and speeches. Examples of correct usage:

"The Fall of the House of Usher" is perhaps Poe's best story.
"Where Are the Snows of Yesteryear?" is a sonnet by Villon.
The forty-second chapter of <u>Moby Dick</u> is "The Whiteness of the Whale."
Did you read John Snow's article "Convergent Evolution"?

Note in the third example that the title of a book is underlined (italicized in print; see below, UNDERLINING).

3. Words used as words may be enclosed in quotation marks, or they may be underlined (italicized), according to preference. Examples of correct usage:

The word "jabberwocky" was coined by Lewis Carroll.
Is the word <u>scuttlebutt</u> slang?

4. Use quotation marks to enclose a word used in an unusual or ironic sense:

Hollywood stars feel they must belong to the "right set."

Here the writer means that the stars' conception of the right set is not his conception.

5. Use single quotation marks to enclose a unit within a unit already enclosed in quotation marks. Example:

Professor Fleenor's review calls the story "an ingenious adaptation of Poe's 'Cask of Amontillado.'"

Note that the period comes within both the single and the double quotation marks.

6. Avoid enclosing slang words and phrases in quotation marks as an apology for their use.

POOR USAGE: The heroine of the novel is a "floozy" who likes to "paint the town red."

If you feel a word or phrase is worth using, use it without apology. Note the difference between this questionable use of quotation marks and their legitimate use in number 4 above.

7. Do not use quotation marks to enclose a title used as a heading. When the title of an essay is mentioned within written discourse, it is enclosed in quotation marks, but when it is used as a heading it is not so enclosed. Of course, a title may have within it a unit enclosed in quotation marks. Examples:

TITLE AS HEADING: Loopholes in the Usury Laws
TITLE AS HEADING: A Study of Milton's "On His Blindness"

Quotation Marks and Other Punctuation

Quotation marks are used to enclose not only direct quotations but also certain other kinds of units that appear within written discourse. In general, these units, explained below, are not parenthetic but are integral parts of the sentence structure.

A mark of punctuation that belongs to an enclosed unit is placed within the quotation marks, as in this example:

Ruth asked, "Have you read *As I Lay Dying?*"

Note that a period is not used in addition to the question mark, even though the whole sentence is a statement rather than a question.

A comma or period is placed within quotation marks even when it is not a part of the enclosed unit. Example:

"Let sleeping dogs lie," a proverb from *Poor Richard's Almanac*, should have been "let sleeping babies lie."

The comma and the period after *lie* and *lie* are not parts of the quoted units, but they are still placed within the quotation marks.

Other marks of punctuation are put outside the quotation marks when they do not belong to the enclosed unit, as in these examples. Note that the quoted units are themselves questions.

Do you really think "the better part of valor is discretion"?
Why did she say, "Don't read *Sanctuary*"?

Underlining

In print, italics (*words printed like these in parentheses*) are used to distinguish certain kinds of written units from the main body of discourse. In longhand or typing, italics are designated by **underlining**.

1. The titles of books, plays, long poems, magazines, newspapers, musical compositions, and works of art and the names of ships and aircraft are underlined in college writing. The whole title, not just individual words, should be underlined. Examples of correct usage:

Faulkner's last novel was The Reivers.
W. Somerset Maugham's most famous play is The Circle.
The New Yorker is one of American's most sophisticated magazines.
The Mona Lisa was brought to America for display.

2. Foreign words and phrases that have not been fully anglicized are underlined. Examples:

The sine qua non of astrological forecasting is ambiguity.
The raison d'être for his becoming a celebrity is unknown.

3. Words used as words may be underlined or enclosed in quotation marks, according to preference. Example of correct usage:

The word autointoxication was once important in medical terminology.

James, where John had had <u>had had</u>, had had <u>had</u>; <u>had had</u> had
had the teacher's approval.
Was his use of "tomato" slang?

A TIP ON USAGE Permissible abbreviations are *Dr., Mr., Mrs., Ms.,
Sr., Jr.*; college degrees, such as *Ph.D., M.A.,* and *A.B.*; and governmental agencies and established organizations and foundations, such
as *UNESCO, CIA,* and *UMW.*

Normally, you should not abbreviate titles (such as *Prof.* and
Rev.); first names (such as *Benj.* and *Jas.*); states and countries (such
as *Ala.* and *Can.*); days of the week and months of the year such as
Tues. and *Jan.*); streets and avenues (*St.* and *Ave.*); *Xmas;* weights
and measures (such as *lb., in.,* and *yd.*); and common words (such as
yrs. and *govt.*). Avoid the ampersand (&) unless it is part of a
company's name.

A MINI-EXERCISE Write two meaningful sentences, using the following two constructions correctly. Use each construction in the
second half of each sentence.

1. Henry and I: _____

   _____

   _____

2. Henry and me: _____

   _____

   _____

A TIP ON USAGE Use *beside* to mean "at the side of" and *besides* to
mean "in addition to" or "except."

WRONG: We brought everything **beside** beer.
RIGHT: **Besides** beer, we need pot.
RIGHT: The keg is **beside** the pickup.

A MINI-EXERCISE Discuss what is illogical about the construction
of these sentences:

1. Puppy love is when you are attracted to someone but have no
   deep affection for that person.
2. Organic farming is where you do not use any commercially produced fertilizer to grow your crops.

Exercise 30

QUOTATION MARKS AND UNDERLINING

DIRECTIONS *Write five intelligent sentences of fifteen or more words each using these constructions in this order: (1) the title of a book; (2) the title of a short story; (3) the Latin words meaning, "It does not follow" (your teacher will tell you what they are); (4) two words used as words and not for their meaning; and (5) the title of a short poem within a brief direct quotation (which you make up).*

1. _____

_____

_____

_____

2. _____

_____

_____

_____

3. _____

_____

_____

_____

4. _____

   _____

   _____

   _____

5. _____

   _____

   _____

   _____

A MINI-EXERCISE   Write meaningful sentences using the following
pair of words correctly.

1. a. everyday: _____

   _____

   _____

   _____

   b. every day: _____

   _____

   _____

   _____

Lesson

31 COLLOQUIALISMS; SLANG; NONSTANDARD EXPRESSIONS

Errors in usage are sometimes made in the **social level** of words and phrases. These errors may be considered under three headings: **colloquialisms, slang,** and **nonstandard expressions.**

Colloquialisms

A colloquialism is a word or expression on an informal level. The word *colloquial* comes from a Latin term meaning "conversation"; it has nothing to do with a particular locale or region. Orginally, a colloquialism was judged suitable for conversation but not for writing. Now it is just an expression suitable for informal writing or conversation.

A colloquialism, then, is not an error in and of itself. Only when it is **out of place** (that is, when it is used in formal or semiformal writing) can it be considered an error. But it is not always easy to tell when an expression is out of place, for there are levels of colloquialisms. For example, the phrase *join up* is colloquial for *enlist,* but it is certainly a good expression that might be used in almost any writing. On the other hand, we have such a colloquial expression as *kind of* for *quite* or *rather,* as in

> I'm kind of tired.
> I'm rather tired.

Most people would recognize *kind of* as too informal for any usage except the most informal conversation. It would be considered an error in college writing. Thus only low-level colloquialisms can be judged as errors.

193

Here are some low-level colloquialisms that should be avoided. The improper colloquialism in each sentence is italicized. A more appropriate expression is placed in parentheses after each sentence.

Your recipe was *real* good. (quite)
I'll see you *inside of* a week. (within)
He didn't know *but what* the other car would stop. (but that)
Do you *reckon* it will rain? (suppose)
He *got* sick at the last minute. (became)
The murderer was *hung* at dawn. (hanged)
Most everybody had his assignment completed. (almost)
She is *kind of* pretty. (rather)
It looks *like* it might rain. (as if)
Lots of people sleep only five hours a night. (many)
The crowd was *nowhere near as* large as expected. (not so)
He was *plenty* worried. (quite)
I *put in* much time on the project. (spent)
The teacher *put across* his idea well. (expressed)
I'm *awfully* sorry you can't come. (very)
I have *around* twenty-five snakes in my collection. (about)
I tried to *show up* Tom when he pretended to be the best player.
   (expose)
She *sure* is intelligent. (surely)
Try and come on time. (try to)
I was *mighty* worried. (very)
Be *sure and* vote. (sure to)
I'm *terribly* concerned about your health. (quite)

The colloquial expressions italicized in these sentences are not **bad** language in the sense that they are incorrect. They are just **inappropriate** in all but the most informal conversation. In that kind of language they are perfectly acceptable.

Slang

Although everybody knows what slang is, it is hard to define. In general, it is unconventional language invented for specific occasions or uses. Most slang terms are short-lived, but slang itself is in widespread use in ordinary conversation. Often the line between slang and colloquialisms is not very clear.

   Like colloquialisms, slang is bad language only when **inappropriately** used. Some slang terms are so vigorous and expressive that they find effective use in good writing in such magazines as *Harper's* and *The*

Atlantic. For example, the following slang terms have appeared in these magazines: *stashed away, flopped, dishes up, payoff, spilling the beans,* and *gift of gab.* Other slang expressions are so weak and ineffective that they really should be avoided in any writing. For example, *guys and gals, right on, cool it,* and *zonked* would probably be inappropriate in any college writing. In a middle range are such expressions as *bomb, clobber, gizmo goof off, all that jazz, the greatest,* and *sweat out.*

In general, you should be wary about using slang in your college writing. If you think an expression will be especially effective, you may use it wisely, but for the most part slang should be avoided.

Following are some slang terms currently in use in California. As an amusing exercise, see how many you know (perhaps only a few, for slang is usually both regional and short-lived), and decide which ones you think might be effective in college writing. Add slang expressions that are in use in your part of the country.

quail	jam	junk
bread	pop	camp
turned on	hooked	wheelie
cookie	tracks	travel agent
baked	bag	fuzz
turn off	bombed out	sacked out
good call	crash	chop
dudly	slick	scarf
jacked up	peel out	catnip
trainpuller	pole	hooker
make out	plastic	chopper
split	foxie lady	gross out
skate	bug off	bird out
rap	up tight	kill it
zit	flake off	bummer
shag	out of sight	burn artist
dig it	hang-up	scratch
pig	drag	clicking
pad	rip off	bitching
burned	dog it	bananas

Nonstandard Expressions

Nonstandard is the language of the uneducated masses. It is language unaffected by education. Many so-called ungrammatical expressions are nonstandard: *I done it, he seen me, ain't that good, them potatoes, don't have no,* and so forth. Obviously, such **nonstandard** constructions should be avoided in all college writing.

There are many nonstandard words and phrases that should be avoided. They are not slang, although some of them approach being colloquial. Here are some of the more common ones:

broadcasted
bust, busted, bursted
nowheres, anywheres
being as, being that
irregardless
anyways
pretty near all
ain't
all the farther
at (after *where*)
hadn't ought to
hisself, theirselves
learn (for *teach*)
leave (for *let*)
nohow
this here, that there

Few high school graduates use such nonstandard expressions, and so they are not an important factor in college writing.

A TIP ON USAGE   Avoid the incorrect double negatives *don't hardly*, *can't hardly*, and *can't scarcely*.

RIGHT: **I can hardly** (or **can scarcely**) tolerate fifty minutes of Professor Graybo's lectures.

Exercise 31

COLLOQUIALISMS; SLANG;
NONSTANDARD
EXPRESSIONS

DIRECTIONS *In the following sentences cross out any inappropriate colloquialisms, slang, or vulgate expressions, and in the blanks provided write more appropriate expressions.*

1. Did you receive your invite to my party yet?

   _____

2. You can't pass without you study regularly.

   _____

3. I felt sort of bad about having goofed off all day.

   _____

4. Susie offered to learn me how to dance.

   _____

5. You're nowhere near as intelligent as you think you are.

   _____

6. He promised to visit me inside of a week.

   _____

7. Irregardless of the outcome, the team was determined to play a sportsmanlike game.

   _____

8. The valedictorian hadn't ought to of bragged about hisself so much.

   _____

9. Where is the party to be at?

   _____

10. I didn't want to read that there book, nohow.

_____

11. Try and come to the lecture, for it will be terribly interesting.

_____

12. Pretty near all the players caught the flu.

_____

13. Being as it's raining, let's just stay home.

_____

14. That was all the farther I could go on my bicycle.

_____

15. Will you all wait on me while I shave?

_____

16. I'll be mighty contented if you will leave me teach you how to swim.

_____

17. I like to have missed that last fly ball.

_____

18. Did any of your pipes bust in the freeze last night?

_____

19. Yes, two of our pipes busted.

_____

20. Joan has a pleasant manner, but she's kind of icky.

_____

21. "Let's Make a Deal" was lousy last night, but "M*A*S*H" was swell.

_____

22. I wanted a date with Jane in the worst way.

_____

23. Several of the students were plastered at the game.

_____

24. Do you reckon the traitor will be hung?

_____

25. Most everybody was awfully kind to me after my accident.

_____

A MINI-EXERCISE On a separate sheet of paper write five sentences illustrating five different uses of the comma. Specify for each sentence the reason why a comma or commas are used. You can refer to Lessons Seven through Ten.

A MINI-EXERCISE Write meaningful sentences, using the following pairs of words correctly. Do not begin a sentence with one of the words.

1. a. West: _____

   _____

   _____

   b. west: _____

   _____

   _____

2. a. senator: _____

   _____

   _____

   b. Senator: _____

   _____

   _____

Lesson

32 WORDS OFTEN CONFUSED

One source of errors in usage is the confusion of words that sound similar but are different in meaning or that are different in sound but have similar, but not identical, meanings. Following are some of these pairs or trios of words with their meanings.

accept (verb): "to receive willingly"
except (preposition): "not included"
    standard: I will not *accept* your gift.
    standard: No one came *except* the teacher.
    wrong: I cannot *except* such an explanation.

affect (verb): "to have an influence on"
effect (noun): "the influence exerted on something"
effect (verb): "to bring about or cause to happen"
    standard: The new law does not *affect* me.
    standard: The new law has no *effect* on me.
    standard: The convict *effected* an escape from prison.
    wrong: How did the novel *effect* you?
    wrong: What *affect* did the novel have on you?

all ready (adjective): "everyone or everything is prepared.
already (adverb): "at this time or before this time"
    standard: The students are *all ready* to take the test.
    standard: The store is *already* closed.
    wrong: The vote has *all ready* been taken.

all together (adverb): "everyone acts in unison"
altogether (adverb): "wholly or completely"
    standard: Sing *all together* now.
    standard: Your proposal is *altogether* unsatisfactory.
    wrong: Did they come *altogether*?

among (preposition): used when three or more items are designated
between (preposition): used when two items are designated
    standard: We were allowed to choose *among* four tests.
    standard: The money was divided *between* John and me.
    informal: It's difficult to choose *between* the chorus girls.

amount (noun): used to designate a quantity that can't be numbered
number (noun): used to designate a quantity divisible into separate units
    standard: I have a small *amount* of fertilizer left.
    standard: I have a *number* of sacks of fertilizer left.
    informal: I have a small *amount* of sacks left.

anxious (adjective): "uneasy or apprehensive"
eager (adjective): "wanting very much"
    standard: I am *anxious* about the health of my cat.
    standard: I am *eager* to act in the play.
    informal: I am *anxious* to act in the play.

anyway (adverb): "in my case"
any way (noun): "a possible way to do something"
    standard: I didn't want to play the part *anyway*.
    standard: Can you find *any way* to pay the bill?
    wrong: *Any way*, I wasn't offered the job.

colloquialism (noun): "a word or phrase suitable for informal usage"
localism (noun): "a word or phrase used only in one locality"
    standard: In an attempt to be folksy, the politician filled his coast-
            to-coast broadcast with *colloquialisms*.
    wrong: "Larrupting" is a *colloquialism* used in the Blue Ridge
    Mountains.

conscience (noun): "a knowledge or feeling of right and wrong"
conscious (adjective): "aware of alert"
    standard: Your *conscience* should hurt you for kicking that dog.
    standard: Are you *conscious* of my intention?

council (noun): "an official group"
counsel (verb): "to give advice"
counsel (noun): "advice or adviser"
    standard: The *council* voted for the tax increase.
    standard: Will you *counsel* me so that I can enroll properly?
    wrong: My father gave me good *council*.

credible (adjective): "believable"
creditable (adjective): "worthy of praise"
credulous (adjective): "willing to believe readily or easily imposed upon"
 standard: The suspect's explanation was *credible*.
 standard: The team's performance was *creditable*.
 standard: The teacher was so *credulous* that he believed my excuse.

disinterested (adjective): "impartial"
uninterested (adjective): "having no interest in"
 standard: He was a good judge because he was *disinterested*.
 standard: I am *uninterested* in economics.
 wrong: I am *disinterested* in economics.

expect (verb): "to look forward to or to anticipate"
suspect (verb: "to think probable or likely"
 standard: I *expect* to achieve an A in English.
 standard: I *suspect* the teacher will talk about Robert Frost today.
 informal: I *expect* the teacher will talk *about Robert Frost today*.

fewer (adjective): refers to separate items
less (adjective): refers to goods that cannot be divided into separate items
 standard: I own *fewer* books than my brother.
 standard: Alaska has *less* usable land than Texas.

imply (verb): "to suggest or hint"
infer (verb): "to draw a conclusion about"
 standard: Our teacher *implied* that he was dissatisfied with our
  work.
 standard: We *inferred* that our teacher was dissatisfied with our
  work.
 wrong: Our teacher *inferred* that he was dissatisfied with our work.

later (adverb): "at a time after a specified time"
latter (adjective): "nearer the end or the last mentioned"
 standard: The Magna Carta came *later* than the Norman Conquest.
 standard: Our national elections come in the *latter* part of the year.

lay (transitive verb): "to place an object somehwere" (principal parts: *lay, laid, laid*)
lie (intransitive verb): "to be in or take a reclining position" (principal parts: *lie, lay, lain*)
 standard: I will *lie* down this afternoon.
 standard: Yesterday, I *lay* down.
 standard: I have *lain* down every afternoon for the past week.

standard: The book is *lying* on the table.
standard: I will *lay* the book on the table.
informal at best: Don't *lay* there too long.
informal at best: Has he *laid* in bed all day?

liable (adjective): "responsible for or legally bound or likely"
libel (noun): "slanderous reference"
libel (verb): "to slander"
standard: A man is *liable* for debts contracted by his wife.
standard: The gossip columnist was sued for *libel*.
wrong: You are *libel* to catch cold in densely crowded rooms.

maybe (adverb): "perhaps or possibly"
may be (verb): "something might come to pass"
standard: *Maybe* you should take history.
standard: He *may be* an espionage agent.
wrong: That law *maybe* repealed.

passed (verb): past participle of *pass*
past (noun or preposition): "of a former time"
standard: I *passed* English with a *B*.
wrong: I *past* English with a *B*.

principal (adjective or noun): "chief or head of"
principle (noun): "rule, law, or doctrine"
standard: Oslo is the *principal* city of Norway.
standard: What mathematical *principle* does this problem call for?

set (transitive verb): "to place an object in a position" (principal parts:
  set, set, set)
sit (intransitive verb): "to occupy a set or to be in a sitting position"
  (principal parts: *sit, sat, sat*)
standard: *Set* the phonograph on the table.
standard: Will you *sit* in this chair?
standard: I have *sat* here all day.
wrong: The car *set* in the garage.
wrong: He has *set* there all day.

suppose (verb): "to assume or conjecture"
supposed (adjective): "expected or obligated"
standard: I am *supposed* to take chemistry.
wrong: I am *suppose* to take chemistry.

than (conjunction): used to make a comparison
then (adverb): specifies time

standard: He is more intelligent *than* I.
wrong: He is more intelligent *then* I.

there (adverb; expletive): adverb—"a place"; expletive—used to introduce
   sentences
their (possessive pronoun): "belonging to them"
they're (contraction): "they are"

to (preposition; sign of the infinitive): various idiomatic meanings
too (adverb): "to an excessive extent"; "overmuch"
   standard: I was *too* tired to study.
   wrong: I was *to* tired to study.

use (verb): "to utilize"
used (adjective): "accustomed to"
   standard: I am *used* to hard work.
   wrong: I am *use* to hard work.

Exercise 32

WORDS OFTEN CONFUSED

DIRECTIONS *In the following sentences cross out any misused words, and in the blanks provided write in the correct words. Some words may be informally acceptable, but for this exercise cross out such words.*

1. Do you expect your brother will be disinterested in eating at a fast food place?

   _____

2. More than twenty students were suppose to have all ready past the exam.

   _____

3. A large amount of rocks were fallen in the road.

   _____

4. I was so eager to go to the mountains that I couldn't lay in bed past six o'clock.

   _____

5. You shouldn't except gifts from strangers, any way.

   _____

6. Your to kind to infer that he was cheating.

   _____

7. You're principle gave you good council when he told you its' latter then you think.

   _____

8. He did very credible work, for he made less errors than anyone else.

   _____

9. That chair use to set in the attic before we found out who's it was.

   _____

10. May be the expression was a colloquialism used only in Appalachia.

_____

11. The professor inferred that we were too credible to make good debaters.

_____

12. The heavy rain that came latter didn't effect the cotton crop at all.

_____

13. The test was all together to difficult even for the councilor.

_____

14. Your libel to fail if you stay disinterested in your studies.

_____

15. Yesterday I lay my tapes aside, and now I can't find them.

_____

16. I sat the phonograph on the dining table while I went for the large amount of parts that I needed to repair it.

_____

17. One of the principles in the treaty agreement was Poland.

_____

18. The new traffic regulations had a greater effect then they were suppose to.

_____

19. The longer I laid in bed, the less anxious I was to go skiing.

_____

20. Whose suppose to get the largest amount of prizes?

_____

21. Everyone accept the little children was already for the big parade.

_____

23. If I had a choice between power and wealth, I would take the later.

_____

24. You shouldn't lay around loafing; your libel to go broke.

_____

25. Its wagging it's tail more then it use to.

_____

Part Two READING SELECTIONS

Introduction

The following reading selections were chosen both because they present varied topics of general interest and because they are useful in helping you build your vocabulary, one of the most important parts of college studies. It is a proved fact that there is a high correlation between the vocabulary of people and the amount of money they make in their lifetime—the larger one's vocabulary, of course, the more money one usually makes. And also the more one usually enjoys reading, TV watching, and movies.

The words in the vocabulary tests that follow the selections are printed in boldface type in the selections. As you work on the vocabulary tests, *try to determine the word's meaning by its context*—that is, by the way it is used in its sentence. Usually, if you will think, you will come to an understanding of the vocabulary words without resorting to your dictionary. But when you are allowed to, use your dictionary freely if you need to. A good dictionary is probably the most important textbook for almost all college students—and not just in their English courses.

Your instructor will decide how you are to perform the vocabulary tests and the sentence-writing Mini-Exercises that accompany them.

HOW TO READ A BOOK

Mortimer J. Adler and Charles Van Doren

Every book has a skeleton hidden between its boards. Your job is to find 1
it. A book comes to you with flesh on its bare bones and clothes over its
flesh. It is all dressed up. I am not asking you to be impolite or cruel. You
do not have to undress it or tear the flesh off its limbs to get at the firm
structure that underlies the soft. But you must read the book with X-ray
eyes, for it is an essential part of your first **apprehension** of any book
to grasp its structure.

You know how violently some people are opposed to **vivisection**. 2
There are others who feel as strongly against **analysis** of any sort. They
simply do not like to have things taken apart, even if the only instrument
used in cutting up is the mind. They somehow feel that something is being
destroyed by analysis. This is particularly true in the case of works of
art. If you try to show them the inner structure, the **articulation** of the
parts, the way the joints fit together, they react as if you had murdered
the poem or the piece of music.

That is why I have used the **metaphor** of the X-ray. No harm is 3
done to the living organism by having its skeleton lighted up. The patient
does not even feel as if his privacy had been **infringed** upon. Yet the
doctor has discovered the disposition of the parts. He has a visible map
of the total layout. He has an architect's ground plan. No one doubts the
usefulness of such knowledge to help further operations on the living
organism.

Well, in the same way, you can penetrate beneath the moving surface 4
of a book to its rigid skeleton. You can see the way the parts are artic-
ulated, how they hang together, and the thread that ties them into a
whole. You can do this without impairing in the least the **vitality** of the
book you are reading. You need not fear that Humpty-Dumpty will be

all in pieces, never to come together again. The whole can remain in animation while you proceed to find out what makes the wheels go round.

I had one experience as a student which taught me this lesson. Like 5 other boys of the same age, I thought I could write lyric poetry. I may have even thought I was a poet. Perhaps that is why I reacted so strongly against a teacher of English literature who insisted that we be able to state the unity of every poem in a single sentence and then give a **prosaic** catalogue of its contents by an orderly **enumeration** of all its subordinate parts.

To do this with Shelley's *Adonais* or with an ode by Keats seemed 6 to me nothing short of rape and **mayhem**. When you got finished with such cold-blooded butchery, all the "poetry" would be gone. But I did the work I was asked to do and, after a year of analysis, I found otherwise. A poem was not destroyed by such tactics in reading. On the contrary, the greater insight which resulted seemed to make the poem more like a vital organism. Instead of its being an **ineffable** blur, it moved before one with the grace and proportion of a living thing.

That was my first lesson in reading. From it I learned two rules . . . 7 for the first reading of any book. I say "any book." These rules apply to science as well as poetry, and to any sort of **expository** work. Their application will be somewhat different, of course, according to the kind of book they are used on. The unity of a novel is not the same as the unity of a **treatise** on politics; nor are the parts of the same sort, or ordered in the some way. But every book which is worth reading at all has a unity and an organization of parts. A book which did not would be a mess. It would be relatively unreadable, as bad books actually are.

I am going to state these two rules as simply as possible. Then I 8 shall explain them and illustrate them. The first rule can be expressed as follows: *State the unity of the whole book in a single sentence, or at most in several sentences (a short paragraph).*

This means that you must be able to say what the whole book is 9 about as briefly as possible. To say what the whole book is about is not the same as saying what kind of book it is. The word "about" may be misleading here. In one sense, a book *is about* a certain type of subject matter, which it treats in a certain way. If you know this, you know what kind of book it is. But there is another and perhaps more colloquial sense of "about." We ask a person what he is about, what he is up to. So we can wonder what an author is trying to do. To find out what a book is *about* in this sense is to discover its *theme* or main *point*.

Everyone, I think, will admit that a book is a work of art. Further- 10 more, they will agree that in proportions as it is good, as a book and as a work of art, it has a more perfect and **pervasive** unity. They know this to be true of music and paintings, novels and plays. It is no less true of books which convey knowledge. But it is not enough to acknowledge this fact vaguely. You must **apprehend** the unity with definiteness. There is only one way that I know of being sure you have succeeded. You must be able to tell yourself or anybody else what the unity is and in a few words. Do not be satisfied with "feeling the unity" which you cannot express. The student who says, "I know what it is, but I just can't say it," fools no one, not even himself.

The second rule can be expressed as follows: *Set forth the major parts* 11 *of the book, and show how these are organized into a whole, by being ordered to one another and to the unity of the whole.*

The reason for this rule should be obvious. If a work of art were 12 absolutely simple, it would, of course, have no parts. But that is not the case. None of the sensible, physical things man knows is simple in this absolute way, nor is any human production. They are all complex unities. You have not grasped a complex unity if all you know about it is how it is one. You must also know how it is many, not a many which consists of a lot of separate things, but an organized many. If the parts were not organically related, the whole which they composed would not be one. Strictly speaking, there would be no whole at all but merely a collection.

You know the difference between a heap of bricks, on the one hand, 13 and the single house they can constitute, on the other. You know the difference between one house and a collection of houses. A book is like a single house. It is a mansion of many rooms, rooms on different levels, of different sizes and shapes, with different outlooks, rooms with different functions to perform. These rooms are independent, in part. Each has its own structure and interior decoration. But they are not absolutely independent and separate. They are connected by doors and arches, by corridors and stairways. Because they are connected, the partial function which each performs contributes its share to the usefulness of the whole house. Otherwise the house would not be genuinely livable.

The architectural **analogy** is almost perfect. A good book, like a 14 good house, is an orderly arrangement of parts. Each major part has a certain amount of independence. As we shall see, it may have an interior structure of its own. But it must also be connected with the other parts— that is, related to them functionally—for otherwise it could not contribute its share to the intelligibility of the whole.

As houses are more or less livable, so books are more or less readable. 15 The most readable book is an architectural achievement on the part of the author. The best books are those that have the most **intelligible** structure and, I might add, the most apparent. Though they are usually more complex than poorer books, their greater complexity is somehow also a great simplicity, because their parts are better organized, more unified.

That is one of the reasons why the great books are most readable. 16 Lesser works are really more bothersome to read. Yet to read them well— that is, as well as they can be read—you must try to find some plan in them. They would have been better if the author had himself seen the plan a little more clearly. But if they hang together at all, if they are a complex unity to any degree, there must be a plan and you must find it.

Sometimes an author obligingly tells you on the title page what the 17 unity is. In the eighteenth century, writers had the habit of composing elaborate titles which told the reader what the whole book was about. Here is a title by Jeremy Collier, an English divine who attacked the obscenity of the Restoration drama much more learnedly than the Legion of Decency has recently attacked the movies: *A Short View of the Immorality and Profaneness of the English Stage, together with the Sense of Antiquity upon this Argument.* You know from this that Collier recites many **flagrant** instances of the abuse of public morals and that he is going to support his protest by quoting texts from those ancients who argued, as Plato did, that the stage corrupts youth, or, as the early Church fathers did, that plays are seductions of the flesh and the devil.

Sometimes the author tells you the unity of his plan in his preface. 18 In this respect, expository books differ radically from fiction. A scientific or philosophical writer has no reason to keep you in suspense. In fact, the less suspense such an author keeps you in, the more likely you are to sustain the effort of reading him through. Like a newspaper story, an expository book may summarize itself in its first paragraph.

Do not be too proud to accept the author's help if he proffers it, but 19 do not rely too completely on what he says in the preface. The best-laid plans of authors, like those of other mice and men, gang aft agley. Be somewhat guided by the **prospectus** the author gives you, but always remember that the obligation of finding the unity belongs to the reader, as much as having one belongs to the writer. You can discharge that obligation honestly only by reading the whole book.

A TIP ON USAGE For best style, use the *ed* form of *old-fashion*ed, *releas*ed *time, hash*ed *brown*ed *potatoes*, and other such constructions. Avoid *old-fashion, release time*, and so on. Examples:

RIGHT: I bought a full-sized car.
RIGHT: Only fresh-brewed coffee is good.
RIGHT: Here is the Center for the Handicapped (not the *Handicap Center).

A TIP ON USAGE USE NOR, NOT OR, WITH NEITHER.

WRONG: He would have **neither** the president's insight **or** the advantage of good advice.
RIGHT: We need **neither** price controls **nor** a limitation on production.

Exercise 33

DIRECTIONS   *In each blank at the right, write the letter that identifies the correct definition of each of the following words.*

1. **apprehension**: (A) understanding; (B) rejection; (C) grasping; (D) confusion _____
2. **vivisection**: (A) dividing into parts; (B) cutting a living being; (C) operating on a corpse; (D) bisexual _____
3. **analysis**: (A) putting together; (B) enjoying; (C) taking apart; (D) destruction _____
4. **articulation**: (A) taking apart; (B) seeing clearly; (C) regurgitation; (D) joined together _____
5. **metaphor**: (A) a figure of speech saying one thing is something else; (B) abstract thinking; (C) secret meanings; (D) a kind of literal language _____
6. **infringe**: (A) on the edge; (B) trespass; (C) bold and daring; (D) to put fringe on _____
7. **vitality**: (A) liveliness; (B) dullness; (C) offensiveness; (D) creativity _____
8. **prosaic**: (A) interesting; (B) obscene; (C) listed; (D) matter-of-fact _____
9. **enumeration**: (A) a listing; (B) a separation; (C) a naming; (D) a confusion _____
10. **ineffable**: (A) unseen; (B) incompetent; (C) dull; (D) indescribable _____
11. **expository**: (A) poetry (B) fiction; (C) nonfiction; (D) musical _____
12. **pervasive**: (A) perverse; (B) evasive; (C) all-inclusive; (D) unusual _____
13. **analogy**: (A) a comparison; (B) a division; (C) an analysis; (D) a reference _____
14. **intelligible**: (A) clear and easily understood; (B) profound; (C) complex; (D) having high intelligence _____
15. **prospectus**: (A) a gold seeker; (B) a prospect; (C) a view; (D) a summary _____
16. **subordinate**: (A) to make less important; (B) to appoint to a position; (C) to put a border around; (D) to review _____
17. **mayhem**: (A) to clear the throat; (B) to destroy willfully; (C) to dance and frolic; (D) to rebuild _____

18. **treatise**:(A) a treat; (B) an agreement; (C) a formal account; (D) letting someone else pay   _____

19. **apprehend**: (A) to escape: (B) to let go; (C) to understand; (D) to bend out of shape   _____

20. **flagrant**: (A) smelling sweet; (B) to beat; (C) shocking; (D) stinking   _____

A MINI-EXERCISE   Using your dictionary if necessary, write intelligent sentences, using the stated words, some of which come from the preceding vocabulary test. Try to make each sentence contain at least fifteen words.

1. **apprehension:** _____

     _____

     _____

2. **prosaic:** _____

     _____

     _____

3. **pervasive:** _____

     _____

     _____

4. **precise:** _____

     _____

     _____

5. **concise:** _____

     _____

     _____

SIGHT INTO INSIGHT: LEARNING TO SEE

Annie Dillard

I chanced on a wonderful book called *Space and Sight*, by Marius Von 1
Senden. When Western surgeons discovered how to perform safe **cataract**
operations, they ranged across Europe and America operating on dozens
of men and women of all ages who had been blinded by cataracts since
birth. Von Senden collected accounts of such cases; the histories are fascinating. Many doctors had tested their patients' sense **perceptions** and
ideas of space both before and after the operations. The vast majority of
patients, of both sexes and all ages, had, in Von Senden's opinion, no idea
of space whatsoever. Form, distance, and size were so many meaningless
syllables. A patient "had no idea of depth, confusing it with roundness."
Before the operation a doctor would give a blind patient a cube and a
sphere; the patient would tongue it or feel it with his hands, and name
it correctly. After the operation the doctor would show the same objects
to the patient without letting him touch them; now he had no clue whatsoever to what he was seeing. One patient called lemonade "square"
because it pricked on his tongue as a square shape pricked on the touch
of his hands. Of another postoperative patient the doctor writes, "I have
found in her no notion of size, for example, not even within the narrow
limits which she might have **encompassed** with the aid of touch. Thus
when I asked her to show me how big her mother was, she did not stretch
out her hands, but set her two index fingers a few inches apart."

For the newly sighted, vision is pure sensation **unencumbered** by 2
meaning. When a newly sighted girl saw photographs and paintings, she
asked, "'Why do they put those dark marks all over them?' 'Those aren't
dark marks,' her mother explained, 'those are shadows. That is one of the
ways the eye knows that things have shape. If it were not for shadows,

many things would look flat.' 'Well, that's how things do look.' Joan answered. 'Everything looks flat with dark patches.'"

In general the newly sighted see the world as a dazzle of "color- 3 patches." They are pleased by the sensation of color, and learn quickly to name the colors, but the rest of seeing is tormentingly difficult. Soon after his operation a patient "generally bumps into one of these colour-patches and observes them to be **substantial** since they resist him as tactual objects do. In walking about it also strikes him—or can if he pays attention—that he is continually passing in between the colours he sees, that he can go past a visual object, that a part of it then steadily disappears from view; and that in spite of this, however he twists and turns—whether entering the room from the door, for example, or returning back to it—he always has a visual space in front of him. Thus he gradually comes to realize that there is also a space behind him, which he does not see."

The mental effort involved in these reasonings proves overwhelming 4 for many patients. It oppresses them to realize, if they ever do at all, the tremendous size of the world, which they had previously conceived of as something touchingly manageable. It oppresses them to realize that they have been visible to people all along, perhaps unattractively so, without their knowledge or consent. A disheartening number of them refuse to use their new vision, continuing to go over objects with their tongues, and **lapsing** into **apathy** and despair.

On the other hand, many newly sighted people speak well of the 5 world, and teach us how dull our own vision is. To one patient, a human hand, unrecognized, is "something bright and then holes." Shown a bunch of grapes, a boy calls out, "It is dark, blue and shiny. . . . It isn't smooth, it has bumps and hollows." A little girl visits a garden. "She is greatly astonished, and can scarcely be persuaded to answer, stands speechless in front of the tree, which she only names on taking hold of it, and then as 'the tree with the lights in it.'" Another patient, a twenty-two-year-old girl, was dazzled by the world's brightness and kept her eyes shut for two weeks. When at the end of that time she opened her eyes again, she did not recognize any objects, but "the more she now directed her gaze upon everything about her, the more it could be seen how an expression of **gratification** and astonishment overspread her features; she repeatedly exclaimed: 'Oh God! How beautiful!'"

I saw color-patches for weeks after I read this wonderful book. It was 6 summer; the peaches were ripe in the valley orchards. When I woke in the morning, color-patches wrapped round my eyes, **intricately**, leaving not one unfilled spot. All day long I walked among shifting color-patches that parted before me like the Red Sea and closed again in silence, transfigured, wherever I looked back. Some patches swelled and loomed, while others vanished utterly, and dark marks flitted at **random** over the whole dazzling sweep. But I couldn't sustain the illusion of flatness. I've been around for too long. Form is condemned to an eternal **danse macabre** with meaning: I couldn't unpeach the peaches. Nor can I remember ever having seen without understanding; the color-patches of infancy are lost. My brain then must have been smooth as any balloon. I'm told I reached for the moon; many babies do. But the color-patches of infancy swelled as meaning filled them; they arrayed themselves in solemn ranks down distance which unrolled and stretched before me like a plain. The moon rocketed away. I live now in a world of shadows that shape and distance color, a world where space makes a kind of terrible sense. What Gnosticism is this, and what physics? The fluttering patch I saw in my nursery window—silver and green and shape-shifting blue—is gone; a row of Lombardy poplars takes its place, mute, across the distant lawn. That humming oblong creature pale as light that stole along the walls of my room at night, stretching exhilaratingly around the corners, is gone, too, gone the night I ate of the bittersweet fruit, put two and two together and puckered forever my brain. Martin Buber tells this tale: "Rabbi Mendel once boasted to his teacher Rabbi Elimelekh that evenings he saw the angel who rolls away the light before the darkness, and mornings the angel who rolls away the darkness before the light. 'Yes,' said Rabbi Elimelekh, 'in my youth I saw that too. Later on you don't see these things anymore.'"

Why didn't someone hand those newly sighted people paints and 7 brushes from the start, when they still didn't know what anything was? Then may be we all could see color-patches too, the world unraveled from reason, Eden before Adam gave names. The scales would drop from my eyes; I'd see trees like men walking; I'd run down the road against all orders, hallooing and leaping.

SILVER FLASHES

Seeing is of course very much a matter of verbalization. Unless I call my 8 attention to what passes before my eyes, I simply won't see it. If Tinker Mountain erupted, I'd be likely to notice. But if I want to notice the lesser **cataclysms** of valley life, I have to maintain in my head a running description of the present. It's not that I'm observant; it's just that I talk too much. Otherwise, especially in a strange place, I'll never know what's happening. Like a blind man at the ball game, I need a radio.

When I see this way I **analyze** and pry. I hurl over logs and roll 9 away stones; I study the bank a square foot at a time; probing and tilting my head. Some days when a mist covers the mountains, when the muskrats won't show and the microscope's mirror shatters, I want to climb up the blank blue dome as a man would storm the inside of a circus tent, wildly, dangling, and with a steel knife claw a rent in the top, peep, and, if I must, fall.

But there is another kind of seeing that involves a letting go. When 10 I see this way I sway **transfixed** and emptied. The difference between the two ways of seeing is the difference between walking with and without a camera. When I walk with a camera I walk from shot to shot, reading the light on a **calibrated** meter. When I walk without a camera, my own shutter opens, and the moment's light prints on my own silver gut. When I see this second way I am above all an **unscrupulous** observer.

It was sunny one evening last summer at Tinker Creek; the sun was low in the sky, upstream. I was sitting on the sycamore log bridge with the sunset at my back, watching the shiners the size of minnows who were feeding over the muddy sand in **skittery** schools. Again and again, one fish, then another, turned for a split second across the current and flash! the sun shot out from its silver side. I couldn't watch for it. It was always just happening somewhere else, and it drew my vision just as it disappeared: flash! like a sudden dazzle of the thinnest blade, a sparking over a dun and olive ground at chance intervals from every direction. Then I noticed white specks, some sort of pale petals, small, floating from under my feet on the creek's surface, very slow and steady. So I blurred my eyes and gazed toward the brim of my hat and saw a new world. I saw the pale white circles roll up, roll up. Like the world's turning, mute and perfect, and I saw the **linear** flashes, gleaming silver, like stars being born at random down a rolling **scroll** of time. Something broke and something opened. I filled up like a new wineskin. I breathed an air like light; I saw a light like water. I was the lip of a fountain the creek filled forever; I was ether, the leaf in the **zephyr**; I was flesh-flake, feather, bone. 11

When I see this way I see truly. As Thoreau says, I return to my senses. I am the man who watches the baseball game in silence in an empty stadium. I see the game purely; I'm abstracted and dazed. When it's all over and the white-suited players lope off the green field to their shadowed dugouts, I leap to my feet, I cheer and cheer. 12

A TIP ON USAGE   The proper expression is **try to do**, not the lower-level **try and do**.

PREFERRED: I want you to try **to** do your best.

PREFERRED: Please try **to** be mannerly.

POOR STYLE: The pastor wishes you would try **and** come to church rather than play golf.

A TIP ON USAGE   In the "one of those students who . . ." construction, the *who* takes a plural verb because it refers to the plural noun *students*, not to the singular *one*.

RIGHT: He is one of those men who **have** everything.

RIGHT: I'm one of those players who **are** easily upset by tension.

WRONG: John is one of those lovers who **likes** to boast of his conquests.

Exercise 34

DIRECTIONS *In each blank at the right, write the letter that identifies the correct definition of each of the following words.*

1. **cataract**: (A) opacity of the eye; (B) kidney stones; (C) part of the brain; (D) a suture _____
2. **perceptions**: (A) sense of touch; (B) act of listening; (C) deceiving; (D) use of any of the senses _____
3. **encompassed**: (A) used a compass; (B) pointed out; (C) included; (D) by-passed _____
4. **unencumbered**: (A) not numbered; (B) not burdened; (C) not clumsy; (D) not listed _____
5. **substantial**: (A) real; (B) lower; (C) standing; (D) higher _____
6. **lapse**: (A) go jogging; (B) part of the leg; (C) an action; (D) to drift into _____
7. **apathy**: (A) lack of interest; (B) great pleasure; (C) rejection; (D) increase in size _____
8. **gratification** (A) to make good; (B) to intensify; (C) to please; (D) to confuse _____
9. **intricately:** (A) trickily; (B) complexly; (C) cleverly; (D) actually _____
10. **random**: (A) without pattern; (B) stolen; (C) a rare gas; (D) modern _____
11. **danse macabre**: (A) a Scotsman; (B) dance of death; (C) dance of joy; (D) long-lasting dance _____
12. **cataclysm**: (A) a muscle disease; (B) feline condition; (C) sudden shout; (D) violent upheaval _____
13. **analyze**: (A) destroy; (B) put together; (C) take apart; (D) tell a falsehood _____
14. **transfixed**: (A) stuck; (B) went across; (C) transcended; (D) took a drug _____
15. **calibrated**: (A) berated; (B) very small; (C) carefully measured; (D) carelessly designed _____
16. **unscrupulous**: (A) unconscious; (B) not exacting; (C) very careful; (D) not happy _____
17. **skittery**: (A) standing still; (B) near the surface; (C) a small amount; (D) moving swiftly _____
18. **linear**: (A) concerning the moon; (B) above the line; (C) in a line; (D) very near _____

19. **scroll:** (A) a roll of paper; (B) to write; (C) part of the
    head; (D) a dwarf _____
20. **zephyr:** (A) heavier-than-air craft; (B) a breeze; (C) a
    wave; (D) a shout _____

A MINI-EXERCISE   Using your dictionary if necessary, write intelligent sentences, using the stated words. Try to make each sentence
   contain at least fifteen words.

1. a **explicit:** _____

   _____

   _____

   _____

   b. **implicit:** _____

   _____

   _____

   _____

A HANGING
George Orwell

It was in Burma, a sodden morning of the rains. A sickly light, like yellow 1
tinfoil, was slanting over the high walls into the jail yard. We were waiting
outside the condemned cells, a row of sheds fronted with double bars, like
small animal cages. Each cell measured about ten feet by ten and was
quite bare within except for a plank bed and a pot for drinking water. In
some of them brown silent men were squatting at the inner bar, with
their blankets draped round them. These were the condemned men, due
to be hanged within the next week or two.

One prisoner had been brought out of his cell. He was a Hindu, a 2
puny wisp of a man, with a shaven head and vague liquid eyes. He had
a thick, sprouting moustache, absurdly too big for his body, rather like
the moustache of a comic man on the films. Six tall Indian warders were
guarding him and getting him ready for the gallows. Two of them stood
by with rifles and fixed bayonets, while the others handcuffed him, passed
a chain through his handcuffs and fixed it to their belts, and lashed his
arms tight to his sides. They crowded very close about him, with their
hands always on him in a careful, caressing grip, as though all the while
feeling him to make sure he was there. It was like men handling a fish
which is still alive and may jump back into the water. But he stood quite
unresisting, yielding his arms limply to the ropes, as though he hardly
noticed what was happening.

Eight o'clock struck and a bugle call, **desolately** thin in the wet air, 3
floated from the distant barracks. The superintendent of the jail, who was
standing apart from the rest of us, moodily prodding the gravel with his
stick, raised his head at the sound. He was an army doctor, with a grey

toothbrush moustache and a gruff voice. "For God's sake hurry up. Francis," he said irritably. "The man ought to have been dead by this time. Aren't you ready yet?"

Francis, the head jailer, a fat Dravidian in a white drill suit and 4 gold spectacles, waved his black hand. "Yes sir, yes sir," he bubbled. "All iss satisfactorily prepared. The hangman is waiting. We shall proceed."

"Well, quick march, then. The prisoners can't get their breakfast till 5 this job's over."

We set out for the gallows. Two warders marched on either side of 6 the prisoner, with their rifles at the slope; two others marched close against him, gripping him by arm and shoulder, as though at once pushing and supporting him. The rest of us, magistrates and the like, followed behind. Suddenly, when we had gone ten yards, the procession stopped short without any order or warning. A dreadful thing had happened—a dog, come goodness knows whence, had appeared in the yard. It came bounding among us with a loud volley of barks, and leapt round us wagging its whole body, wild with glee at finding so many human beings together. It was a large woolly dog, half Airedale, half **pariah**. For a moment it pranced round us, and then, before anyone could stop it, it had made a dash for the prisoner and, jumping up, tried to lick his face. Everyone stood **aghast**, too taken aback even to grab at the dog.

"Who let that bloody brute in here?" said the superintendent angrily. 7 "Catch it, someone!"

A warder, detached from the escort, charged clumsily after the dog, 8 but it danced and **gambolled** just out of his reach, taking everything as part of the game. A young Eurasian jailer picked up a handful of gravel and tried to stone the dog away, but it dodged the stones and came after us again. Its yaps echoed from the jail walls. The prisoner, in the grasp of the two warders, looked on incuriously, as though this was another formality of the hanging. It was several minutes before someone managed to catch the dog. Then we put my handkerchief through its collar and moved off once more, with the dog still straining and whimpering.

It was about forty yards to the gallows, I watched the bare brown 9 back of the prisoner marching in front of me. He walked clumsily with his bound arms, but quite steadily, with that bobbing gait of the Indian who never straightens his knees. At each step his muscles slid neatly into place, the lock of hair on his scalp danced up and down, his feet printed themselves on the wet gravel. And once, in spite of the men who gripped him by each shoulder, he stepped slightly to avoid a puddle on the path.

It is curious, but till that moment I had never realized what it means 10 to destroy a healthy, conscious man. When I saw the prisoner step aside to avoid the puddle I saw the mystery, the unspeakable wrongness, of cutting a life short when it is in full tide. This man was not dying, he was alive just as we are alive. All the organs of his body were working— bowels digesting food, skin renewing itself, nails growing, tissues forming—all toiling away in solemn foolery. His nails would still be growing when he stood on the drop, when he was falling through the air with a tenth-of-a-second to live. His eyes saw the yellow gravel and the grey walls, and his brain still remembered, foresaw, reasoned—reasoned even about puddles. He and we are a party of men walking together, seeing, hearing, feeling, understanding the same world; and in two minutes, with a sudden snap, one of us would be gone—one mind less, one world less.

The gallows stood in a small yard, separate from the main grounds 11 of the prison, and overgrown with tall prickly weeds. It was a brick erection like three sides of a shed, with planking on top, and above that two beams and a crossbar with the rope dangling. The hangman, a grey-haired convict in the white uniform of the prison, was waiting beside his machine. He greeted us with a **servile** crouch as we entered. At a word from Francis the two warders, gripping the prisoner more closely than ever, half led half pushed him to the gallows and helped clumsily up the ladder. Then the hangman climbed up and fixed the rope round the prisoner's neck.

We stood waiting, five yards away. The warders had formed in a 12 rough circle round the gallows. And then, when the noose was fixed, the prisoner began crying out to his god. It was a high, **reiterated** cry of "Ram! Ram! Ram! Ram!" not urgent and fearful like a prayer or cry for help, but steady, rhythmical, almost like the tolling of a bell. The dog answered the sound with a whine. The hangman, still standing on the gallows, produced a small cotton bag like a flour bag and drew it down over the prisoner's face. But the sound, muffled by the cloth, still persisted, over and over again: "Ram! Ram! Ram! Ram!"

The hangman climbed down and stool ready, holding the lever. 13 Minutes seemed to pass. The steady muffled crying from the prisoner went on and on, "Ram! Ram! Ram!" never faltering for an instant. The superintendent, his head on his chest, was slowly poking the ground with his stick; perhaps he was counting the cries, allowing the prisoner a fixed number—fifty; perhaps, or a hundred. Everyone had changed color. The Indians had gone grey like bad coffee, and one or two of the bayonets were wavering. We looked at the lashed, hooded man on the drop, and listened to his cries—each cry another second of life; the same thought was in all our minds: oh, kill him quickly, get it over, stop that **abominable** noise!

Suddenly the superintendent made up his mind. Throwing up his 14 head he made a swift motion with his stick. "Chalo!" he shouted almost fiercely.

There was a clanking noise, and then dead silence. The prisoner had 15 vanished, and the rope was twisting on itself. I let go of the dog, and it galloped immediately to the back of the gallows, but when it got there it stopped short, barked, and then retreated into a corner of the yard, where it stood among the weeds, looking **timorously** out at us. We went round the gallows to inspect the prisoner's body. He was dangling with his toes pointed straight downwards, very slowly, as dead as a stone.

The superintendent reached out with his stick and poked the bare 16 brown body; it **oscillated** slightly. *"He's* all right," said the superinten- dent. He backed out from under the gallows, and blew out a deep breath. The moody look had gone out of his face quite suddenly. He glanced at his wrist-watch. "Eight minutes past eight. Well, that's all for this morn- ing, thank God."

The warders unfixed bayonets and marched away. The dog, sobered 17 and conscious of having misbehaved itself, slipped after them. We walked out of the gallows yard, past the condemned cells with their waiting prisoners, into the big central yard of the prison. The convicts, under the command of warders armed with lathis, were already receiving their breakfast. They squatted in long rows, each man holding a tin panikin, while two warders with buckets marched round ladling out rice; it seemed quite a homely, jolly scene, after the hanging. An enormous relief had come upon us now that the job was done. One felt an impulse to sing, to break into a run, to snigger. All at once everyone began chattering gaily.

The Eurasian boy walking beside me nodded towards the way we 18 had come, with a knowing smile: "Do you know, sir, our friend [he meant the dead man] when he heard his appeal had been dismissed, he pissed on the floor of his cell. From fright. Kindly take one of my cigarettes, sir. Do you not admire my new silver case, sir? From the boxwalah, two rupees eight annas. Classy European style."

Several people laughed—at what, nobody seemed certain. 19

Francis was walking by the superintendent, talking **garrulously:** 20 "Well, sir, all hass passed off with the utmost satisfactoriness. It was all finished—flick! like that. It iss not always so—oah, no! I have known cases where the doctor wass obliged to go beneath the gallows and pull the prisoner's legs to ensure decease. Most disagreeable!"

"Wriggling about, eh? That's bad," said the superintendent. 21

"Ach, sir, it iss worse when they become **refractory!** One man, I 22 recall, clung to the bars of hiss cage when we went to take him out. You will scarcely credit, sir, that it took six warders to dislodge him, three pulling at each leg. We reasoned with him. 'My dear fellow,' we said, 'think of all the pain and trouble you are causing to us!' But no, he would not listen! Ach, he was very troublesome!"

I found that I was laughing quite loudly. Everyone was laughing. 23 Even the superintendent grinned in a **tolerant** way. "You'd better all come out and have a drink," he said quite **genially.** "I've got a bottle of whisky in the car. We could do with it."

We went through the big double gates of the prison into the road. 24 "Pulling at his legs!" exclaimed a Burmese magistrate suddenly, and burst into a loud chuckling. We all began laughing again. At that moment Francis' **anecdote** seemed extraordinarily funny. We all had a drink together, native and Europeans alike, quite **amicably.** The dead man was a hundred yards away.

Exercise 35

DIRECTIONS *In each blank at the right, write the letter that identifies the correct definition of each of the following words.*

1. **desolately**: (A) in the distance; (B) in an optimistic manner; (C) in a lonely manner; (D) in an incomprehensible manner _____

2. **pariah**: (A) a breed of wolf; (B) something unknown; (C) a social outcast; (D) an unpleasant animal _____

3. **aghast**: (A) silent; (B) showing extreme horror; (C) showing great humor; (D) angry _____

4. **gambolled**: (A) skipped or leaped about; (B) tried to appear controlled; (C) acted stupidly; (D) acted intelligently _____

5. **servile**: (A) very expressive; (B) silent and nonexpressive; (C) submissive and abject; (D) slightly bending _____

6. **reiterated**: (A) very loud; (B) spoken softly; (C) frightened; (D) repeated _____

7. **abominable**: (A) from the stomach; (B) very hateful and disagreeable; (C) unintelligible; (D) inhuman _____

8. **timorously**: (A) timidly or fearfully; (B) threateningly; (C) furiously and angrily; (D) with an idiotic expression _____

9. **oscillated**: (A) vibrated or swung back and forth; (B) gave the appearance of death; (C) gave the appearance of life; (D) snorted _____

10. **garrulously**: (A) seriously; (B) jokingly; (C) in a rambling or wordy manner; (D) in a tone of contempt _____

11. **refractory**: (A) unmanageable or stubborn; (B) completely unresponsive; (C) too responsive; (D) mentally unbalanced _____

12. **tolerant**: (A) idiotic; (B) stupid; (C) meaningless; (D) accepting others' views _____

13. **genially**: (A) indignantly; (B) in a friendly manner; (C) in a vague way; (D) with grave concern _____

14. **anecdote**: (A) a peculiar situation; (B) a counteractant; (C) a brief story; (D) facial expression _____

15. **amicably**: (A) not very socially; (B) in a not very friendly way; (C) in a friendly way; (D) in a manner of forgetting quickly _____

A MINI-EXERCISE   Using your dictionary if necessary, write intelligent sentences, using the stated words, some of which come from the preceding vocabulary test. Try to make each sentence contain at least fifteen words.

1. a. **oscillate:** _____

_____

_____

_____

   b. **osculate:** _____

_____

_____

_____

2. a. **anecdote:** _____

_____

_____

_____

   b. **antidote:** _____

_____

_____

_____

OUTER SPACE TO INNER SPACE: AN ASTRONAUT'S ODYSSEY

Edgar D. Mitchell

In February 1971 I had the privilege of walking on the moon as a member 1 of the Apollo 14 lunar expedition. During the voyage I made a test in **extrasensory perception (ESP)**, attempting to send information **telepathically** to four receivers on earth.

Since then people have asked me why an astronaut would take such 2 an intense interest in psychic research. This question is fair, but it does not **pertain** to the heart of my real interest: understanding the nature of consciousness and the relationship of mind to body that underlies human **potential**. Psychic research is one facet of this larger subject. Therefore, it might be said that my interests have expanded from outer space to include inner space.

When I went to the moon, I was as **pragmatic** a scientist-engineer 3 as any of my colleagues. I'd spent more than a quarter of a century learning the rational-objective-experimental approach to dealing with the universe. But my experience during Apollo 14 had another aspect: It showed me certain limitations of science and technology.

It began with the breathtaking experience of seeing planet earth 4 floating in the immensity of space—the **incredible** beauty of a splendid blue-and-white jewel floating in the vast, black sky. I underwent a religious-like peak experience, in which the presence of divinity became almost palpable, and *I knew* that life in the universe was not just an accident based on random processes. This knowledge, which came directly, **intuitively,** was not a matter of discursive reasoning or logical **abstraction.** It was not deduced from information perceptible by the **sensory** organs. The realization was subjective, but it was knowledge every bit as

Reprinted by permission of G. P. Putnam's Sons, from *Psychic Exploration* by Edgar D. Mitchell. Copyright © 1974 by Edgar D. Mitchell & Associates, Inc.

real and compelling as the objective data the navigational program or the communications system was based on. Clearly, the universe has meaning and direction—an unseen dimension behind the visible creation that gives it an intelligent design and gives life purpose.

Then my thoughts turned to daily life on the planet. With that my 5 sense of wonderment gradually turned into something close to **anguish**. I realized that at that very moment people were fighting wars; committing murder and other crimes; lying, cheating, and struggling for power and status; abusing the environment by polluting the water and air, wasting natural resources, and ravaging the land; acting out of lust and greed; and hurting others through intolerance, bigotry, prejudice, and all the other failings that add up to man's inhumanity to man.

It was also painfully apparent that the millions of people suffering 6 in conditions of poverty, ill health, misery, fear, and near-slavery did so in large measure because of economic exploitation, political domination, religious and ethnic persecution, and a hundred other demons that spring from the human ego. Science, for all its technological feats, did not yet— more likely could not, in its present form—deal with these problems stemming from man's self-centeredness.

The **magnitude** of the overall problem seemed staggering. How had 7 the world come to such a critical situation—and why? Even more important, what could be done to correct it? How could the highest development of our objective reason, **epitomized** by factual science, be wedded to the highest development of our subjective intuition, epitomized by ethical religion?

As I survey the challenge facing humanity today, I see only one 8 answer: *a transformation of consciousness*. Man must rise from his present ego-centered consciousness to find universal harmony, starting within himself and proceeding outward through his relations with other people and the environment to his relation with the **cosmos**. Otherwise, man will continue to move deeper into **chaos** and crisis toward a destruction of his own making.

My interest in consciousness research began about nine years ago, 9 when I first looked at parapsychology. I was quite skeptical—and ignorant—about the whole field. But, to be frank, I was actually searching for concepts that would explain the meaning of life—**holistic** concepts that I had not found during years of searching in religion, philosophy, and science.

So I started looking into extrasensory perception, psychokinesis, 10 mediumship. and other **phenomena**. To my surprise, my disbelief about the validity of these occurrences began to disappear. As one trained to evaluate on the basis of **empirical** data, I could not possibly avoid the implications of the evidence of psychic research. To anyone with an open mind, it should now be clear that people have faculties associated with— but not limited to—their known sensory systems. The contemporary scientific model of man as simply a complex organization of organic molecules is insufficient for explaining consciousness. Human beings are more than mere lumps of flesh. They have a dimension that **transcends** the entity of the person and takes them into the category of the transperson.

That concept, of course, takes us right back into religion and phi- 11 losophy. It presents a sound reason for religious beliefs—a rational basis for explaining why people throughout history have persisted in claiming that the physical world has a spiritual foundation. But it takes a change of consciousness if we are to "see" that foundation.

To help bring about that change, we need to study the nature of 12 consciousness in all its **manifestations**. The value-free rational-objective-experimental mode of Western science, based on materialism, is not sufficient by itself for coping with the ever-increasing planetary crises besetting civilization. The intuitive-subjective-experiential mode characteristic of religion and Eastern traditions has much to contribute to the study of mind and consciousness. Noetics, which seeks to use the best of both approaches and to discover an acceptable value system, can play an important role in leading the way to solutions and in helping others to make the same discovery that I made in outer space.

Like mystical and religious experiences, psychic experiences can 13 help a person become more aware and, when they are properly developed in an ethical framework, less self-centered. Psychic development is not a **panacea**, and it does not assure spiritual growth. But it is useful in objectively oriented thinking, because it can be a key to unlock the missing experiential component with which to expand awareness. It can play an important role in helping people become conscious of their participation in the continuing miracle of creation. It can be a major element in the long-sought formula for enriching human minds, transforming society, and generally aiding nature in the great work of evolving the race to a higher state of consciousness.

A MINI-EXERCISE   Explain how commas could change meaning in these sentences:

1. My son George has been elected president of his class.
2. This bushel of onions came from the first planting of its species in America in 1975.

Exercise 36

DIRECTIONS *In each blank at the right, write the letter that identifies the correct definition of each of the following words.*

1. **odyssey**: (A) a journey; (B) a restaurant; (C) something odd; (D) a decision _____
2. **telepathically** (A) by telephone; (B) from mind to mind; (C) sadly; (D) far away _____
3. **pertain**: (A) rather pretty; (B) to show; (C) relate to; (D) understand _____
4. **potential**: (A) powerful; (B) almost; (C) improbable; (D) possible _____
5. **pragmatic**: (A) automatic; (B) intrinsic; (C) fanciful; (D) practical _____
6. **incredible**: (A) unbelievable; (B) unusual; (C) undecided; (D) understandable _____
7. **intuitive**: (A) interestingly; (B) to reason carefully; (C) to know nothing; (D)to know without reasoning _____
8. **abstraction**: (A) a general idea; (B) a specific example; (C) a small area; (D) a hospital device _____
9. **sensory**: (A) a Japanese whiskey; (B) using any of the senses; (C) having good sense; (D) about scents _____
10. **anguish**: (A) pride; (B) torment; (C) pressure; (D) extinguish _____
11. **magnitude**: (A) size; (B) shape; (C) distance; (D) attracts metal _____
12. **epitomized**: (A) put in a pit; (B) to sum up; (C) to subtract from; (D) to join with _____
13. **cosmos**: (A) a harmonious universe; (B) total disorganization; (C) partial disruption; (D) the solar system _____
14. **chaos**: (A) a harmonious universe; (B) total disorganization; (C) the solar system (D) partial disruption _____
15. **holistic**: (A) very religious; (B) full of wholes; (C) seeing all the parts; (D) parting all the seams _____
16. **empirical**: (A) a large kingdom; (B) tyrannical; (C) based on rules; (D) based on observation _____
17. **transcends**: (A) sends far away; (B) tries again; (C) goes beyond; (D) reconsiders _____
18. **manifestations**: (A) something hidden; (B) something shown; (C) something guessed at; (D) something new _____

19. **panacea:** (A) a cooking vessel; (B) a sailing vessel; (C) a universal cure-all; (D) a universal illness _____
20. **phenomena:** (A) occurrences or events; (B) frauds or fakes; (C) money or gold; (D) men or women _____

A MINI-EXERCISE   Read the following statement by a tenth-grade student, and then answer the questions that follow.

> In my experience, the smartest kids in a class cheat as much as or more than the "dumb" ones. They realize that cheating is the easiest way out of the monotony of schoolwork, and they can rationalize their actions many ways. It is the best way to assure good grades, to relieve the pressure, and, besides, everybody does it—including adults and possibly the kids' own parents.

1. Is it more wrong to steal one thousand dollars than to steal ten cents?
2. Is it more wrong to shoplift in a friend's small store than at a national supermarket chain?
3. Is it more wrong for a bright student to cheat than a dull student?
4. *Why* is it wrong to cheat?

VERBAL KARATE, A MARITAL ART

Jack Smith

In our concern here with the **declarative** question—which is a seeming 1
question that actually is intended to make a statement—we overlooked
another common form of speech that is similar in form but different in
character and purpose.

The declarative question is good-natured and helpful. Its character 2
is **diffidence**; its purpose is to give useful information. ("This is Jim
Jones? The TV repairman?") But the character of this new form is false
innocence, and its purpose is **ridicule** and dominance.

The form has been identified by R. W. Prouty of Westlake Village, 3
who defines it as "a question-statement that is much used by people in
positions of authority (including wives and mothers).

"I first realized this," he explains, "in a high school woodworking 4
class when one of the students cut the tip of his finger off with a power
saw. The instructor rushed over and asked, 'Why did you do that?' What
he really meant, of course, was 'That was a stupid thing to do.'

"This question-statement does not require an answer, but most of 5
us try anyway. Fortunate is he who has a **valid** and believable response
ready . . . It seems to me that personal relationships are often strained
by the use of this type of question."

Of course this form of statement-question is so familiar that more 6
examples than those Prouty has supplied are hardly needed. I think,
though, that Prouty's term—the question-statement—is inadequate to
suggest its underlying wickedness. Perhaps it could more accurately be
called the **interrogative** put-down.

Certainly it is among the most common of weapons, and is especially 7
useful in situations where one wishes to **demoralize** an **adversary**—
often a loved one—without seeming to have meant any harm.

The interrogative put-down is known to every married couple, I 8
suspect, and is perhaps more often employed by those who are in general
on good terms with one another than by those who are not. Those who

---

quarrel openly have no need for the disguised thrust of the interrogative put-down.

It is a sign of our **mutual** affection, I would say, and not a symptom 9 of some submerged hostility, that my wife almost always resorts to the interrogative put-down to let me know that I have done something stupid, such as driving past our turnoff on the freeway again. What she usually says is: "Where are you going?"

This suggests genuine curiosity. She had been expecting me to take 10 the usual turnoff, but I have gone past it, and now, excited by the prospect of adventure, she simply can't wait to find out where I'm taking her. How exciting, she seems to imply, to have an unpredictable mate!

Of course I know the old interrogative put-down when I hear it. I'm 11 not fooled by its mask of innocence. What she really means is, "Well, you've done it again. You really *are* getting absentminded.

Naturally she doesn't wish to come right out and say I'm getting 12 absentminded, because absentminded is a code word for **senile**, which ordinary kindness does not allow her to say. So she simply says "Where are you going?" and the message is received.

★

I'm afraid I do the same thing, especially in matters of the table. 13 She is a good cook: not showy, not fussy, but good, and she is willing to experiment and risk disaster. But she has her pride.

For example, just the other evening I asked her, after sampling an 14 unfamiliar dish: "This is chicken?"

I'm sure she recognized it at once as an interrogative put-down, 15 meaning that I knew very well it was chicken but I didn't like the way it was prepared and I didn't want her to try it again.

Her answer was very clever, neither openly resentful nor **bellig-** 16 **erent**: yet it offered me no recognizable advantage, no chance for a fol-lowup. She might have said, for example, "What do you think it is?" That would have been a *counter* interrogative put-down, meaning "Are you so uncivilized you don't know chicken when you taste it?"

But of course that would have given me an excellent opening. "**Mar-** 17 **inated** herring?" I might have asked, which would have been a *counter-*counter interrogative put-down, meaning "This chicken is so bad it tastes like herring." Two interrogative put-downs in a row, unblocked, are usu-ally enough to achieve the desired result, which is to establish one's superiority for the remainder of the evening.

But alas, what she actually said was: "Does the stereo really have 18 to be that loud?"

Simply brilliant. Not only was it a counter interrogative put-down, 19 meaning "Are you deaf?" (i.e., senile), but a **non sequitur** as well. The old one-two.

There was nothing to do but turn down the stereo and eat my dinner. 20 Whatever it was.

Exercise 37

DIRECTIONS *In each blank at the right, write the letter that identifies the correct definition of each of the following words.*

1. **marital**: (A) about war; (B) about marriage; (C) about the sea; (D) a military rank _____
2. **martial**: (A) about war; (B) about marriage; (C) about the sea; (D) a military rank _____
3. **declarative**: (A) a document; (B) a statement; (C) a clarification; (D) a confusion _____
4. **mutual**: (A) an insurance company; (B) having something in common; (C) going in different directions; (D) meeting in a strange place. _____
5. **ridicule**: (A) very small; (B) a kind of net; (C) to make fun of; (D) to enjoy very much. _____
6. **adversary**: (A) bad luck or misfortune; (B) to advertise or show; (C) a friend or acquaintance; (D) a foe or enemy. _____
7. **diffidence**: (A) confidence; (B) difference; (C) shyness; (D) brashness _____
8. **valid**: (A) difficult to see; (B) silly or foolish; (C) unusually confusing; (D) logically sound _____
9. **interrogative**: (A) a statement; (B) a clarification; (C) a question; (D) an answer _____
10. **demoralize**: (A) to misbehave; (B) to deprive of spirit; (C) to issue demerits; (D) to demolish _____
11. **thrust**: (A) a push; (B) part of the anatomy; (C) a small bird; (D) evidence _____
12. **senile**: (A) old; (B) happy; (C) without interest; (D) dead _____
13. **belligerent**: (A) fat; (B) warlike; (C) ancient; (D) related to _____
14. **marinated**: (A) went to sea; (B) soaked in a liquid; (C) had a cold drink; (D) indulged heavily _____
15. **non sequitur**: (A) cannot be seen; (B) glittering ornament; (C) off the topic, illogical; (D) unable to write _____

A MINI-EXERCISE Using your dictionary if necessary, write intelligent sentences, using the stated words, one of which comes from the preceding vocabulary test. Try to make each sentence contain at least fifteen words.

1. a. **compulsion:** _____

   _____

   _____

   _____

   b. **demoralize:** _____

   _____

   _____

   _____

THE BOYS' AMBITION

Mark Twain

When I was a boy, there was but one permanent ambition among my 1
comrades in our village[1] on the west bank of the Mississippi River. That
was, to be a steamboatman. We had **transient** ambitions of other sorts,
but they were only transient. When a circus came and went, it left us all
burning to become clowns; the first negro minstrel show that ever came
to our section left us all suffering to try that kind of life; now and then
we had a hope that, if we lived and were good, God would permit us to
be pirates. These ambitions faded out, each in its turn; but the ambition
to be a steamboatman always remained.

Once a day a **cheap, gaudy** packet arrived upward from St. Louis, 2
and another downward from Keokuk. Before these events, the day was
glorious with expectancy; after them, the day was a dead and empty thing.
Not only the boys, but the whole village, felt this. After all these years
I can picture that old time to myself now, just as it was then: the white
town drowsing in the sunshine of a summer's morning; the streets empty,
or pretty nearly so; one or two clerks sitting in front of the Water Street
stores, with their splint-bottomed chairs tilted back against the walls,
chins on breasts, hats slouched over their faces, asleep—with shingle-
shavings enough around to show what broke them down; a sow and a
litter of pigs loafing along the sidewalk, doing a good business in watermelon rinds and seeds; two or three lonely little freight piles scattered
about the "levee"; a pile of "skids" on the slope of the stone-paved wharf,
and the **fragrant** town drunkard asleep in the shadow of them; two or
three wood flats at the head of the wharf, but nobody to listen to the
peaceful lapping of the wavelets against them; the great Mississippi, the
majestic, the magnificent Mississippi, rolling its mile-wide tide along,

"The Boys' Ambition" from *Life on the Mississippi* by Mark Twain (Harper & Row). reprinted
by permission of Harper & Row, Publishers, Inc.

[1]Hannibal, Missouri.

shining in the sun; the dense forest away on the other side; the "point" above the town, and the "point" below, bounding the river-glimpse and turning it into a sort of sea, and withal a very still and brilliant and lonely one. Presently a film of dark smoke appears above one of those remote "points"; instantly a negro drayman famous for his quick eye and prodigious voice, lifts up the cry, "S-t-e-a-m-boat a-comin' !" and the scene changes! The town drunkard stirs, the clerks wake up, a furious clatter of drays follows, every house and store pours out a human contribution, and all in a twinkling the dead town is alive and moving. Drays, carts, men, boys, all go hurrying from many quarters to a common center, the wharf. Assembled there, the people fasten their eyes upon the coming boat as upon a wonder they are seeing for the first time. And the boat is rather a handsome sight, too. She is long and sharp and **trim** and pretty; she has two tall, fancy-topped chimneys, with a gilded device of some kind swung between them: a fanciful pilot-house, all glass and "ginger-bread," perched on top of the "texas" deck behind them; the paddle-boxes are gorgeous with a picture or with gilded rays above the boat's name; the boiler-deck, the hurricane-deck, and the texas deck are fenced and ornamented with clean white railings; there is a flag gallantly flying from the jack-staff; the furnace doors are open and the fires glaring bravely; the upper decks are black with passengers; the captain stands by the big bell, calm, imposing, the envy of all; great volumes of the blackest smoke are rolling and tumbling out of the chimneys—a husbanded grandeur created with a bit of pitch-pine just before arriving at a town; the crew are grouped on the forecastle; the broad stage is run far out over the port bow, and an envied deck-hand stands picturesquely on the end of it with a coil of rope in his hand; the pent stem is creaming through the gauge-cocks; the captain lifts his hand, a bell rings, the wheels stop; then they turn back, churning the water to foam, and the steamer is at rest. Then such a scramble as there is to get aboard, and to get ashore, and to take in freight and to discharge freight, all at one and the same time; and such a yelling and cursing as the mates **facilitate** it all with! Ten minutes later the steamer is under way again, with no flag on the jack-staff and no black smoke issuing from the chimneys. After ten more minutes the town is dead again, and the town drunkard asleep by the skids once more.

My father was a justice of the peace, and I supposed he possessed 3 the power of life and death over all men, and could hang anybody that offended him. This was distinction enough for me as a general thing; but the desire to be a steamboatman kept intruding, nevertheless. I first wanted to be a cabin-boy, so that I could come out with a white apron on and shake a table-cloth over the side, where all my old comrades could see me; later I thought I would rather be the deck-hand who stood on the end of the stage-plank with the coil of rope in his hand, because he was particularly **conspicuous**. But these were only daydreams—they were too heavenly to be **contemplated** as real possibilities. By and by one of our boys went away. He was not heard of for a long time. At last he turned up as apprentice engineer or "striker" on a steamboat. This thing shook the bottom out of all my Sunday-school teachings. That boy had been **notoriously** worldly, and I just the reverse; yet he was **exalted** to this eminence, and I left in obscurity and misery. There was nothing generous about this fellow in his greatness. He would always manage to have a rusty bolt to scrub while his boat tarried at our town, and he would sit on the inside guard and scrub it, where we all could see him and envy him and **loathe** him. And whenever his boat was laid up he would come home and swell around the town in his blackest and greasiest clothes, so that nobody could help remembering that he was a steamboatman; and he used all sorts of steamboat technicalities in his talk, as if he were so used to them that he forgot common people could not understand them. He would speak of the "labboard" side of a horse in an easy, natural way that would make one wish he was dead. And he was always talking about "St. Looy" like an old citizen; he would refer casually to occasions when he was "coming down Fourth Street," or when he was "passing by the Planter's House," or when there was a fire and he took a turn on the brakes of "the old Big Missouri"; and then he would go on and lie about how many towns the size of ours were burned down there that day. Two or three of the boys had long been persons of consideration among us because they had been to St. Louis once and had a vague general knowledge of its wonders, but the day of their glory was over now. They **lapsed** into a humble silence, and learned to disappear when the ruthless "cub"-engineer approached. This fellow had money, too, and hair-oil. Also an ignorant silver watch and a showy brass watch-chain. He wore a leather belt and used no suspenders. If ever a youth was cordially admired and hated by his comrades, this one was. No girl could withstand his charms. He "cut out" every boy in the village. When his boat blew up at last, it diffused a **tranquil** contentment among us such as we had not known for months. But when he came home the next week, alive, renowned, and appeared in church all battered up and bandaged, a shining hero, stared at and wondered over by everybody, it seemed to us that the **partiality** of Providence for an undeserving reptile had reached a point where it was open to criticism.

    This creature's career could produce but one result, and it speedily 4 followed. Boy after boy managed to get on the river. The minister's son became an engineer. The doctor's and the postmaster's sons became "mud clerks"; the wholesale liquor dealer's son became a barkeeper on a boat; four sons of the chief merchant, and two sons of the county judge, became pilots. Pilot was the grandest position of all. The pilot, even in those days of trivial wages, had a princely salary—from a hundred and fifty to two hundred and fifty dollars a month, and no board to pay. Two months of his wages would pay a preacher's salary for a year. Now some of us were left **disconsolate**. We could not get on the river—at least our parents would not let us.

So, by and by, I ran away. I said I would never come home again till   5
I was a pilot and could come in glory. But somehow I could not manage it. I went meekly aboard a few of the boats that lay packed together like sardines at the long St. Louis wharf, and humbly inquired for the pilots, but got only a cold shoulder and short words from mates and clerks. I had to make the best of this sort of treatment for the time being, but I had comforting day-dreams of a future when I should be a great and honored pilot, with plenty of money, and could kill some of these mates and clerks and pay for them.

A TIP ON USAGE   For best style use *anxious* to mean "beset with anxiety" or "uneasy" and *eager* to mean "strongly desirous of" or "anticipating with pleasure."

PREFERRED: I was **eager** to make first string on the football team.
PREFERRED: I was **eager** to be alone with Charlotte.
INFERIOR STYLE: I was **anxious** to pass the rumor on.
RIGHT: I was **anxious** about the health of my mother.

A MINI-EXERCISE   Consulting the rules in Lessons Seven through Ten and Lessons Twenty-nine and Thirty if necessary, explain the need for all the marks of punctuation used in the following paragraph.

Shortly after dark on the night of the twelfth, the Air Defense Command radar station at Ellsworth AFB, just east of Rapid City, had received a call from the local ground Observer Corps filter center. A lady spotter at Black Hawk, about 10 miles west of Ellsworth, had reported an extremely bright light low on the horizon, off to the northeast. The radar had been scanning an area to the west, working a jet fighter in some practice patrols, but when they got the report they moved the sector scan to the northeast quadrant. There was a target exactly where the lady reported the light to be. The warrant officer, who was the duty controller for the night, told me that he'd studied the target for several minutes. He knew how weather could affect radar but this target was "well defined, solid, and bright." It seemed to be moving, but very slowly. He called for an altitude reading, and the man on the height-finding radar checked his scope. He also had the target—it was at 16,000 feet.[1]

---

[1] From *The Report on Unidentified Flying Objects* by Edward J. Ruppelt.

Exercise 38

DIRECTIONS   *In each blank at the right, write the letter that identifies the correct definition of each of the following words.*

1. **transient**: (A) beyond and above; (B) sent away; (C) temporary; (D) reluctant   _____
2. **gaudy**: (A) joyous; (B) showy; (C) thin; (D)unwholesome   _____
3. **fragrant**: (A) overripe; (B) a hobo; (C) foul tasting; (D) pleasant smelling   _____
4. **trim** (A) cut into pieces; (B) tricky; (C) neat; (D) messy   _____
5. **gilded**: (A) gold-covered; (B) quite bald; (C) unable to reproduce; (D) old and rusty   _____
6. **facilitate**: (A) make easier; (B) make more difficult; (C) make out of tin; (D) cover with moisture   _____
7. **conspicuous**: (A) with special effort; (B) carefully hidden; (C) easily noticed; (D) absent   _____
8. **contemplated**: (A) cohabited; (B) used a template; (C) thought about; (D) became annoyed   _____
9. **notorious**: (A) unfavorably well-known; (B) little used; (C) bad smelling gas; (D) loud and clumsy   _____
10. **exalted**: (A) shouted aloud; (B) executed; (C) raised above others; (D) sent away from home   _____
11. **loathe**: (A) hate; (B) love; (C) fear; (D) dismay   _____
12. **lapsed**: (A) ran faster than another; (B) spoke with difficulty; (C) declined temporarily; (D) sat on another   _____
13. **tranquil**: (A) peaceful; (B) a medicine; (C) a slanted railroad; (D) a writing instrument   _____
14. **partiality**: (A) part of; (B) favoritism; (C) amount; (D) a small portion   _____
15. **disconsolate**: (A) happy; (B) gloomy; (C) angry; (D) seeking revenge   _____

A MINI-EXERCISE   Using your dictionary if necessary, write intelligent sentences, using the stated words. Try to make each sentence contain at least fifteen words.

1. a. **condescension:** _____

_____

_____

  b. **patronizing:** _____

_____

_____

2. a. **perpetuate:** _____

_____

_____

  b. **perpetrate:** _____

_____

_____

SHARING THE WEALTH

S. I. Hayakawa

The new deal **effected** a great many changes in Americans' attitudes 1
toward their government. I do not quarrel about its necessity at the time.
But I'd like to discuss its consequences and to ask the question. What is
government for?

For a long time, the function of government has been to maintain 2
national security, to preserve domestic order and **tranquility**, to regulate
trade, and to write and administer the laws. At no time did the people
of the United States amend the Constitution to say that another function
of government is to redistribute income.

That, however, is the principal function of government today. Roy 3
Ash, former director of the Office of Management and Budget, has pointed
out that transfer payments—payments for aid to families with dependent
children, food stamps, Medicaid, housing **subsidies**, supplementary Social Security income programs, social services, and the like—comprise
one-half of federal expenditures. We are reaching the point, he said, where
there will soon be more people benefiting from federal-government payments than taxpayers to carry the load.

How did we get ourselves into this fix? One trouble is that, the way 4
the rules are written for most social programs, more and more people find
themselves entitled to payments—and the rules continue to be written
so that even larger numbers become eligible. The food-stamp program,
for example, began in 1964 and served 400,000 people at a cost of $35
million. Now it serves nearly 19 million people at a cost of $5.7 billion.

The **momentum** in the direction of additional services is such that 5
further increases in benefit—and therefore in taxes—seem almost **inevitable**. The producers of goods and services will have to give up more
than half their earnings to support the **beneficiaries** of the system.

As for the beneficiaries, they will remain discontented, since many 6
of their benefits will come not in cash, but in kind—such as medical care,
day-care services, and educational grants-in-aid.

In brief, everyone is going to be unhappy—both those who are taxed 7
and those who benefit from the taxes—which means the whole country.
When there are more beneficiaries of transfer payments than there are
taxpayers, we shall really have changed the social system!

I believe that we all accept the principle that an **affluent** society 8
must do what it can to prevent hunger and misery, and also to provide
equality of opportunity to those who have been denied it. But how far can
a society go in the redistribution of wealth without changing the very
nature of society? I think this is a problem that we've got to face. I do not
think that a majority in Congress are trying to face it, or realize that it
is a problem, because so many of them are still hard at work at this
business of redistributing income.

All that reminds me of what happened in the universities during 9
the 1960s and 1970s—events that I witnessed from a ringside seat. During
this period we had a fashion of giving A's to every student—there were
no failures. The effect on academic life was **devastating**. When **illiterate**
or lazy students could get an A average, good students stopped studying.
The result was a profound change in academic life: formerly dropouts
were those who failed in their studies; in the 1960s and 1970s most of the
dropouts were the most gifted and brilliant students, who found that
college had become meaningless.

What happens in the schools is not unlike what happens in society 10
at large when the penalties of **improvidence**, laziness, or ignorance are
not just softened, but removed. When there is no such thing as failure,
there is no such thing as success either. Motivation, the desire to excel,
the urge to accomplishment—all these disappear. The **dynamism** of society is lost.

This, I'm afraid, is the direction in which our society has been going 11
steadily for many years. The biggest losers are the brightest and most
capable men and women. But the average person is a loser too. Faced
with no challenge, assured of a comfortable living whether they work or
not, such persons become willing dependents, content with a **parasitical**
relationship to the rest of society.

What is significant in our time is that there is a whole class of people 12
interested in encouraging this parasitism. Many welfare officials and
social workers are threatened with a loss of their power if there is a
marked reduction in the number of their clients, so they are motivated
to increase rather than decrease welfare dependency.

Politicians, too, have flourished by getting increased federal grants 13
for this or that disadvantaged group. They go back to their **constituents**
and say. "Look what I've done for you, and get reelected. These are the

officeholders who are far more interested in being reelected than in doing what is good for people, good for the economy, good for the nation.

If everybody is rewarded just for being alive, you get the same sort 14 of effect as you do when you reward every student just for being enrolled. You destroy not only education, you destroy society by giving A's to everyone. This is a philosophical consideration that bothers me very much as I sit in the United States Senate and see its great budget **allocations** going through.

The United States is a profit-oriented industrial society. Because we 15 are **capable** of the mass production of consumer goods, we have mass consumption—and advertising to stimulate that consumption. The unintended revolution created by mass production and mass consumption has come close to producing a classless society in America. Executives and workingmen alike drive Comets and Cadillacs, drink Coke and Schlitz and Old Grand-Dad, eat Nabisco wafers and Hormel ham, and watch the Johnny Carson show.

There is no "ruling class." Anyone can become President, including 16 a graduate of Harvard (John F. Kennedy), of Southwest State Teachers College (Lyndon B. Johnson), of Whittier College (Richard M. Nixon), or of no college at all (Harry S. Truman)—and, after attaining that lofty height, he can still be **impeached**.

And the poor of America are not poor by world standards. Our welfare 17 clients live far better than the working people of more than half the world.

We are people of plenty. We have become so through our energy, 18 our inventiveness, our encouragement of **initiative**. Yet with the **prevailing** political philosophy of rewarding the unsuccessful and punishing the creators of our national abundance, there is no guarantee that we shall continue to be people of plenty. Washington is full of power-hungry **mandarins** and bureaucrats who distrust abundance, which gives people freedom, and who love scarcity and "zero growth," which give them power to assign, **allocate**, and control. If they ever win out, heaven help us! Americans do not know how to live with scarcity.

Exercise 39

DIRECTIONS *In each blank at the right, write the letter that identifies the correct definition of each of the following words.*

1. **tranquility**: (A) a state of calm; (B) a state of glory; (C) a state of anxiety; (D) a state of union   _____
2. **subsidy**: (A) below the surface; (B) an undersea city; (C) a government payment; (D) the purchase price   _____
3. **momentum**: (A) brief period of time; (B) speed of movement; (C) antacid tablet; (D) form of government   _____
4. **inevitable**: (A) unavoidable; (B) untrue; (C) not living; (D) erased or obliterated   _____
5. **beneficiary**: (A) a good, kind person; (B) a person in religious orders; (C) a person who diets; (D) a person who receives benefits   _____
6. **affluent**: (A) waste water; (B) wealthy; (C) flows easily; (D) a loud noise   _____
7. **devastating**: (A) laying waste to; (B) making larger; (C) selling an estate; (D) settling down   _____
8. **improvidence**: (A) referring to God; (B) not referring to God; (C) thrifty; (D) wasteful   _____
9. **dynamism**: (A) generating electricity; (B) force or vigor; (C) refusing to die; (D) rule by a small group   _____
10. **parasitical**: (A) growing by itself; (B) thought transference; (C) dependent upon another; (D) a restatement of an idea   _____
11. **constitutent**: (A) a piece of the action; (B) someone represented by an elected official; (C) a person exhibiting perverse behavior; (D) an absolutely ridiculous assumption   _____
12. **allocations**: (A) a certain portion of expenses; (B) all of the locations; (C) a distant site; (D) a mathematical variable   _____
13. **impeached**: (A) put a peach into; (B) challenged with misconduct; (C) removed from office; (D) incarcerated   _____
14. **initiative**: (A) sign one's initials; (B) start from the beginning; (C) basic intelligence; (D) ability to follow through   _____
15. **mandarin**: (A) a Chinese official; (B) a civil servant with great powers; (C) an elaborate literary style; (D) a dialect of an Oriental language   _____

16. **illiterate**: (A) unable to speak; (B) unable to read; (C) unable to write; (D) unable to read *and* write. _____

17. **prevailing**: (A) unusual; (B) hostile; (C) most common; (D) tallest _____

18. **allocate**: (A) fence in; (B) distribute; (C) collect; (D) put in a crate _____

19. **capable**: (A) can do; (B) can't do; (C) ought to; (D) should _____

20. **effected**: (A) caused to happen; (B) changed; (C) made another ill; (D) acted silly. _____

A MINI-EXERCISE   In the blanks provided, write the correct form of the pronoun or pronouns given below the blanks. For example, the possible forms of *they* are *they, them, their, theirs,* and *themselves.*

1. It was Louis _____ who borrowed _____.
   (he) *(she)*

2. The coach was annoyed at _____ fumbling the ball.
   (you)

3. You should order _____ mushrooms to prevent
   (them or those?)
   _____ being poisoned.
   (you)

4. It was they _____ who visited the sick dog said to be
   (they)
   _____.
   (they)

5. You shouldn't interfere with _____ style of dress.
   (he)

6. The library _____ didn't stock _____
   (it) *(that or those?)*
   type of book.

7. Henry's father saw _____ swimming and objected to
   (he)
   _____ swimming at that hour.
   (he)

8. Is there anything wrong with _____, asking
   (you)
   _____ kind of question?
   (this or these?)

9. Just between you and _____, Morris is smater than
   (I)
   _____.
   (I)

10. Was the package for Joe and _____, or is it that
    (I)
    _____ not telling?
    (your or you're?)

IN DEFENSE OF SIN
Phyllis McGinley

Mothers, even the wisest of them, are **improvident** creatures; they never 1
really believe their children will grow up. It isn't that they do not plan.
Their lives are feverish with planning, the paths behind them littered
with discarded maps and charts and abandoned strategies. It is simply
that parenthood is such a hand-to-mouth existence, such a series of skir-
mishes won (or lost), that they can only live, like soldiers in the field,
from day to day.

Sufficient unto the hour is the crisis thereof. Babies must cut molars, 2
kindergartners start off to school, little boys break windows, and little
girls their hearts at dancing class. Each peril has to be faced as it is
encountered—the first fib, the measles, the naughty word, the sprained
ankle, and the explanation of sex. Puppies get run over, teachers are
unjust, cronies turn out to be faithless; and every event is an emergency
for which there can be no real preparation except love and common sense.

And then suddenly a mother looks about her and her children are 3
children no longer. This is a curious moment, compounded in almost equal
portions of **exhilaration**, panic, and surprise. In the ascent of her particular Everest, she has reached a sort of plateau, and there is triumph
in that. But as she peers back at the trail by which she has come—at all
the little peaks surmounted and chasms crossed—what a safe and pleasant
climb it appears in **retrospect**!

Even the most desperate situation had this consolation—that how- 4
ever inadequate her hand, it was there to be reached for. She could **interpose** herself between the child and life.

Now that must change. Our daughters (for since I have only daugh- 5
ters, I must speak of the gender I know best) must climb the rest of the
way very nearly unaccompanied, and it wrings the heart. Perhaps they

From *The Province of the Heart* by Phyllis McGinley. Copyright 1954 by Phyllis McGinley.
Reprinted by permission of The Viking Press.

have not quite recovered from adolescence. They are still unsure of themselves. They still keep diaries, which they lock away in secret drawers. They worry about their complexions and are touchy about their friends and take a gentle suggestion as a personal affront. But they have driving licenses and a clothes allowance; and the boys they bring home are growing up to their ears and speak **condescendingly** to adults in manly voices. Next year or the year after will bring college or a job. It will also bring either love or its **facsimile**.

What then shall I, what shall any mother, give them for an **amulet** 6 against the dangerous journey they must take alone? For we know, unfashionable as it may be to say so, that the dangers are real. Thousands of textbooks, editorials in the press; papers read to learned societies, a whole new profession of consultants on the matter, often attached to the schools—all these, plus the conversation of the young themselves, attest their genuineness.

Surely no one would be **naïve** enough to think that little biological 7 chats about conception and bodily structure are sufficient. Our daughters have known for a long time just how babies are born, and have accepted, we hope, their theoretical knowledge of sex gravely and sweetly. But the tides of spring run strong. Home ties are breaking off, and to the confusion of new voices and circumstances and the competition for popularity will be added the pulse of their own blood. Curiosity, even, will have its urgent pull.

Admitted that **illicit** sexual adventure is a peril, at least for what 8 used to be called "marriageable girls," what memorable word can we teach them that they can repeat like an **incantation** if the tide should become a threatening flood?

I have talked this over with friends and psychologists. I have read 9 the brochures and the textbooks. I have also thought about the problem deeply, and I know what I, for one, shall do. It's a very **iconoclastic** thing; it has not been mentioned at all in any of the dozens of pamphlets and tomes I have dipped into. But it seems sanest. I shall remind my daughters simply that there is such a thing as right and such a thing as wrong. I shall commit the dreadful heresy of talking about sin.

Sin has always been an ugly word, but it has been made so in a new 10 sense over the last half-century. It has been made not only ugly but **passé**. People are no longer sinful, they are only immature or underprivileged or frightened or, more particularly, sick. And I think it has no doubt been helpful to some unfortunates to find themselves so considered. But my daughters and yours are fairly brave and certainly privileged and more mature than we might have hoped; and if their souls had been sick, we should have known it before this. My children would believe themselves mortally insulted to have their **misdemeanors** classified as illness. In our household we have never been afraid of sin as a common noun.

In fact, although until now we have never used the word in con- 11
nection with matters of sex, we have found it a subject of fruitful discussion. We think it is sinful to slander our neighbors. We believe that
stealing and cheating and bearing false witness are sins. We think dishonest politicians are sinners. Once, when intolerance raised its una-
trractive head, we disposed of it readily. We refused to repeat all the
windy arguments that have become the standard **clichés**; we just said
that anti-Semitism, like every other artificial bias against one's fellow
man, is a sin. And that—as nearly as is humanly possible—was that.

Oddly enough I find little opposition to this last stand among the 12
schoolbook **coterie**. If they decline to mention sin in connection with
prejudice, they do consent to speak of "**erroneous** social thinking." But
not once, in any text, did I come across a reference to either right or wrong
in regard to the great act of love. Most of the books naturally **deplore**
sexual experiment. They use all the commonplace arguments. They point
out the physical dangers, the emotional involvement, the inconveniences
and distresses of **furtive** passion.

And while some writers I find **inane** to the point of vulgarity (One 13
author even suggested coy things to say to "break off a petting session"),
others have set down superbly reasoned appeals for chastity. But how
strong is reason against a tidal wave? I think conscience proves a superior
shelter. My daughters shall be told that there exist a moral law and an
ancient commandment and that they do wrong to flout them.

And now against my critics (who will be many if they are well versed 14
in the gospel that had its ultimate evangelist in Dr. Kinsey) I should like
to argue the wholesomeness of treating extramarital relations as sinful.
For this is what I do consider such teaching—wholesome and even
effective.

To begin with, sin implies goodness, and the young love goodness 15
with all their hearts. We all know what idealists they are, how fiercely
they react against injustice and cruelty, how they hate hypocrisy and
cant. To take away their delight in virtue, to tell them that they must
withstand temptations because temptations are merely urges toward immature behavior, is to give them stones when they pant for bread. It is
to weaken the muscles of their characters.

In the second place, it is confusing. I think we have all argued too 16
much with our children in this generation. It has been drummed into our
ears that we must explain the reasons behind every taboo, and we in turn
have drummed these reasons into their ears until they are nearly deaf-
ened. I remember my older daughter, when she was small, once listening
quietly to my careful **dissertation** on why some action was not to be
tolerated. Finally she burst out, "Oh Mother, why don't you just tell me
not to for once and stop explaining!" Just so. It is simpler to treat sex
morally than reasonably. Moreover, believing in sin is a kind of tactful

armor. A girl might find, in a given situation, that it was better to tell a young man that he was doing wrong than that he was being a social dunce. His self-esteem would suffer less.

"But how about guilt?" ask my opponents. "When the young believe **17** in sin, they must necessarily feel guilty if they commit it. Is not that destructive?"

From my **fallible** viewpoint, I do not think so. For sin implies for- **18** giveness. One who has done a wrong can be sorry and recover. If he is generous enough, he can even forgive himself. But how does one go about forgiving oneself for a lapse in taste or a **gaucherie**? We have all committed sins in our lives, meanness and angers and lies. But most of us have forgotten them easily. What we find hard to forget or to forgive are the silly things we have said, the times we have been awkward and **doltish**. It is one of my articles of psychological faith that a girl (and perhaps the same thing applies to a boy) would find life less broken apart after a misguided love affair if she could feel that she had been sinful rather than a fool. And I hope that all our daughters are sure enough of parental love not to let a sense of guilt destroy them in silence.

Now all this does not mean that because I am, like Coolidge's min- **19** ister, against sin, I am also against sex or that my girls will get that impression. On the contrary, they will believe, I hope, that it is one of the moving graces of the world, far too magnificent a gift to be carelessly handled. We three women in our house are proud of being women. We feel a little sorry for men, who can never bear children or be wives. so when I mention the moral standard, they will understand that it is for the sake of protecting this magnificence that mankind has slowly, strugglingly, been building for several thousand years. Fashions in morals **fluctuate**. Puritan rigor gives way to Restoration license, and that in turn drowned in Victorian severity. It is possible that much of our own permissive nonsense will be frowned on by the generation now growing up. But right and wrong do not really alter, nor do their consequences. And of this my daughters must be aware.

So what in the end shall I tell my daughters about chastity before **20** marriage? Of *course*, I shall be sensible and point out the ordinary social penalties attached to any other conduct. I shall touch on the possible pregnancy, the untidiness, and the heartbreak. But I shall also say that love is never merely a biological act but one of the few miracles left on earth, and that to use it cheaply is a sin.

In fact that is what I have already told them. **21**

A TIP ON USAGE   For good style, avoid the low-level *hadn't ought to*. PREFERRED: We **shouldn't** be careless in the chemistry laboratory. POOR STYLE: You **hadn't ought to** criticize your good friends.

A TIP ON USAGE   Avoid the nonsensical phrase *in this day* **in** *age*. Instead, use *in this day* **and** *age* if you use this cliché at all.

Exercise 40

DIRECTIONS *In each blank at the right, write the letter that identifies the correct definition of each of the following words.*

1. **improvident**: (A) selfish; (B) wayward, wandering; (C) lacking in foresight, having no thrift; (D) devoted to children _____
2. **exhilaration**: (A) disappointment; (B) disgust; (C) state of being aglow with happiness; (D) state of being taken aback _____
3. **retrospect**: (A) public; (B) a view of the past; (C) a thinking of oneself; (D) self-congratulation _____
4. **interpose**: (A) to back off from; (B) to rush into; (C) to put between; (D) to be pushy _____
5. **condescending**: (A) in a mumbling way; (B) in incomprehensible language; (C) speaking down to or making a display of courtesy; (D) speaking as equals _____
6. **facsimile**: (A) direct opposite; (B) severe hate; (C) affection which is not love; (D) a copy or imitation of _____
7. **amulet**: (A) a charm to protect against evil; (B) a bracelet, (C) an expense account; (D) advice _____
8. **naïve** (A) stupid; (B) highly intelligent; (C) crazy, unbalanced; (D) lacking in wordly experience _____
9. **illicit**: (A) mutually agreeable; (B) highly pleasurable; (C) not pleasurable; (D) unlawful or unauthorized _____
10. **incantation**: (A) a parable; (B) a biblical quotation; (C) magic words; (D) reasonable words _____
11. **iconoclastic**: (A) unheard of; (B) silly; (C) highly appropriate; (D) attacking cherished beliefs _____
12. **passé**: (A) unacceptable; (B) out-of-date; (C) unreasonable; (D) immoral _____
13. **misdemeanor**: (A) a minor offense; (B) a major offense; (C) religious transgression; (D) act of mental illness _____
14. **cliché**: (A) mode of explanation; (B) incorrect explanation; (C) a trite or overused expression; (D) an argument _____
15. **coterie**: (A) publishers; (B) explanation; (C) a small group of those devoted to a person or cause; (D) those who accept something uncritically _____

16. **erroneous**: (A) unreligious; (B) logical; (C) debatable; (D) incorrect   _____

17. **deplore**: (A) to advocate; (B) to steer clear of; (C) to try to explain; (D) to show regret for   _____

18. **furtive**: (A) secret or evasive; (B) excessive; (C) openly expressed; (D) brought to a conclusion   _____

19. **inane**: (A) inaccurate; (B) pompous; (C) empty of meaning; (D) offensive or obscene   _____

20. **cant**: (A) sin; (B) insincere behavior accompanied by pleasant actions; (C) meaningless explanation; (D) hypocritical expression of piety   _____

21. **dissertation**: (A) a speech or essay making a point; (B) objection to; (C) a scolding; (D) an impatient explanation   _____

22. **fallible**: (A) subject to change; (B) subject to error; (C) subject to attack; (D) not to be disputed   _____

23. **gaucherie**: (A) error in logic; (B) an awkward action; (C) a forgivable mistake; (D) a boastful action   _____

24. **doltish**: (A) mean; cruel; (B) like a stupid person; (C) like an animal; (D) clumsy and stumbling   _____

25. **fluctuate**: (A) derive from God; (B) do not derive from God; (C) change or shift about; (D) remain subject to debate   _____

THE SECOND WAVE OF FEMINISM
Edward D. Eddy, Jr.

Today I want to talk about women. Surprisingly, this is still a risky 1
business to undertake with a predominantly male audience. Many American men continue to enjoy their little snickers about "the fairer sex, God
bless 'em." The basically sentimental male just doesn't like to give up his
blonde, brunette, or redhead on a pedestal.

For twelve years, I've been serving as president of the fourth oldest 2
women's college in the nation. The fact that many of you know less than
you should about Chatham attests to the low priority which this nation,
your companies, and probably you have given over the years to the education of women. But times are changing, and it seems particularly
appropriate for this organization to have as its first speaker of the new
year one of the oldest living male presidents of one of the oldest existing
female colleges.

What are some of the changes which will have a direct effect on your 3
corporation or profession? Let me cite one **graphic** illustration: Partly
due to the economy and partly due to the **stimulus** of the Federal government, education for a career has become a primary thrust of the
American school system. Swept along with this wave—indeed, in some
instances, riding its crest—are the women of America.

As recently as three to five years ago when I talked with graduating 4
high school students, the young women would ask me. "Can you take a
course in art in your freshman year in college? I think I'd like to explore
it." Today these students say, "I intend to be an artist." Or the question
of a few years ago might have been: "Maybe I'll major in political science.
Do you think it might be useful if I ever wanted a job?" The high school
senior of 1973 says, "I am going to be a lawyer or an urban specialist, so
I'll need some political science."

Published by permission of the author.

This distinct change in the attitude of the high school senior is 5
happening among women of almost every age and background. Many
women are asking why they cannot make a contribution beyond that of
mother and wife as their husbands automatically do beyond that of husband and father. Mature women are returning to the workforce and returning to school to resume their education in increasing numbers. Recent
reports indicate they make above-average students because their motivation tends to be rather high. These women, too, want to be lawyers,
artists and **urban** specialists. Not every one will be working full-time but
each is intent on making a substantial contribution.

The young woman of today is intent on seeking self-fulfillment and 6
being independent and self-directed. She feels that she can win that independence and gain that direction by becoming a skilled, competent
professional. Thus more and more young women are looking for careers
in business, government, social agencies, the arts and the professions as
their way of "making it" in a world of work which is still a man's world.
(And if you have any doubt about the man's world, glance around you to
count the number of women who are here today.)

Some people contend, of course, that this is a man's world because 7
the woman's place is in the home. For the male **chauvinist** there is only
brief comfort in that myth. The labor statistics show that 75% of all women
alive today will be gainfully employed at some point in their lives. Furthermore, the percentage of women who work is mushrooming. In 1920,
only 23% of American women were working at any given time. Now the
figure is almost 45%.

Of course "work" for many of these women means employment in 8
a **menial** low-paying, and usually dead-end job. Thirty-four per cent of
all employed women today are clerical workers. The **median** earnings
of women working full time are about 57% of the earnings of men, down
from 64% in 1955.

The women who do contribute in their work far beyond their defined 9
responsibilities—and there are many such women—are seldom rewarded
or promoted. Such a person must be content with the occasional recognition that, when the chips are down, she is the unofficial mainstay.
Stewart Brand, the creator of the Whole Earth Catalog, has observed that
in his experience "every working organization has one over-worked, un-
der-paid woman in the middle of things carrying most of the load." In all
likelihood, on her mantelpiece at home is the silver ashtray—she probably
doesn't smoke and never did—with the message that in 1950 she was
named Secretary of the Year in her division.

The statistics I've cited and the living examples are all too familiar 10
to you. But what may not be so familiar will be the increasing number
of women who are looking actively for advancement or for a new job in
your offices. This woman may be equipped with professional skills and

perhaps valuable experience. She will not be content to be Executive Assistant to Mr. Seldom Seen or the Assistant Vice President's Girl Friday, who is the only one who comes in on Saturday.

She is the **symbol** of what I call the Second Wave of Feminism. She is the modern woman who is determined *to be*. 11

Her forerunner was the radical feminist who interpreted her trapped position as a female as oppression by the master class of men. Men, she believed, had created a domestic, **servile** role for women in order that men could have the career and the opportunity to participate in making the great decisions of society. Thus the radical feminist held that women through history had been oppressed and dehumanized, mainly because man chose to exploit his wife and the mother of his children. Sometimes it was deliberate exploitation and sometimes it was the innocence of never looking beneath the **pretensions** of life. 12

The radical feminists found strength in banding together. Coming to recognize each other for the first time, they could explore their own identities, realize their own power, and view the male and his system as the common enemy. The first phases of feminism in the last five years often took on this militant, class-warfare tone. Betty Friedan, Gloria Steinem, Germaine Greer, and many others hammered home their ideas with a persistence that aroused and intrigued many of the brightest and most able women in the country. Consciousness-raising groups allowed women to explore both their identities and their dreams—and the two were often found in direct conflict. 13

What is the **stereotyped** role of American women? Marriage. A son. Two daughters. Breakfast. Ironing. Lunch. Bowling, maybe a garden club or for the very daring, non-credit courses in ceramics. Perhaps an occasional cocktail party. Dinner. Football or baseball on TV. Each day the same. Never any growth in expectations—unless it is growth because the husband has succeeded. The **inevitable** question: "Is *that* all there is to life?" 14

The rapid growth of many feminist organizations **attests** to the fact that these radical feminists had touched some vital nerves. The magazine "Ms." was born in the year of the death of the magazine "Life." But too often the consciousness-raising sessions became ends in themselves. Too often sexism reversed itself—and man-hating was encouraged. Many women found themselves as unhappy with the fanatical feminist as they had been with the male chauvinist. 15

It is not difficult, therefore, to detect a trend toward moderation. Consciousness-raising increasingly is regarded as a means to independence and fulfillment, rather than a ceremony of fulfillment itself. Genuine independence can be realized through competence, through finding a career, through the use of education. Remember that for many decades the education of women was not supposed to be useful. 16

In what Gloria Steinem might call a chauvinist statement, Andre 17
Malraux has proclaimed, "A man is what he does." Now, as if for the first
time, the question is posed to all women: "What are you going to do?
What are you going to be?" The modern woman begins to answer, but it
is not the answer to which we are accustomed. She says, "I have chosen
to be a wife and mother." Or "I have chosen to pursue a career in business . . . to be a doctor . . . to run a lab . . . to go into politics."

A woman should have—must have—the same **options** as a man. 18
She must choose the life she wants for herself; competing on an equal
basis with men. This is the Second Wave of Feminism.

Two and one-half years ago Chatham College decided to back what 19
seemed to be a national trend toward coeducation. It chose to remain a
women's college. With this decision came a renewed commitment that the
Chatham experience should take constant **cognizance** of the changing
role of modern women. We knew that the traditional liberal arts college
was in danger of being regarded as **irrelevant**. but we also knew that,
with the second wave of feminism, a college enrolling women could become
very revelant indeed both for the women enrolled and for the society
served.

Chatham has remained a liberal arts college but with a difference. 20
A true liberal education is not narrowly vocational in nature. Instead,
it enables the graduate to follow a variety of options. Chatham's changes
have included the introduction of highly flexible curriculum which forces
each student to help design her own education. Under the guidance of a
faculty advisor, she begins to choose the program—and possibly the life
pattern—which best suits her as an individual.

The college calendar includes a one-month **interim** program during 21
January. A student may take an intensive course in one area of special
interest or may design her own project. During this January, for example,
Chatham women are working all over the world on projects they designed
or in courses they chose. One Chatham student is an intern at the American Embassy in London; 15 students are observing and assisting in an
open school in England; eight have joined a group studying Spanish in
Mexico. Nine Chatham students are working in the Florida Keys on a
marine biology project. In Pittsburgh a student is at Pittsburgh National
Bank, focusing on international finance; another young woman is working
for PPG Industries, using mathematical models in distribution systems.
At the Cleft Palate Clinic at Presbyterian Hospital a student is doing
laboratory work in preparation for a career as a doctor.

Many of these students will have received guidance and field place- 22
ment help through the Pittsburgh-Chatham Program, a foundation-spon-
sored experiment in bringing the city and the liberal arts college in closer
working relationship.

For many years Chatham has attracted to Pittsburgh over two-thirds 23
of its students from across the nation. A large percentage of these women—

some of the sharpest and most creative America has to offer—remain in the Pittsburgh area or return after a few years elsewhere. The pool of talent is substantial. We stand at the threshold of a new era when, for the first time, the needs of a city—of business, industry, the professions, the arts—can be met in a far more substantial way by the products of liberal education for women.

Recently, Nora Ephron, the *Esquire* columnist, attended her 10th 24 reunion at her New England alma mater. She reported that, as a feminist, she felt very out of place. Her particular college obviously had neglected its responsibility to "force young women to define themselves before they **abdicate** the task and become defined by their husbands." She concluded that her alma mater was irrelevant. "This college," she wrote, "is about as meaningful to the educational process in America as a perfume factory is to the national economy."

I assure you that Pittsburgh's Chatham college is no perfume factory. 25 Its relevance is tied to an educational experience which forces the student to begin to make choices about her own future as she follows an academic pattern which she has helped to chart. A college for women must enable the student to cope realistically with the problems and possibilities of being a women today. And being a woman today has no stereotype.

Don Quixote, the man of La Mancha, tilted at windmills in the quest 26 for his supposedly impossible dream. The woman graduate today, intent on realizing her goal to be an economist, an administrator, the head of a chain of stores, or whatever from among her options, will also be tilting at windmills of another kind. She will be fighting the lingering myths which surround the employment of women. You probably have others to add to my list. Let's see what we can put together as a start:

Myth Number One You can't count on a woman to appear on the job. 27 First there are those times in the month and then those emotional outbursts. Nonsense. Studies show that the women's absentee rate is the same as men's.

Myth Number Two You can't keep a women in a job. She will leave to 28 get married or to have a baby. Untrue. Statistics show that men leave companies just as often as women do.

Myth Number Three A woman just isn't ambitious in her work. Up to 29 this point, why should she be, if she ends up only with a silver ashtray on the mantle? Don't judge yesterday's ambition by tomorrow's determination. Give the woman a chance to move up—and watch not only her ambitious develop but the onset of anxiety among the men.

Myth Number Four A woman is never mobile and can't be considered 30 for transfer to a better job in another city. False. Many women in business today are moving their families. And their husbands are following the lead of the wife to another location.

Myth Number Five The independent, self-directed woman is a home- 31 wrecker. As soon as she begins to think for herself, she loses interest in her husband and her family. This is false, too. A study of divorce rates shows that divorce is more common among housewives than among career women. A bright, active woman usually finds her whole life is more fulfilling if she has a chance to "be somebody" outside of the narrow confines of the home. And the horizons of the home are expanded in the process.

Myth Number Six   A woman just can't wear two hats and do a decent 32 job. How can she be a mother and a top lawyer, a manager and a happy wife? The cruelty of this question is easy to spot if we merely ask it about a man: How can that man be a decent father and husband if he is a good lawyer, an efficient manager?

Myths are misty to spot but curiously easy to hide behind. Many 33 companies will use these myths to avoid a genuine response to women seeking careers. Instead, they will rely on **tokenism** as the easy way out. Tokenism is, of course, counterproductive. It doesn't accomplish anything to hire a women merely to bow to some outer-directed or self-imposed quota, or in the belief that such an act is a noble nod to social obligations. If a women is to be productive, she must be given the same opportunity as a man. And this includes all of the responsibility which accompanies a position, as well as the chance to rise to the highest possible position.

Let's resist having our appetite satisfied with half a loaf. Some of 34 us can be enthusiastic about hiring women—so long as we have the middle-level managerial spots as the goal. The Second Wave of Feminism—woman's concentration on a career as a basis for independence— will be successful only when a capable woman is regarded as a natural choice for the presidency of United States Steel or the United States of America.

That day perhaps isn't as far off as many men suspect. It will be 35 hastened by those very factors which make women such a vital new resource for business and the professions. These women are ground-breakers, pioneers. They are no longer content to follow the traditional routes of social service, teaching, and **dietetics**. They expect to enter any career that a man with similar skills and capabilities can pursue.

As a pioneer, this new woman has made a conscious decision to 36 become an exception. And she, more often than not, is exceptional. As a highly motivated individual, she wants all of the responsibilities given to a man with her talents. She's the kind of woman who rises above the traditional male and female roles to function as a capable person, regardless of sex. She's the kind of women who need not rely on titles, pecking orders, and the size of the lettering on the office door. She is interested in getting the job done—if only because for so many years women like her have been denied any role in the making of corporate decisions at any level.

We have talked rather politely up to this point about the education 37 and employment of women. Maybe now is the time to face the harsh picture of reality. If any business or industry henceforth wishes to do business with the United States government or to manufacture and distribute products which are purchased by women as consumers, that firm is under the gun. Not only does it have to employ more women and in more responsible roles, but it will make good business sense to do so.

My question, then, is why doesn't it make good business sense also 38 to appoint the best women you can find, to assist in their education, and to realize from them the immense amount of insight and competence which they have to offer?

I hope that you will, indeed, take a second look, or a third and fourth 39 one, at the women in your organization and at the level of women you plan to hire in the future. You will be surprised at what the Second Wave of Feminism will bring you. You won't be able to fall back on the myths, to hide behind the alleged "maleness" of heavy industry, mercantile operations, banking, real estate management, middle business, or whatever it is that your life is dedicated to. Only men will suffer from the threat to the masculinity of their jobs. Women will be too busy doing those jobs to worry about the sex in them.

Perhaps now you can sense why I feel so strongly that there is a 40 genuine **mandate** for strong colleges for women in our nation and especially in cities like Pittsburgh. The mandate is to prepare those who have been tagged as second-class citizens so that, when they go out into the world, they can have all of the choices of first-class citizens.

It is not our job at Chatham to fire up the goals in women so that 41 they will not be contented with anything less than the top office or the Nobel prize. But we do want to make sure that IF the Chatham woman has such aspirations, she may follow her dream with all of the advantages of any college graduate.

Exercise 41

DIRECTIONS *In each blank at the right, write the letter that identifies the correct definition of each of the following words.*

1. **graphic**: (A) proved true; (B) highly important; (C) giving a clear and effective picture; (D) being full of lines   _____
2. **stimulus**: (A) a subsidy of money; (B) a dictatorial decree; (C) an organized program; (D) something that quickens action   _____
3. **urban**: (A) generalized; (B) pertaining to money; (C) pertaining to cities; (D) pertaining to male activities   _____
4. **chauvinist**: (A) an opportunist; (B) one who is zealous and belligerant about his or her own cause; (C) one who acts illegally; (D) one who does not understand the rights of others   _____
5. **menial**: (A) pertaining to tasks calling for little ability; (B) pertaining to work a particular person hates; (C) having to do with bedpans; (D) unjust; improper   _____
6. **median**: (A) the part that is spendable; (B) money earned by work rather than capital; (C) situated in the exact middle; (D) being in the lower half   _____
7. **symbol**: (A) an advance guard; (B) the best part of; (C) the originator of; (D) something representing something else   _____
8. **servile**: (A) pertaining to the home; (B) pertaining to having babies; (C) slavishly submissive; (D) resentful   _____
9. **pretension**: (A) something alleged or of doubtful truth; (B) financial standings; (C) the real meaning of; (D) the higher aspects of   _____
10. **stereotyped**: (A) pertaining to the arts; (B) conventional; in a fixed form; (C) common or usual; (D) most cherished   _____
11. **inevitable**: (A) final; (B) first; (C) most important; (D) unavoidable   _____
12. **attest**: (A) to allude to; (B) to make the most of; (C) to explain a difficult subject; (D) to claim or show the truth of   _____

13. **option**: (A) rate of pay; (B) governmental protection; (C) right to choose; (D) ability to achieve   ———

14. **cognizance**: (A) notice of; (B) action leading to a result; (C) paternal interest in; (D) agreement to   ———

15. **irrelevant**: (A) of low quality; (B) of declining quality; (C) not to be applicable or of use to; (D) overrated   ———

16. **interim**: (A) intensely active; (B) without guidance; (C) an intervening period; (D) something not of lasting importance   ———

17. **abdicate**: (A) to give up formally; (B) to handle badly; (C) to handle successfully; (D) to trade for something else   ———

18. **tokenism**: (A) high pay; (B) low pay; (C) evasion; (D) something of pretended high but only small value   ———

19. **dietetics**: (A) the raising of a family; (B) science of preparing food; (C) clerical work; (D) ministering to the poor   ———

20. **mandate**: (A) male desire; (B) desire for males; (C) a federal law; (D) an authoritative order or demand   ———

A MINI-EXERCISE Using your dictionary if necessary, write intelligent sentences, using the stated words, one of which comes from the preceding vocabulary test. Try to make each sentence contain at least fifteen words.

1. a. **urban**: _____

    _____

    _____

    _____

   b. **suburbia**: _____

    _____

    _____

    _____

A LAST WORD FROM THE FIRST AMERICANS

Vine Deloria, Jr.

> I am Deganawidah and with the Five Nations'
> confederate lords I plant the Tree of the Great
> Peace . . . If any man or any nation . . . shall show a
> desire to obey the laws of the Great Peace . . . they may
> trace the roots to their source . . . and they shall be
> welcomed to take shelter beneath the Tree.—Preamble to
> the Constitution of the United Nations (Iroquois), circa
> 1455

An old Hopi at Oraibi in Arizona, a community that was established about 1150 A.D. and discovered by Coronado 400 years later, was heard to remark not long ago that a 200th anniversary is not exactly an event without **precedent**. Most traditional medicine men have sacred drums, pipes and wampum that are nearly twice that age, so the white man's **concept** of **longevity** is not really bowling people over on the reservations. And the Papagos and Pueblos, remembering the 200–plus years of Spanish occupation and seeing no Spanish officials around today, do not fear the American entrenchment on their lands as a **perpetual** presence. 1

Perhaps the chief puzzlement among Indians about the nationwide celebration is their amazement at the white man's idea of progress. About the only thing this continent lacked when the whites first stepped ashore was a poverty class of the peasant type. From the direction in which the 2

---

country is now proceeding, it would seem that the white man is finally making up for this deficiency. The island of Manhattan, which operated at a profit for thousands of years, has lately been running so badly and at such a **deficit** that an old Potawatomi said recently that the sale of the island "was the best deal we ever made." Indians wonder how the white man could have achieved such startling moral and economic bankruptcy in only 200 years. The evolution of American statesmen from Washington and Jefferson to Nixon and Kissinger seems to defy the theory of progress, and in view of modern taxing policies, the celebration of a revolution against unjust taxation appears the height of folly.

When the pony express began its famous run through the lands of 3 the Plains Indians, it took 10 days to deliver a letter from St. Joseph, Mo., to Sacramento, Calif., and the mail cost $10 an ounce. Today it doesn't cost quite as much (although we are given to understand that new postal raises are in order once again), but it still can take just as long. In the old days, the pony express had to fight its way past Indian war parties; today the tribes along the way would even be happy to assist the mailmen if they could be assured that their mail would be delivered in a reasonable time.

Many whites want Indians to participate in the regional celebrations 4 on the theory that everyone in America shares the same view of American history. Indians respond with a gentle reminder that one reason there are so many national cemeteries scattered around the country is that some of the citizens took land theft unkindly a few decades ago. The Sioux and Cheyenne, for example, have proposed that Custer Battlefield National Monument should be **redesignated** "A Tribute to Sioux and Cheyenne Marksmanship," and it seems to be the general Indian **consensus** that the Washington Monument should be renamed the Indian Memorial because it represents the shaft the Indians got when the white man came to this continent.

The Mohawks now occupy lands claimed by the State of New York 5 at Eagle Bay; their first crop has been harvested, and they are well into their second ceremonial year in their new living quarters, having cleverly obtained a map of New York State, dated 1768, which clearly identifies the upper half of the state as being reserved for the Iroquois. The state avoids a confrontation with them, presumably because it is not yet certain whether it is bankrupt and whether loss of additional lands could bring the whole **flimsy** structure of state government toppling down.

Professional sports teams that **appropriated** Indian names for 6 themselves did singularly miserable jobs last season, thus adding to the confusion of newspaper readers when news about Wounded Knee and the occupation of the monastery in Wisconsin was reported in the back pages along with sports. The headline, "Chiefs Lose to Raiders," could easily cover either a football game or a report on a conference between tribal

officals and the Department of the Interior over strip mining. The tribes-
men feel that if sports teams are going to steal Indian names, they ought
to do at least as well as the Apaches did against the prospectors in Arizona
a century ago.

As part of its **bicentennial** celebration, the United States Army last 7
spring presented testimony on a bill before the Senate Judiciary Committee, which seeks **belated compensation** to Indian victims of the
Wounded Knee massacre. The **gist** of the Army's argument was that the
Indians started the conflict and therefore provided justification for the
killing of women and children some miles from the scene of the crime.
Even though this position clashes with statements of Nelson A. Miles,
Commanding General of the Army in the 1890's, the more recent Army
success with My Lai massacre, including the high lecture fees obtained
by Lieutenant Calley after his release, provides good reason for the slant
of its testimony before the Senate Committee.

As the **pageants** relive America's past this year, one wonders what 8
would have happened had the American Revolution failed. From the
Indian viewpoint, the Boston Tea Party, always depicted as one of the
braver acts that started the hostilities, was at least partly an attempt to
escape liability by ensuring that the Indians would take the rap in case
the protest backfired. The idea that the colonists might have lost the
whole thing and provoked an extensive war between the tribes and Great
Britain is not lost on Indians today. And the consensus is that, had the
tribes fought England, they might well have won, and the British Empire
would have collapsed a couple of centuries before it did. As it is, the
United States, according to its tradition, has always promptly rewarded
its **vanquished** enemies with economic aid, following a war; and since
Indians have never received any aid of this kind, the natural conclusion
must be that they probably won all those Indian wars after all.

The courts are jammed with cases dealing with Indian treaty rights 9
in this year of anniversary joy, and several will determine the ownership
of large tracts of land. There is, consequently, a kind of creeping paralysis
among the judges, as a proper way to deny the Indians title to their land
is being considered. In short, little has changed in two centuries that
would bring the several tribes into the celebration with enthusiasm.

Looking forward to the next hundred years, Indians are depressed 10
but still optimistic. We have brought the white man a long way in nearly
500 years—from a childish search for mythical cities of gold and fountains
of youth to the simple recognition that lands are essential for human
existence. With the Forest Service now adopting Indian methods of forest
maintenance, it is possible that before long other Indian procedures will
be adopted.

Among the old people who represent the traditional views of the 11
tribes, there is a saying that one does not judge a person until one has

walked a moon in his moccasins. So we cannot render a final judgment after only two centuries of American existence. But one thing the white man would do well to remember. One does not steal another's moccasins in order to walk in them.

A TIP ON USAGE Don't use the incorrect correlative conjunction *both . . . or*. Use instead *both . . . and*.

> WRONG: Piazzi can deliver diplomatic messages in **both** Italian **or** Russian.

Exercise 42

DIRECTIONS *In each blank at the right, write the letter that identifies the correct definition of each of the following words.*

1. **precedent:** (A) comes first; (B) comes last; (C) a democratic ruler; (D) an example _____
2. **concept:** (A) an idea; (B) an example; (C) a gathering; (D) a guess _____
3. **longevity:** (A) being great; (B) great expectations; (C) a long life; (D) much levity _____
4. **perpetual:** (A) based on orders; (B) based on observation; (C) lasting a long time; (D) lasting briefly _____
5. **deficit:** (A) a shortage; (B) an amount; (C) an excess; (D) a degree _____
6. **consensus:** (A) a government report; (B) a general agreement; (C) disturbing statistics; (D) concern _____
7. **redesignated:** (A) resigned; (B) designed again; (C) signed anew; (D) named again _____
8. **flimsy:** (A) strong; (B) funny; (C) whimsy; (D) weak _____
9. **appropriated:** (A) restored; (B) removed; (C) took away; (D) gave _____
10. **bicentennial:** (A) every century; (B) twice in a century; (C) every two centuries; (D) every three centuries _____
11. **compensation:** (A) sensation; (B) repayment; (C) combination; (D) deployment _____
12. **belated:** (A) said; (B) overdue; (C) on time; (D) painful _____
13. **gist:** (A) a guest; (B) almost; (C) nearly correct; (D) main idea _____
14. **vanquished:** (A) conquered; (B) disappeared; (C) vandalized; (D) made flat _____
15. **pageant:** (A) to call out; (B) a colorful display; (C) part of a book; (D) a servant _____

A MINI-EXERCISE Using your dictionary if necessary, write intelligent sentences, using the stated words, some of which come from the preceding vocabulary test. Try to make each sentence contain at least fifteen words.

1. a. **cynical:** _____

   _____

   _____

   b. **belated:** _____

   _____

   _____

2. a. **abominable:** _____

   _____

   _____

   b. **pageant:** _____

   _____

   _____

CAN ANIMALS "SPEAK"?

Carl Sagan

"Beasts abstract not," announced John Locke, expressing mankind's pre- 1
vailing opinion throughout recorded history. . . . Abstract thought, at least
in its more **subtle** varieties, is not an invariable accompaniment of everyday
life for the average man. Could abstract thought be a matter not of kind but
of degree? Could other animals be capable of abstract thought but more
rarely or less deeply than humans?

We have the impression that other animals are not very intelligent. 2
But have we examined the possibility of animal intelligence carefully
enough? In discussing communication with the animals, the French phi-
losopher Montaigne remarked, "The defect that hinders communication
betwixt them and us, why may it not be on our part as well as theirs?"

There is, of course, a considerable body of **anecdotal** information 3
suggesting chimpanzee intelligence.

Until a few years ago, the most extensive attempt to communicate 4
with chimpanzees went something like this: A newborn chimp was taken
into a household with a newborn baby, and both would be raised together—
twin cribs, twin **bassinets**, twin high chairs, twin potties, twin diaper
pails, twin baby-powder cans. At the end of three years, the young chimp
had, of course, far outstripped the young human in manual **dexterity**,
running, leaping, climbing and other motor skills. But while the child
was happily babbling away, the chimp could say only, and with enormous
difficuty, "Mama," "Papa," and "cup." From this it was widely concluded
that in language, reasoning and other higher mental functions, chimpanzees were only **minimally** competent: "Beasts abstract not."

But in thinking over these experiments, two psychologists, Beatrice 5
and Robert Gardner, at the University of Nevada realized that the phar-
ynx and larynx of the chimp are not suited for human speech.

The Gardners hit upon a brilliant idea: Teach a chimpanzee Amer- 6
ican sign language, known by its **acronym, Ameslan,** and sometimes as
"American deaf and dumb language" (the "dumb" refers, of course, to the
inability to speak and not to any failure of intelligence). It is ideally suited
to the immense manual dexterity of the chimpanzee. It also may have all
the **crucial** design features of verbal languages.

There is by now a vast library of described and filmed conversations, 7
employing Ameslan and other gestural languages, with Washoe, Lucy,
Lana and other chimpanzees studied by the Gardners and others. Not
only are there chimpanzees with working vocabularies of 100 to 200 words;
they are also able to distinguish among nontrivially different grammatical
patterns and **syntaxes.** What is more, they have been remarkably in-
ventive in the construction of new words and phrases.

On seeing for the first time a duck land quacking in a pond, Washoe 8
gestured "water bird," which is the same phrase used in English and
other languages, but which Washoe invented for the occasion. Having
never seen a spherical fruit other than an apple, but knowing the signs
for the principal colors, Lana, upon spying a technician eating an orange,
signed "orange apple." After tasting a watermelon, Lucy described it as
"candy drink" or "drink fruit," which is essentially the same word form
as the English "water melon." But after she had burned her mouth on
her first radish, Lucy forever after described them as "cry hurt food." A
small doll placed unexpectedly in Washoe's cup **elicited** the response
"Baby in my drink." When Washoe soiled, particularly clothing or furniture, she was taught the sign "dirty," which she then extrapolated as
a general term of abuse. A rhesus monkey that evoked her displeasure
was repeatedly signed at: "Dirty monkey, dirty monkey, dirty monkey."
Occasionally Washoe would say things like "Dirty Jack, gimme drink."
Lana, in a moment of creative annoyance, called her trainer "You green
shit." Chimpanzees have invented swear words. Washoe also seems to
have a sort of sense of humor; once, when riding on her trainer's shoulders
and, perhaps **inadvertently,** wetting him, she signed: "Funny, funny."

Boyce Rensberger is a sensitive and gifted reporter for the *New York* 9
Times whose parents could neither speak nor hear, although he is in both
respects normal. His first language, however, was Ameslan. He had been
abroad on a European assignment for the *Times* for some years. On his
return to the United States, one of the first domestic duties was to look
into the Gardners' experiments with Washoe. After some little time with
the chimpanzee, Rensberger reported, "Suddenly I realized I was conversing with a member of another species in my native tongue." The use
of the word tongue is, of course, **figurative:** it is built deeply into the

structure of the language (a word that also means "tongue"). In fact, Rensberger was conversing with a member of another species in his native "hand." And it is just this **transition** from tongue to hand that has permitted humans to regain the ability—lost, according to Josephus, since Eden—to communicate with the animals.

At an early stage in the development of Washoe's verbal abilities, 10 Jacob Bronowski and a colleague wrote a scientific paper denying the significance of Washoe's use of gestural language because, in the limited data available to Bronowski, Washoe neither inquired nor negated. But later observations showed that Washoe and other chimpanzees were perfectly able both to ask questions and to deny **assertions** put to them. And it is difficult to see any significant difference in quality between chimpanzee use of gestural language and the use of ordinary speech by children in a manner that we unhesitatingly attribute to intelligence. In reading Bronowski's paper I cannot help but feel that a little pinch of human **chauvinism** has crept in, an echo of Locke's "Beasts abstract not." In 1949, the American anthropologist Leslie White stated unequivocally: "Human behavior is symbolic behavior; symbolic behavior is human behavior." What would White have made of Washoe, Lucy and Lana?

These findings on chimpanzee language and intelligence have an 11 intriguing bearing on "Rubicon" arguments—the contention that the total brain mass, or at least the ratio of brain to body mass, is a useful index of intelligence. Against this point of view it was once argued that the lower range of the brain masses of microcephalic humans overlaps the upper range of brain masses of adult chimpanzees and gorillas; and yet, it was said, **microcephalics** have some, although severely impaired, use of language—while the apes have none. But in only relatively few cases are microcephalics capable of human speech. One of the best behavioral descriptions of microcephalics was written by a Russian physician, S. Korsakov, who in 1893 observed a female microcephalic named "Masha." She could understand a very few questions and commands and could occasionally reminisce on her childhood. She sometimes chattered away, but there was little **coherence** to what she uttered. Korsakov characterized her speech as having "an extreme poverty of logical associations." As an example of her poorly adapted and **automaton**-like intelligence, Korsakov described her eating habits. When food was present on the table, Masha would eat. But if the food was abruptly removed in the midst of a meal, she would behave as if the meal had ended, thanking those in charge and **piously** blessing herself. If the food were returned, she would eat again. The pattern apparently was subject to indefinite repetition. My own impression is that Lucy or Washoe would be a far more interesting dinner companion than Masha, and that the comparison of microcephalic humans with normal apes is not inconsistent with some sort of "Rubicon" of intelligence. Of course, both the quality and the quantity of neural connections are probably vital for the sorts of intelligence that we can easily recognize.

Because adult chimpanzees are generally thought (at least by zoo- 12 keepers) to be too dangerous to retain in a home or home environment, Washoe and other verbally accomplished chimpanzees have been involuntarily "retired" soon after reaching puberty. Thus we do not yet have experience with the adult language abilities of monkeys and apes. One of the most intriguing questions is whether a verbally accomplished chimpanzee mother will be able to communicate language to her offspring. It seems very likely that this should be possible and that a community of chimps initially competent in gestural language could pass down the language to subsequent generations.

Where such communication is essential for survival, there is already 13 some evidence that apes transmit extragenetic or cultural information. Jane Goodall observed baby chimps in the wild emulating the behavior of their mothers and learning the reasonably complex task of finding an appropriate twig and using it to prod into a termite's nest so as to acquire some of these tasty delicacies.

Differences in group behavior—something that it is very tempting 14 to call cultural differences—have been reported among chimpanzees, baboons, macaques and many other primates. For example, one group of monkeys may know how to eat bird's eggs, while an **adjacent** band of precisely the same species may not. Such primates have a few dozen sounds or cries, which are used for intra-group communication, with such meanings as "Flee; here is a predator." But the sound of the cries differs somewhat from group to group: there are regional accents.

I would expect a significant development and elaboration of language 15 in only a few generations if all the chimps unable to communicate were to die or fail to reproduce. Basic English corresponds to about 1,000 words. Chimpanzees are already accomplished in vocabularies exceeding 10 percent of that number. Although a few years ago it would have seemed the most **implausible** science fiction, it does not appear to me out of the question that, after a few generations in such a verbal chimpanzee community, there might emerge the memoirs of the natural history and mental life of a chimpanzee, published in English or Japanese (with perhaps an "as told to" after the by-line).

If chimpanzees have consciousness, if they are capable of abstrac- 16 tions, do they not have what until now has been described as "human rights"? How smart does a chimpanzee have to be before killing him constitutes murder? What further properties must he show before religious missionaries must consider him worthy of attempts at conversion? But chimpanzees *can* abstract. Like other mammals, they are capable of strong emotions. They have certainly committed no crimes. I do not claim to have the answer, but I think it is certainly worthwhile to raise the question: Why, exactly, all over the civilized world, in virtually every major city, are apes in prison? The **cognitive** abilities of chimpanzees force us, I think, to raise searching questions about the boundaries of the community of beings to which special ethical considerations are due, and can, I hope, help to extend our **ethical** perspectives downward through the taxa on Earth and upwards to extraterrestrial organisms, if they exist.

Exercise 43

DIRECTIONS *In each blank at the right, write the letter that identifies the correct definition of each of the following words.*

1. **abstract:** (A) able to generalize; (B) able to speak; (C) able to perform simple tasks; (D) able to remember _____
2. **Ameslan:** (A) a railroad; (B) a sign language; (C) American English; (D) a Russian province _____
3. **subtle:** (A) below; (B) obvious; (C) mentally clever; (D) unintentional _____
4. **anecdotal:** (A) cure for poison; (B) lengthy poem; (C) a proverb; (D) a brief story _____
5. **bassinet:** (A) a baby bed; (B) a small hound; (C) a kind of flute; (D) a diaper _____
6. **minimally:** (A) left-handed; (B) the largest; (C) the smallest; (D) in the middle _____
7. **dexterity:** (A) skill; (B) laziness; (C) confusion; (D) happiness _____
8. **acronym:** (A) the opposite of a word; (B) a word used in anger; (C) a word made from initials; (D) a word that is untrue _____
9. **crucial:** (A) a metal container; (B) shaped like a circle; (C) a small doughnut; (D) a critical decision _____
10. **syntax:** (A) a grammatical pattern; (B) a tax on sin; (C) a synthesis; (D) a government organization _____
11. **elicited:** (A) covered up; (B) omitted; (C) made moist; (D) brought forth _____
12. **inadvertently:** (A) on purpose; (B) by accident; (C) repeatedly; (D) seldom _____
13. **figurative:** (A) real or actual; (B) involving a figure of speech; (C) involving exercise; (D) figuring it out _____
14. **transition:** (A) move from one state to another; (B) to go beyond; (C) a covering up; (D) a situation _____
15. **assertion:** (A) a kind of sweet food; (B) another situation; (C) a weak question; (D) a strong statement _____
16. **chauvinism:** (A) liking women; (B) hating women; (C) excessive patriotism; (D) self-love _____

17. **intriguing:** (A) destroying; (B) fascinating; (C) unsettling; (D) revolting _____

18. **microcephalic:** (A) under a microscope: (B) relating to snails; (C) of small brain size; (D) relating to certain human organs _____

19. **coherence:** (A) sticking together; (B) pulling apart; (C) getting bald; (D) money from a relative _____

20. **automaton:** (A) a small appliance; (B) a robot; (C) a food-supplying machine; (D) a kind of vehicle _____

21. **piously:** (A) carefully; (B) easily; (C) offensively; (D) religiously _____

22. **adjacent:** (A) distant from; (B) a military title; (C) hidden by; (D) next to _____

23. **implausible:** (A) cannot be seen; (B) cannot be heard; (C) cannot be believed; (D) cannot happen _____

24. **cognitive:** (A) joined together; (B) having small wheels; (C) confused or hidden; (D) known or perceived _____

25. **ethical:** (A) right or wrong; (B) moral or immoral: (C) correct or incorrect; (D) honest or dishonest _____

FROM "CIVIL DISOBEDIENCE"
Henry David Thoreau

I heartily accept the motto—"That government is best which governs 1
least"; and I should like to see it acted up to more rapidly and system-
atically. Carried out, it finally amounts to this, which also I believe—
"That government is best which governs not at all"; and when men are
prepared for it, that will be the kind of government which they will have.
Government is at best but an **expedient**; but most governments are
usually, and all governments are sometimes, inexpedient. The objections
which have been brought against a standing army, and they are many
and weighty, and deserve to prevail, may also at last be brought against
a standing government. The standing army is only an arm of the standing
government. The government itself, which is only the mode which the
people have chosen to execute their will, is equally liable to be abused
and **perverted** before the people can act through it. Witness the present
Mexican war, the work of comparatively a few individuals using the
standing government as their tool; for, in the outset, the people would
not have consented to this measure.

This American government—what is it but a tradition, although a 2
recent one, endeavoring to transmit itself **unimpaired** to posterity, but
each instant losing some of its **integrity**? It has not the vitality and force
of a single living man; for a single man can bend it to his will. It is a sort
of wooden gun to the people themselves. But it is not the less necessary
for this; for the people must have some complicated machinery or other,
and hear its din, to satisfy that idea of government which they have.
Governments show us how successfully men can be imposed on, even
impose on themselves, for their own advantage. It is excellent, we must
all allow. Yet this government never of itself furthered any enterprise,

Originally published by Houghton Mifflin Company.

but by the alacrity with which it got out of its way. *It* does not keep the country free. *It* does not settle the West. *It* does not educate. The character **inherent** in the American people has done all that has been accomplished; and it would have done somewhat more, if the government had not sometimes got in its way. For government is an expedient by which men would fain succeed in letting one another alone; and, as has been said, when it is most expedient, the governed are most let alone by it. Trade and commerce, if they were not made of India-rubber, would never manage to bounce over the obstacles which legislators are continually putting in their way; and, if one were to judge these men wholly by the effects of their actions and not partly by their intentions, they would deserve to be classed and punished with those mischievous persons who put obstructions on the railroads.

But, to speak practically and as a citizen, unlike those who call 3
themselves no-government men, I ask for, not at once no government, but *at once* a better government. Let every man make known what kind of government would command his respect, and that will be one step toward obtaining it.

After all, the practical reason why, when the power is once in the 4
hands of the people, a majority are permitted, and for a long period continue, to rule is not because they are most likely to be in the right, nor because this seems fairest to the minority, but because they are physically the strongest. But a government in which the majority rule in all cases cannot be based on justice, even as far as men understand it. Can there not be a government in which majorities do not **virtually** decide right and wrong, but conscience?—in which majorities decide only those questions to which the rule of expediency is applicable? Must the citizen ever for a moment, or in the least degree, resign his conscience to the legislator? Why has every man a conscience, then? I think that we should be men first, and subjects afterward. It is not desirable to cultive a respect for the law, so much as for the right. The only obligation which I have a right to assume is to do at any time what I think right. It is truly enough said, that a corporation has no conscience; but a corporation of conscientious men is a corporation *with* a conscience. Law never made men a whit more just; and, by means of their respect for it, even the well-disposed are daily made the agents of injustice. A common and natural result of an undue respect for law, is that you may see a file of soldiers, colonel, captain, corporal, privates, powder-monkeys, and all, marching in admirable order over hill and dale to the wars, against their wills, ay, against their common sense and consciences, which makes it very steep marching indeed, and produces a **palpitation** of the heart. They have no doubt that it is a damnable business in which they are concerned; they are all peaceably inclined. Now, what are they? Men at all? or small movable forts and magazines, at the service of some **unscrupulous** man

in power? Visit the Navy-Yard, and behold a marine, such a man as an American government can make, or such as it can make a man with its black arts—a mere shadow and **reminiscence** of humanity, a man laid out alive and standing, and already, as one may say, buried under arms with funeral accompaniments.

The mass of men serve the state thus, not as men mainly, but as 5 machines, with their bodies. They are the standing army, and the militia, jailors, constables, posse comitatus, and so forth. In most cases there is no free exercise whatever of the judgment or of the moral sense; but they put themselves on a level with wood and earth and stones; and wooden men can perhaps be manufactured that will serve the purpose as well. Such command no more respect than men of straw or a lump of dirt. They have the same sort of worth only as horses and dogs. Yet such as these even are commonly **esteemed** good citizens. Others—as most legislators, politicians, lawyers, ministers, and office-holders—serve the state chiefly with their heads; and, as they rarely make any moral distinctions, they are as likely to serve the Devil, without *intending* it, as God. A very few, as heroes, patriots, martyrs, reformers in the great sense, and *men*, serve the state with their consciences also, and so necessarily resist it for the most part; and they are commonly treated as enemies by it . . . .

How does it become a man to behave toward this American govern- 6 ment to-day? I answer, that he cannot without disgrace be associated with it. I cannot for an instant recognize that political organization as *my* government which is the *slave's* government also.

All men recognize the right of revolution; that is, the right to refuse 7 allegiance to, and to resist, the government, when its tyranny or its inefficiency are great and unendurable. But almost all say that such is not the case now. But such was the case, they think, in the Revolution of '75. If one were to tell me that this was a bad government because it taxed certain foreign commodities brought to its ports, it is most probable that I should not make an ado about it, for I can do without them. All machines have their friction. . . . But when the friction comes to have its machine, and oppression and robbery are organized, I say, let us not have such a machine any longer. In other words, when a sixth of the population of a nation which has undertaken to be the refuge of liberty are slaves, and a whole country is unjustly overrun and conquered by a foreign army, and subjected to military law, I think that it is not too soon for honest men to rebel and revolutionize. What makes this duty the more urgent is the fact that the country so overrun is not our own, but ours is the invading army. . . .

Unjust laws exist: shall we be content to obey them, or shall we 8 endeavor to amend them, and obey them until we have succeeded, or shall we **transgress** them at once? Men generally, under such a government as this, think that they ought to wait until they have persuaded the majority to alter them. They think that, if they should resist, the remedy would be worse than the evil. But it is the fault of the government itself that the remedy *is* worse than the evil. *It* makes it worse. Why is it not more apt to anticipate and provide for reform? Why does it not cherish its wise minority? Why does it cry and resist before it is hurt? Why does it not encourage its citizens to be on the alert to point out its faults, and *do* better than it would have them? Why does it always crucify Christ, and excommunicate Copernicus and Luther, and pronounce Washington and Franklin rebels? . . .

I do not hesitate to say, that those who call themselves Abolitionists 9 should at once **effectually** withdraw their support, both in person and property, from the government of Massachusetts and not wait till they constitute a majority of one, before they suffer the right to prevail through them. I think that it is enough if they have God on their side, without waiting for that other one. Moreover, any man more right than his neighbors constitutes a majority of one already.

I meet this American government, or its representative, the state 10 government, directly, and face to face, once a year—no more—in the person of its tax-gatherer; this is the only mode in which a man situated as I am necessarily meets it; and it then says distinctly, Recognize me; and the simplest, most effectual, and, in the present posture of affairs, the indispensablest mode of treating with it on this head, of expressing your little satisfaction with and love for it, is to deny it then. My civil neighbor, the tax-gatherer, is the very man I have to deal with—for it is, after all, with men and not the parchment that I quarrel—and he has voluntarily chosen to be an agent of the government. How shall he ever know well what he is and does as an officer of the government, or as a man, until he is obliged to consider whether he shall treat me, his neighbor, for whom he has respect, as a neighbor and well-disposed man, or as a maniac and disturber of the peace, and see if he can get over this obstruction to his neighborliness without a ruder and more **impetuous** thought of speech corresponding with his action. I know this well and if one thousand, if one hundred, if ten men whom I could name—if ten *honest* men only—ay if *one* HONEST man, in this State of Massachusetts, *ceasing to hold slaves*, were actually to withdraw from this copartnership, and be locked up in the county jail therefore, it would be the abolition of slavery in America. For it matters not how small the beginning may seem to be: what is once well done is done forever. . . .

Under a government which imprisons any unjustly, the true place 11 for a just man is also a prison. The proper place to-day, the only place which Massachusetts has provided for her freer and less desponding spirits, is in her prisons, to be put out and locked out of the State by her own act, as they have already put themselves out by their principles. It is there that the fugitive slave, and the Mexican prisoner on parole, and the Indian come to plead the wrongs of his race should find them; on that separate, but more free and honorable ground, where the State places those who are not *with* her, but *against* her the only house in a slave State in which a free man can abide with honor. If any think that their influence would be lost there, and their voices no longer afflict the ear of the State, that they would not be as an enemy within its walls, they do not know by how much truth is stronger than error, nor how much more eloquently and effectively he can combat injustice who has experienced a little in his own person. Cast your whole vote, not a strip of paper merely, but your whole influence. A minority is powerless while it **conforms** to the majority; it is not even a minority then; but it is irresistible when it clogs by its whole weight. If the alternative is to keep all just men in prison, or give up war and slavery, the State will not hesitate which to choose. If a thousand men were not to pay their tax-bills this year, that would not be a violent and bloody measure, as it would be to pay them, and enable the State to commit violence and shed innocent blood. This is, in fact, the definition of a peaceable revolution, if any such is possible. If the tax-gatherer, or any other public officer, asks me, as one has done, "But what shall I do?" my answer is, "If you really wish to do anything, resign your office." When the subject has refused allegiance, and the officer has resigned his office, then the revolution is accomplished. But even suppose blood should flow. Is there not a sort of blood shed when the conscience is wounded? Through this wound a man's real manhood and immortality flow out, and he bleeds to an everlasting death. I see this blood flowing now. . . .

Exercise 44

DIRECTIONS *In each blank at the right, write the letter that identifies the correct definition of each of the following words.*

1. **expedient:** (A) a means of control; (B) an ineffective means of control; (C) a means to an end regardless of right; (D) a human invention ____
2. **perverted:** (A) treated badly; (B) turned to an improper use; (C) forced to act honestly; (D) treated well ____
3. **unimpaired:** (A) without its money removed; (B) trying to remain honest; (C) hurriedly; (D) in sound shape or as it is ____
4. **integrity:** (A) honesty; (B) unity; (C) wealth; (D) dishonesty ____
5. **impose:** (A) to force upon others or on oneself; (B) to enrich others or oneself; (C) to fail miserably; (D) to treat gently ____
6. **inherent:** (A) acquired by hard work; (B) acquired by study; (C) inborn; (D) given by others ____
7. **virtually:** (A) with honesty or virtue; (B) without the slightest doubt; (C) for all practical purposes; (D) without the use of conscience ____
8. **palpitation** (A) a physical aching; (B) a quivering or trembling; (C) complete stoppage; (D) a gleeful feeling ____
9. **unscrupulous:** (A) politically strong; (B) not in office by election; (C) in office by fraudulent election; (D) unprincipled or immoral ____
10. **reminiscence:** (A) outline of; (B) a recalling of past events; (C) substitute for; (D) a suggestion but not a reality ____
11. **esteemed:** (A) considered good on the basis of false information; (B) made true; (C) held in high opinion or of great value; (D) secretly scorned ____
12. **transgress:** (A) to make operable; (B) to forget about; (C) to violate or go against; (D) to obey without reverence for ____

13. **effectually:** (A) financially; (B) for a short time; (C) forever; (D) in an effective manner _____

14. **impetuous:** (A) rashly hasty; (B) deliberately hasty; (C) carefully planned; (D) effective _____

15. **conform:** (A) to go against; (B) to circumvent or go around; (C) to comply with or go along with; (D) to imitate _____

A MINI-EXERCISE Using your dictionary if necessary, write intelligent sentences, using the stated words, some of which come from the preceding vocabulary test. Try to make each sentence contain at least fifteen words.

1. a. **perverted:** _____

_____

_____

_____

b. **converted:** _____

_____

_____

_____

2. a. **inherent:** _____

_____

_____

_____

b. **coherent:** _____

_____

_____

_____

ABOLISHING GRADES

William Glasser, M.D.

If we educate students to think, should we grade them? If we could be 1
sure that each child would learn to think and solve problems to the best
of his ability, grades would make no sense. Those who argue for grades
maintain this rarely happens, that without grades students would have
little **incentive** to learn. I believe that the kind of education offered
(relevance and thinking) and the way it is offered (involvement) have
much more to do with incentive than grades. When school offers little
material that is **relevant** and requires little more than memorization,
grades provide incentive for some students who get A's and B's; for those
who do not get B or better, however, grades are a signal to give up. Those
who get C or below consider themselves failures and stop working. They
become part of the large group (in my estimate, over 50 percent in an
average secondary school) who are learning very little.

Because grades emphasize failure much more than success and be- 2
cause failure is the basis of almost all school problems, I recommend a
system of reporting a students' progress that totally eliminates failure.
That is, *I suggest that no student ever at any time be labeled a failure or
led to believe he is a failure through the use of the grading system.* As
stated above, a student who believes he is a failure usually refuses to
work in school. Because failure is never motivating, when we eliminate
failure we cannot harm a child who is failing under the present grading
system. Although he may not suddenly start learning when we stop labeling him a failure, at least we leave the door open for a change of heart
later on when he may wish to start working and learning. If we label
him a failure, often even once, there is less chance that he will ever start

From pp. 95–97, 103–105, in *Schools Without Failure* by William Glasser, M.D. Copyright
© 1969 by William Glasser, Inc. Reprinted by permission of Harper & Row, Publishers,
Inc.

to learn. To keep a child working in school, we must let him know, beginning in kindergarten, that from the standpoint of grades or labels, *it is not possible to fail*. Whether or not any individual student wants to study, he is in a school where he sees many others who do work and enjoy learning. Kept in close contact with successful students in the **heterogeneous** class, he is stimulated to think during relevant class discussions. In this situation it is easier to succeed than to fail.

There is nothing **radical** about not labeling people as failures. In 3 the armed forces, in athletics, in the arts, and in fact in most jobs, simple or complex, total failure is rarely of concern. Rather, we concern ourselves with levels of success; almost everyone succeeds to some degree in any job. Only in school are we so definitely labeled failure. Education partly explains its refusal to stop the labeling of countless children as failures by "it's tradition." This tradition discourages many little first graders struggling to make some sense out of a school situation they don't understand. Once a child receives the failure label and sees himself as a failure, he will rarely succeed in school. If, instead of quickly labeling a child a failure, we work with him patiently, he may begin to learn and, in a year or two, catch up. We have gained everything, lost nothing, by abandoning failure.

There are of course more arguments than tradition for continuing 4 the present system—arguments about **incentive**, about fairness to better students, and about controlling the unruly. There are arguments that parents want the grade system and that colleges demand it. I maintain, nevertheless, that the price of failure associated with the present system outweighs even the most **valid** of these arguments.

I haven't met a child **incapable** of thinking and participating to 5 some degree in school if we let him know we value what he can contribute. One of the best class meetings I have ever had in terms of thoughtful participation was with a group of mentally **retarded** children in a central-city school class in which their teacher helped them to experience success. I haven't met a small child who believes he is a total failure, but I have met some adolescents and adults who do. Having learned failure in school, they now give up all effort to think and to work effectively. They are defeated by failure. To correct this too-common bad situation, children, from the time they enter school, should be promised that they will not fail; to make this promise **valid**, they must not be labeled failures through failing grades. From the time they enter school they must think in terms of success, not failure. We cannot achieve this goal using the present grading system.

Appreciating the value of a good education, the better student is 6 willing to work hard, to try harder courses (in high school and college), and to learn because he enjoys it. I would like to suggest, therefore, two somewhat different systems of reporting a student's progress, neither of which employs traditional A-B-C-D-F grades. One system is to be used in the first six grades, the other in the next six.

During the first six grades, except for an occasional adjustment for 7 a student who had nothing in common with his class, all students pass each year. Grade levels may or may not be emphasized. (The ungraded school, with which I have had no experience and so cannot discuss, is not essential to my argument.) Children are grouped only by age into heterogeneous classes and moved ahead each year for six years until they finish the sixth grade. Because there is no failure and no attempt to rate students against each other or against a rigid standard, report cards as we know them are not needed. To satisfy the parents understandable interest in their children's progress, a written report is made emphasizing what the chid is doing and where he needs to improve.

A report such as this one is sent home by the teacher at least twice 8 during the school year. It need not be sent home at the same time for all students (an impossible burden on the teacher, but is spaced out, say, over the last six weeks of each semester. Thinking more deeply about their children so that they can write about them, teachers discover much more about them than they do using the present **superficial** grade ratings. The report is discussed individually with each student; parents are invited to join the conference, which are student, not parent, centered. As with the written reports, the conferences are spread over the last six weeks of each semester.

On this narrative kindergarten to sixth-grade (K–6) report form, 9 there is recognition for students who do superior (S) work. This is reported in a separate paragraph at the end of the K–6 form. what does a student do to get an S? The principles of the S grade are exactly the same for elementary, junior high, or senior high school: for an S, a student does extra, superior school work on his own. If time allows, he may present his work to the class for both the enlightenment and the comments of the class. Final evaluation of the work, however, is made by the teacher. Presenting work to the class acts as a **stimulus** for more students to attempt work on their own. In addition, when a student attempts an S, he agrees to devote some time each week to help those students who are not doing well. As an example, a student doing satisfactory work in history may wish, at any grade level from primary through high school, to investigate some area of history that seems important and relevant to him and then to explain and defend his work. If his teacher judges the work superior, he receives an S in history. The student takes responsibility for his educational effort, sets his own standards, and does the extra work.

Using the superior system, extra effort is rewarded and education 10 breaks out of the narrow **confines** of present practice. Superior work will come from students who at present rarely do anything more outstanding than memorize enough facts to get A's. In this system, S is not phony; it represents basic achievement plus increased initiative and responsibility. An S requires enough work so that students are satisfied to work for an S in one course each semester rather than the present meaningless competition for many A's. This system does much to rid education of the cut and dried **sterility** of learning details that have no value other than leading to an A or B. Teachers and students are continually alert for new ideas or new variations of old ideas.

It is important, however, that the superior (S) grade not be confused 11 with the A of our present system. To explain the differences, we need look again at the present system. A student with 96 may get an A and a student with 76 may get a C. Although both students pass, the A student remembers considerably more (at least for a short time) than the C student. Using S, a whole new avenue is opened equally to all students doing passing work. The choice of trying for an S is solely the student's responsibility. First deciding whether he wants to try, he then decides how to try. He must use **judgment**, make a decision, and think about implementing his decision. The extra work for an S is done **concurrently** with the regular class work. Most important also is the restriction that only one S is allowed per semester, thus eliminating the possibility of S becoming a substitute for A.

The grading system that has just been described applies to the first 12 six grades. In junior and senior high school, where students no longer have one teacher all day but rather a different teacher for each course, several modifications are required. The narrative form of report filled out by the single heterogeneous classroom teacher is replaced by a form filled out by each teacher. Although it somewhat resembles the present report card, it differs considerably in emphasis and details. As in the first six grades, there is no failure, but all students pass every course attempted. Teachers set standards and *pass only those who achieve these standards*. If a teacher sets his standards too high, students avoid his courses or so many students fail to pass that parents complain. If a teacher sets standards too low, other teachers who have these students in more advanced courses of the same subject complain. For these reasons, somewhat similar standards are maintained throughout the school. Three possible report cards using the recommended system are shown:

History—S	History—P	History—P
English—P	English—P	English—P
Algebra—P	Algebra—P	Algebra—)*
Spanish—P	Spanish—P	Spanish—)*
Excellent Student	*Good Student*	*Poor Student*

A student who does not achieve the standards set by the teacher is 13 eligible to take the course again. He is never marked "fail." A talk with

---

*There is no record on the official transcript of these attempts in Algebra and Spanish.

his teacher can give the student an idea of whether or not to try again or of what he needs to do to pass. No record of his inability to pass a course is entered into his permanent transcript. School records are kept only of the courses passed and the courses passed with a superior grade. Each individual student, however, is asked to keep his report cards to present as he takes courses over again. These report cards are the only record of whether or not he has taken a course previously. If he does not pass after two tries, he must **petition** a faculty committee to allow him to take the course a third time. When a student leaves a school, he destroys his records. Although students who change schools may thus get a few extra tries, it is a small price to pay compared with transferring the damning no-pass record.

By using the reporting system outlined here, the destructive quality 14 of our present grading system can be eliminated. Students who are slower, who may have had misfortunes in their home or family, who were ill, or who were not interested at any one particular time all have a chance to express increased or renewed motivation through taking the course again and doing well a second or even a third time. A school can find out about unsuccessful attempts at courses at other schools only if the student voluntarily shows his earlier report cards; the official record only shows what he passed, not how many times a course was attempted. As in the elementary school, a student is allowed to elect to try for only one superior a semester and, in electing to try, he must make himself available to help others who are having difficulty.

Using a system that does not contain failure, students are encour- 15 aged to try hard courses. Education is thus expanded. A student need not drop a course because he fears a low grade. Even if he does not pass, he can continue through the rest of the semester to assimilate a certain amount of skill and knowledge, perhaps enough to allow him to pass the second time if he tries the course again.

If the pass-superior system is put into effect, standards will have to 16 be reexamined. Our present attempt to keep standards high is ineffective. Teachers present too much material and hold students responsible for learning more than they can **assimilate**. In courses such as chemistry, physics, advanced math, economics, or literature, a few able students keep up, but the rest fall behind and learn next to nothing. Recognizing that most of the students in these classes are incapable of performing at the required level, teachers give many C's and D's. In doing so, teachers achieve a perfect marriage between unrealistic standards and inadequate grades. Rather than take the honest approach—fail the students who know nothing (and almost all students who get C or less in any high school course know nothing in that course)—teachers temporize and give many of these students a C, getting both parties off the hook. The teachers rationalize that they taught a good course because few students failed.

The C students rationalize that they did average work when in fact they learned next to nothing. The D students, who learned nothing, at least do not have to repeat the agony of sitting all semester in a class where they have no idea what is going on. The system is preserved, the only loss is education.

Exercise 45

DIRECTIONS *In each blank at the right, write the letter that identifies the correct definition of each of the following words.*

1. **incentive:** (A) to burn; (B) a pleasant odor: (C) a beginning; (D) arousing to action _____
2. **relevant:** (A) religious; (B) confused or hidden; (C) to the point; (D) very important _____
3. **heterogeneous:** (A) all of the same kind; (B) of different kinds; (C) a kind of milk; (D) sexual _____
4. **radical:** (A) far to the left; (B) far to the right; (C) moderate; (D) any extreme _____
5. **valid:** (A) logical, well-founded; (B) silly or foolish; (C) difficult to see; (D) unusually confusing _____
6. **incapable:** (A) cannot wear a cap; (B) generally unable; (C) unwilling to do something; (D) reluctant _____
7. **superficial:** (A) very powerful; (B) a crack in the earth; (C) on the surface; (D) in the depths _____
8. **stimulus:** (A) part of a flower; (B) a small drop; (C) something that depresses; (D) something that excites _____
9. **confines:** (A) limits; (B) charges a fee; (C) goes together; (D) terminates or ends _____
10. **assimilate:** (A) to put together: (B) to take apart; (C) to take in, absorb; (D) to imitate _____
11. **retarded:** (A) made over; (B) slowed down; (C) increased; (D) turned around _____
12. **sterility:** (A) virility; (B) decent; (C) lifelessness; (D) happiness _____
13. **petition:** (A) a request; (B) a list; (C) a divider; (D) a separation _____
14. **judgment:** (A) a large sum of money; (B) any kind of guess; (C) a statement of approval or disapproval: (D) a general agreement with existing conditions _____
15. **concurrently:** (A) following something else in time; (B) going before something else in time; (C) flowing, as a stream; (D) happening at the same time as something else _____

FROM "SELF-RELIANCE"
Ralph Waldo Emerson

What I must do is all that concerns me, not what the people think. This 1
rule, equally **arduous** in actual and in intellectual life, may serve for
the whole distinction between greatness and meanness. It is the harder,
because you will always find those who think they know what is your
duty better than you know it. It is easy in the world to live after the
world's opinion; it is easy in solitude to live after our own; but the great
man is he who in the midst of the crowd keeps with perfect sweetness the
independence of solitude.

The objection to conforming to **usages** that have become dead to you 2
is, that it scatters your force. It loses your time and blurs the impression
of your character. If you maintain a dead church, contribute to a dead
Bible-society, vote with a great party either for the government or against
it, spread your table like base housekeepers,—under all these screens I
have difficulty to detect the **precise** man you are. And, of course, so much
force is withdrawn from all your proper life. But do your work, and I shall
know you. Do your work, and you shall reinforce yourself. A man must
consider what a blind man's buff is this game of **conformity**. If I know
your sect, I **anticipate** your argument. I hear a preacher announce for
his text and topic the **expediency** of one of the institutions of his church.
Do I not know beforehand that not possibly can he say a new and spon-
taneous word? Do I not know that, with all this **ostentation** of examining
the grounds of the institution, he will do no such thing? Do I not know
that he is pledged to himself not to look but at one side—the permitted
side, not as a man, but as a parish minister? He is a retained attorney,
and these airs of the bench are the emptiest **affectation**. Well, most men
have bound their eyes with one or another handkerchief, and attached

Originally published by Houghton Mifflin Company.

themselves to some one of these communities of opinion. This conformity makes them not false in a few particulars, authors of a few lies, but false in all particulars. Their every truth is not quite true. Their two is not real two, their four not the real four; so that every word they say **chagrins** us, and we know not where to begin to set them. Meantime nature is not slow to equip us in the prison-uniform of the party to which we **adhere**. We come to wear one cut of face and figure, and acquire by degrees the gentlest **asinine** expression. There is a **mortifying** experience in particular, which does not fail to wreak itself also the general history; I mean "the foolish face of praise," the forced smile which we put on in company where we do not feel at ease in answer to conversation which does not interest us. The muscles, not spontaneously moved, but moved by low **usurping** willfulness, grow tight about the outline of the face, with the most disagreeable sensation.

For nonconformity the world whips you with its displeasure. And 3 therefore a man must know how to estimate a sour face. The bystanders look **askance** on him in the public street or in the friend's parlour. If this **aversion** had its origin in contempt and resistance like his own, he might well go home with a sad countenance, but the sour faces of the multitude, like their sweet faces, have no deep cause, but are put on and off as the wind blows and a newspaper directs. Yet is the discontent of the multitude more **formidable** than that of the senate and the college. It is easy enough for a firm man who knows the world to brook the rage of the cultivated classes. Their rage is **decorous** and **prudent**, for they are timid as being very **vulnerable** themselves. But when to their feminine rage the indignation of the people is added, when the ignorant and the poor are aroused, when the unintelligent brute force that lies at the bottom of society is made to growl and mow, it needs the habit of **magnanimity** and religion to treat it godlike as a trifle of no concernment.

The other terror that scares us from self-trust is our consistency; a 4 reverence for our past act or word, because the eyes of others have no other data for computing our orbit than our past acts, and we are loth to disappoint them.

But why should you keep your head over your shoulder? Why drag 5 about this corpse of your memory, lest you contradict somewhat you have stated in this or that public place? Suppose you should contradict yourself; what then? It seems to be a rule of wisdom never to rely on your memory alone, scarcely even in acts of pure memory, but to bring the past for judgment into the thousand-eyed present, and live ever in a new day. In your metaphysics you have denied personality to the Deity: yet when the devout motions of the soul come, yield to them heart and life, though they should clothe God and shape and color. Leave your theory, as Joseph his coat in the hand of the harlot, and flee.

A foolish consistency is the hobglobin of little minds, adored by little 6
statesmen and philosophers and divines. With consistency a great soul
has simply nothing to do. He may as well concern himself with his shadow
on the wall. Speak what you think now in hard words, and to-morrow
speak what to-morrow thinks in hard words again, though it contradict
every thing you said to-day. "Ah, so you shall be sure to be misunderstood."
Is it so bad, then, to be misunderstood? Pythagoras was misunderstood,
and Socrates, and Jesus, and Luther, and Copernicus, and Galileo, and
Newton, and every pure and wise spirit that ever took flesh. To be great
is to be misunderstood.

Exercise 46

DIRECTIONS *In each blank at the right, write the letter that identifies the correct definition of each of the following words.*

1. **arduous:** (A) applicable; (B) of great value; (C) very difficult; (D) enjoyable

2. **usages:** (A) customary practices; (B) useless modes of behavior; (C) things out of fashion; (D) distasteful modes of behavior

3. **precise:** (A) exact; (B) honest; (C) devious, dishonest; (D) likable

4. **conformity:** (A) a striving to be rich; (B) a striving to be superior; (C) a willingness to behave like the crowd; (D) a willingness to be different

5. **anticipate:** (A) to understand clearly; (B) clearly not to understand; (C) to enjoy; (D) to know in advance or to expect

6. **expediency:** (A) basic beliefs of; (B) the organization of; (C) the quick achieving of an end without regard to right; (D) religious tone

7. **ostentation:** (A) a pretending without real action; (B) showiness; (C) careful observation; (D) poor mental effort

8. **affectation:** (A) legal maneuvering; (B) citing poor reasons for; (C) artificiality of behavior; (D) attempt to be liked

9. **chagrins:** (A) deceives; (B) enlightens; (C) confuses; (D) embarrasses or humiliates

10. **adhere:** (A) to reinstate oneself; (B) to reject; (C) to be devoted to; (D) to be elected to

11. **asinine:** (A) like an angel; (B) like a devil; (C) like a clergyman; (D) like an ass

12. **mortifying:** (A) killing; exterminating; (B) affecting with shame; (C) causing to be joyful; (D) causing to reject

13. **usurping:** (A) slowly growing; (B) quickly growing; (C) poorly thought out; (D) seizing without right

14. **askance:** (A) sidewise; (B) head on; (C) with approval; (D) without understanding

15. **aversion:** (A) approval of; (B) disapproval of or extreme dislike of; (C) a turning inward; (D) surprise at _____

16. **formidable:** (A) mysterious; (B) fully understandable; (C) exciting fear by reason of strength; (D) having a clear form _____

17. **decorous:** (A) angry; (B) restrained; (C) proper and in good taste; (D) wise _____

18. **prudent:** (A) cautious and careful to avoid errors; (B) particularly violent; (C) only mildly violent or raging; (D) having high morals _____

19. **vulnerable:** (A) weak because of low morals; (B) reasonably strong; (C) self-assured; (D) unprotected or capable of being hurt _____

20. **magnanimity:** (A) state of being high-minded; (B) state of being low-minded; (C) state of being religius; (D) state of being cooperative in all things _____

A MINI-EXERCISE   Using your dictionary if necessary, write intelligent sentences, using the stated words.

1. a. **arduous:** _____

_____

_____

_____

   b. **ardent:** _____

_____

_____

_____

THE DRIVER EDUCATION MYTH

Edward A. Tenney

For the past twenty-five years, the auto industry has declared its love for 1
mankind by urging the school system of every state to put a stop to "the
senseless slaughter on our highways." This means to this end is Driver
Education, and millions of dollars are spent **annually** on its promotion.
Despite the lack of any real statistics, the industry, which includes organized tourism and auto insurance, sturdily **proclaims** that among graduates of Driver Ed, accidents, injuries and death on the road are reduced
by 50 percent and more.

Our children will become good, safe motorists, the theory goes, by 2
taking this course at thirteen in states which issue the adult license at
fourteen. In other states, the course is given the year before the children
become **eligible** for licenses. And it **instills** in its students such excellent
vehicular manners that parents, relatives and friends learn safety by
example. The child driver soon converts father and mother from their
driving sins, and thus traffic **prudence** will spread until our whole society
becomes **immune** to preventable accidents.

For the gist of the Driver Ed doctrine is that accidents do not happen; 3
they are caused. Good people are rewarded by being safe; bad people are
punished by suffering accidents which crush, kill, mutilate, paralyze and,
on occasion, leave the evildoer idiotic for the remainder of his days. Those
who die are memorialized in a pamphlet entitled: *The Dishonor Roll*
published by an insurance company.

Teachers and students alike recognize that this pseudo-religious talk 4
and teaching is silly. There are various nicknames for Driver Education.
It is called the "Mickey Mouse Course" because the safety movies show
Mickey Mouse **sprites** tempting drivers to do good or evil things. It is

From *The Nation*, April 20, 1964. Reprinted with permission.

sometimes called a "gut" course because it makes few demands upon intelligence, and a "frill" because it is said to be an ornament dangling from the regular curriculum.

But whether Mickey Mouse, gut, or frill, Driver Ed commands the 5 respect neither of the faculty which teaches it nor the children who are taught. No responsible scientist in or out of high school or college, no important figure in any part of the country, no leader of **integrity** or **eminence, asserts** that the course as presently taught from one end of the country to the other has any **ascertainable** effect upon the death rate, or upon the accident rate, or upon the violations rate, or upon the character for good or evil of the children who take the course. According to Dr. Leon J. Goldstein of the Division of Accident Prevention in the U.S. Public Health Service: "No conclusions can be drawn as to whether driver education is or is not effective."

The endlessly repeated statement that it reduces accidents and in- 6 juries by 50 percent is **patently** false, as the statistics clearly show. Although many millions of our children have now been "immunized" against preventable accidents, and although these millions now **saturate** the driving population in the 15–24 age group, the record of this group shows no **substantial** improvement. In the decade 1952–62, according to figures of the National Safety Council, the 15–24 group increased the number of us which it kills per 100,000 from 38.5 to 39.7. In the 25–44 age group the rate declined from 24.8 in 1952 to 22.5 in 1962. In other words, the group which had less exposure to Driver Ed improved more. The teen-agers become deadlier by the year. In 1958, they (7.2 percent of the United States drivers) had 12.5 percent of all accidents; in 1962 they (7.1 percent of the whole) had 14.7 percent of these accidents. Nationally, 6 percent more of us were killed in 1962 than in 1961, and again 6 percent more in 1963 than in 1962. We boosted the number of dead by motor accidents from 38,091 in 1961, to 43,400 in 1963. In a period when Driver Ed should have been pushing the number of deaths steadily down, they were going steadily up.

The most startling illustration of this tendency is to be seen in 7 Michigan. The state has long boasted of its semi-compulsory Driver Ed law which issues adult licenses at 16 to children who have taken the course. Children not so taught cannot obtain licenses until they are 18. Each year the state receives a medal and citation because it enrolls 100 percent of its potential child enrollment. Michigan once boasted of its intention to have the best traffic safety record in the nation: "The state which is first in autos should also be first in safety." In the years 1962–63 motorized deaths in Michigan rose from 1529 to 1847. The national rate rose 14 percent in that time; Michigan's rose 20 percent.

Among a good many close observers of safety the impression grows 8 that the Mickey Mouse course may actually be one cause of the increase in traffic deaths. The *American Legion Magazine* has published a substantial study of teen-age death and accident rates which compared states with much Driver Ed against states which had little or none. The latter had lower rates. A report by the Texas Board of Insurance shows that, of the insured group studied, those who had been exposed to Driver Ed had 12 percent more accidents than those who had not.

Why, in the face of such evidence, do the propaganda drums continue 9 to boom for Driver Ed? Why does the old myth that traffic deaths and injuries are reduced by 50 percent continue to appear in the press? Why is it that when a school board calls a special meeting to consider dropping Mickey Mouse, the room is jammed with his ardent admirers, armed with charts and pamphlets to show how large are the cash savings to everyone, how wonderful is the decline in juvenile delinquency?

Actually there is no mystery. Those in the safety business know that 10 Driver Ed is a branch of Consumer Ed; and that although the value of Driver Ed may be unproved, that of Consumer Ed is beyond question. The motor car needs to be made into a status symbol at the earliest possible age. Every leader in auto insurance, in auto making, in auto selling, in trucking, in tires and in dozens of associated businesses, including the National Safety Council, the American Automobile Association, the National Education Association now knows, or ought to know, that the propaganda for Driver Ed goes on, not because it has any **detectable** power to save lives, but because it is the cheapest kind of advertising. It pays off by getting adult licenses into the hands of children.

Twenty-five years ago the leadership of this massive industry may 11 have believed that a genuine scientific discovery had been made and that it really might save as much as 50 percent immunity against traffic accidents. Perhaps these industrialists really felt that money spent on this **alleged** discovery was genuine **philanthrophy**. Time would tell— meanwhile they were certain that they would be tapping a great new market.

Driver education really put the children on the road by giving them 12 licenses, by **dispelling** the fears of their parents, by making the auto a teen-age status **symbol**. Thus as Driver Ed expanded so did the sale of cars, gas, oil, tires, insurance, motel rooms and acessories.

But now that time has shown that children are not immunized to 13 any **discernible** degree, one might suppose that the leadership in this industry would acknowledge the fact and act accordingly. Quite aside from injury and death, it is common knowledge that access to cars harms children intellectually by **diverting** their attention from their studies, morally by exposing them to the unchaperoned temptations of liquor and love, socially by developing superiority complexes, economically by keeping them in debt, physically by depriving them of exercise. If General Motors, Ford, Chrysler would now stop sending fleets of new cars into the schools each fall by way of their dealers, school boards might send the old cars to the junkyards and stop exploiting the children.

But only an old-fashioned American idealist would really expect any 14 such responsible leadership from the automobile industry. Having, perhaps **unwittingly**, sold a bill of goods in the name of safety and having persisted in selling it for the profit, having thus established a reputation as a lover of safety and a protector of youth, the industry is in a tight spot. If the facts became known, Detroit might be accused of **callous** disregard for the welfare of American boys and girls—and that, to put it mildly, would be bad public relations.

General Motors appears to recognize the spot on which it so gingerly 15 sits. It has undertaken an immense advertising campaign on the theme, *General Motors Is People*. This almost idiotic slogan appears inspired by the desire to make people believe that a warm heart beats deep in the corporate bosom, that G.M. is really concerned with the general welfare.

Many safety-minded people remember how smug General Motors 16 was when in 1956 it outsold Ford. That was the year when Ford emphasized safety and G.M. dazzled the public with chrome and charm. As G.M. boasted later, "Ford sold safety, but we sold cars." Some observers hold G.M. primarily responsible for the failure of American auto makers to produce a safe car, one designed to "package the occupant." Such a car, we are told, can be built and really might reduce deaths and injuries by 50 percent in ten years' time if its principles were universally adopted. But such a car exists only on the drawing boards of the safety engineers.

Instead of joining with Ford in 1956 in an intense competition to 17 see which corporation could produce the stronger, safer car, G.M. sold charm, speed and danger, and shortly thereafter put on an advertising campaign for Driver Ed with the slogan: "The Cars Are Safer. The Roads Are Safer. The Rest Is Up to You."

We are told that the removal of Driver Ed from the schools would 18 drastically reduce the number of drivers and produce a recession so intense as to frizzle your hair. Children, it is true, are great consumers of secondhand cars, and assist greatly in the process of **dynamic obsolescence**— that is, they drive them into the ground or smash them into scrap. But the removal of Driver Ed from the schools would produce no recession provided the auto industry awakened to its own responsibility. This responsibility is, first, to put on the market a full range of models designed primarily for the safety of the occupant. And, second, the responsibility is to educate the people to use them. If the leadership accepted this obligation, the National Safety Council, The National Education Association, The American Automobile Association would fall in line and a real safety movement would get under way.

Exercise 47

DIRECTIONS *In each blank at the right, write the letter that identifies the correct definition of each of the following words.*

1. **annually:** (A) uselessly; (B) usefully; (C) yearly; (D) monthly _____
2. **proclaim:** (A) to lie about; (B) to tell the truth about; (C) to publish in newspapers; (D) to declare or announce _____
3. **eligible:** (A) having possession of; (B) not having possession of; (C) legally qualified; (D) not legally qualified _____
4. **instill:** (A) to train formally; (B) to put into or introduce into; (C) to give complete knowledge of; (D) to withhold from _____
5. **prudence:** (A) caution to avoid errors; (B) a system of laws; (C) a system of social behavior; (D) good manners _____
6. **immune:** (A) indifferent to; (B) protected from; (C) knowledgeable about; (D) ignorant of _____
7. **sprites:** (A) instructors; (B) cartoon characters; (C) goblins or ghostly spirits; (D) hirelings _____
8. **integrity:** (A) industry in general; (B) the auto industry; (C) honesty; (D) great intelligence _____
9. **eminence:** (A) great intelligence; (B) power; (C) high rank; (D) the political system _____
10. **assert:** (A) to prove; (B) to state positively; (C) to believe without proof; (D) to undertake or take action _____
11. **ascertainable:** (A) very important; (B)negligible; (C) able to be learned with certainty; (D) caused by positive action _____
12. **patently:** (A) officially; (B) unofficially; (C) perhaps true; (D) clearly and obviously _____
13. **saturate:** (A) to cause harm to; (B) to prevent harm from coming to; (C) to drink; (D) to fill completely or to be dominant in _____
14. **substantial:** (A) financial; (B) pertaining to insurance; (C) solid or of real worth; (D) subject to scientific proof _____
15 **detectable:** (A) official; (B) capable of being discovered; (C) unofficial; (D) having material substance _____

16. **alleged:** (A) asserted to be true without proof; (B) secret; (C) having no truth in it; (D) officially adopted   ————

17. **philanthropy:** (A) scientific proof; (B) earnest behavior; (C) deed of charity; (D) official meddling   ————

18. **dispel:** (A) to prove false; (B) to divert to other thoughts; (C) to confirm; (D) to drive away   ————

19. **symbol:** (A) something that represents something else; (B) desired object; (C) something of influence; (D) a musical instrument   ————

20. **discernible:** (A) being a large proportion of; (B) recognizable; (C) desirable; (D) predicted   ————

21. **divert:** (A) to change one thing for another; (B) to turn aside or away from; (C) to reduce; (D) to increase   ————

22. **unwittingly:** (A) in an attempt to make profit; (B) in an attempt to do public good; (C) unknowingly; (D) with cynicism   ————

23. **callous:** (A) profitable; (B) unprofitable; (C) hardened in feelings; (D) political   ————

24. **dynamic:** (A) having force and energy; (B) being automatic; (C) planned in advance; (D) completely unplanned   ————

25. **obsolescence:** (A) the quality of going out-of-date; (B) improvement in quality; (C) quick change in quality; (D) getting rid of   ————

A MINI-EXERCISE Explain what is wrong with the pronoun reference in this sentence:

Bick also told trustees that the on-call pay should be restored because interns [doctors] feel **this** is distracting from their other training.

Part Three WRITING ASSIGNMENTS

Introduction

Part I of this text is intended to help you make your writing correct. This part is intended to help make it effective. The nine assignments represent most of the major kinds of writing. Each kind is first defined for you. Then practical instructions are given to guide you in writing each kind of theme. Following the instructions is a model student theme with commentary, the whole being a further guide for you to use in your own writing. The themes have been revised and improved beyond the original, but they all represent the kind of writing you can aspire to. Finally, a specific writing assignment is given.

Before beginning each of your assignments, study the instructions and the model theme. Your instructor may discuss them with you in class. He may also omit a few of the assignments in order to give you more practice in some of the others. Probably Assignment Five, the expository essay, is the one you need most practice in. But all the assignments will give you valuable training in preparing for a college career.

Writing Assignment

1 COLLEGE WRITING, AN OVERVIEW

Writing is intended to communicate to the reader, never to confuse him. The writer may wish to communicate a variety of things: to tell a story or relate an event, to describe a scene or a person, to explain his thoughts about a matter that may be of minor consequence or of major importance, to tell someone how to do something, to define something in detail, or to persuade the reader to believe or accept an idea. When a description is vague or unclear, when a narrative or definition is confusing, or when the persuasion fails to convince, the writer has failed to communicate well.

College writing, in fact, all effective writing, is purposeful. The effective writer always has a specific goal: the narrative should be of some significance, the character sketch should emphasize one dominant trait, the explanation or persuasion should have a clear and understandable goal. To write an effective theme or essay, you need to start by developing but two elements: a precise **topic** and a clear **statement** about the topic.

Developing a Topic

Most topics in college are determined by the nature of the course for which you are writing the essay. For a class in geology, you may be writing about oil. For a class in sociology, you may be required to write about the differences between city and farm children. You have your choice and selection in the **limiting** of the topic. Because an **effective** essay will cover all aspects of the topic, it would be impossible to write all about *oil* in less than several hundred thousand words, clearly impossible. You must, then, **limit** the topic. Some examples of topics and possible limitations follow:

Topic	Limitation
Oil	synthetic oils
City and farm children	differences in educational opportunities.
	differences in health
Natural parks	Yosemite

311

Making a Statement

Once you have decided on the limitation of your topic, the next step is to make a **statement** about the topic. The statement will give direction and purpose to your essay. Some examples:

Limited topic	Statement
Synthetic oils	are too expensive to replace natural petroleum.
Rural children	have better general health than city children.
Yosemite National Park	is the most beautiful in the nation.

The topic plus the statement is a clear, declarative sentence. This sentence is often called the **thesis** or controlling thought. Once you have developed a useful thesis statement, all you have to do is gather the information and select the examples, and the essay will almost write itself. Without a clear thesis statement, you may ramble vaguely from point to point and lose the purpose and goal of your writing.

ASSIGNMENT   Select any three of the following large, general topics, and limit them so that they might be written about in an essay of a few hundred words.

a. **Mountains** _____

_____

b. **A relative** _____

_____

c. **Crime** _____

_____

d. **Advertising** _____

_____

e. **Automobiles** _____

f. **Education** _____

Now, pick any two of your limited topics, and write a clear, understandable statement for each. Refine and revise your topic statement (thesis) until it tells the reader both what you are going to write about and what you are going to say about it. Your instructor may ask you to write a brief essay from your thesis statement.

Writing Assignment

2 DESCRIPTION

Description is the kind of writing that tells how something looks, feels, sounds, smells, or tastes. Writers of description put into words impressions that their five senses have registered in their mind (or similar impressions that they create in their imagination). They write about colors, shapes, textures, motions, noises, stenches, and so on. Normally, description is not written just for its own sake but to supplement other kinds of writing. It appears most frequently in storytelling, being used to establish setting and to help make the characters seem real. It is also often used in informative writing for the purpose of clarification, such as in an explanation of how to assemble a model airplane. But the writing of pure description— that which is not intended to supplement some other kind of writing—is a good exercise for composition students, for it gives training in techniques that apply to all kinds of good writing. Other kinds of themes that you write will often contain patches of description. In writing a theme of description, you should observe the following techniques. And incidentally, you need not avoid the pronoun *I*.

Organize your theme on the basis of *units of impression*   After you have chosen the subject of your description—such as a particular dormitory room—you should jot down the three to five **units of impression** (they are, in effect, **main points**) that you will develop, such as these:

1. The furniture in the room
2. The wall decorations of the room
3. The books and other evidence of schoolwork
4. The evidences of recent human habitation, such as food scraps

Each of these units of impression will then be developed in **one** paragraph. Do NOT include two units of impression in one paragraph. As for length, your paragraphs may range from as few as 25 to 30 words to as many as 150 to 175. But each should describe just one unit of impression.

Here is another example of this kind of organization. Let us say the subject of your description is a professor. Your units of impression might be these:

314

1. Her physical characteristics, including her speech
2. Her distinctive style of dress and how she varies it
3. Her mannerisms, both in class and on the campus
4. Her reactions to various situations and persons in class or in conferences with students

Again, you would develop each of these units of impression in one paragraph. Of course, you may not think of the units of impression in the exact order that you will want to present them. Thus after you jot down the three to five units you will develop, you should arrange them in the order you prefer.

Have your opening sentence establish the totality of your subject matter Ignore your title when you compose your opening sentence, and have that sentence express clearly what your paper will be about. Here is a suitable opening for the first topic suggested above:

> The dormitory room of my best boyfriend is not exactly a picture of suburban luxury. Its furniture might even be called dilapidated.

Now the reader knows what you are going to describe, and, with the second sentence, you are ready immediately to begin describing the furniture as your first unit of impression. *Do NOT have your opening sentence stand as a separate paragraph.* Instead, make it the first sentence of your first paragraph, with the second (or, occasionally, third) sentence establishing what the first unit of impression will be, as illustrated. Your closing sentence, which also should not be a separate paragraph but just the last sentence of the last paragraph, should simply sound a note of finality, like this:

> My friend's dormitory room, then, is quite serviceable, but it would shock his parents.

Such a sentence simply sounds like an ending.

Be selective of details and avoid wordiness Description, of course, is made up of details. But if writers try to express every detail of whatever scene they are describing, they will bore their readers, and their writing will sound wordy. The good writer of description knows how to select details in order to give the *appearance* of reality, NOT the actual full reality. For example, suppose you are describing one of your classrooms, and suppose one of your units of impression is the group of students gathered for a learning experience. Would you tell the color of hair and eyes of every girl, the exact dress of each boy, and so on? No, you should select details to give your reader the feel of reality, not the full reality. In this respect a generalization about the casual dress of the male students could serve as one detail. For example, you might write this sentence in your paragraph about the appearance of the students who are sitting in the classroom:

> The boys are all dressed in a casual fashion that would scandalize their grandparents, for their trousers are faded, unpressed, and ragged at the cuffs (or where the cuffs would be) and their T-shirts all seem to have been sent to a mechanic's school.

A detail in description is not necessarily one that cannot be broken down into smaller details. Generalizations as details are an important part of description.

Also, in describing details of your scene avoid the pitfall of using too many adjectives, for too many will bog down a piece of description and prevent sharpness of scene. For example, compare these two phrases:

1. the pink-petaled honeysuckle with its beckoning boughs
2. the pink-petaled, gaudy, luxuriant honeysuckle with its uneven, twisted, brittle, yet beckoning boughs

In the flow of a paragraph, the crisp first phrase would be more pleasing to the reader than the overloaded second phrase. Be sure to give what seems to be a full picture of your scene, but do not get bogged down in adjectives.

Use vivid, sensory phrasing Sensory phrasing is that which puts **images** (or pictures) in our minds as we read. **Visual imagery** is most important in description, for we mostly describe what we see. But also images of feeling, hearing, smelling, and tasting can appear in description. The idea, of course, is to try to make your reader *see* (or feel, hear, smell, or taste) what you see. The words a writer chooses determine the quality of his imagery.

One important point is that not only adjectives but also verbs and nouns may be vividly descriptive. Think, for example, how much more descriptive *haggle, banter, jabber, chatter, yak*, and so on are than the bland verb *talk* or how much more image-forming *stagger, limp, stroll, strut*, and so on are than just *walk*. Also, remember that the verb *to be* is hardly image-forming at all. Try to use vivid verbs rather than *is, was, will be*, and so on. Nouns, too, have varying descriptive values. Compare, for example, *torches* with *lights, billows* with *waves*, and *girdle* with *foundation garment*. The first words in these pairs are distinctly more vivid.

As much as you can, make your word choice in description as **specific** as possible rather than general. A general word covers many more details than does a specific word. For example, *torment* is much less specific than *jeer at*. Also make your word choice as **concrete** as possible, rather than abstract. In this sense, concrete means an image-forming word, such as *pimply*, whereas an abstract word, which does not name anything tangible, does little, if any, image-forming. An example of an abstract word is *communistic*.

Attempt to create a few figures of speech Two figures of speech are most used in description. One is **simile**, in which two essentially unlike things are compared with the use of a comparative word, such as *like* or *as*. For example, "The rays of sunshine were like golden shafts from heaven" is a simile. The second major figure of speech is **metaphor**, which is the same as simile except that a direct identification is made without the use of a comparative word. For example, "The rays of sunshine were golden shafts from heaven" is a metaphor. The technical difference between the two is unimportant.

Figures of speech are especially desirable in description because they are usually specific and concrete and are usually image-forming. They contribute vividness to description. However, do not use figures of speech to excess, for they can then become tiresome and cloying. Also avoid **clichés**. A cliché (often a figure of speech) is a worn-out, overused expression, such as *pretty as a picture* or *the crack of dawn*. Most student writers use too many clichés.

Choose to be either a stationary or a moving observer Writers of description, of course, describe what they observe (or imagine). Often they describe what they see from a fixed position, as they probably would if describing a dormitory room. Sometimes, however, a scene to be described—such as a whole campus—calls for the writer to shift positions, thus getting new perspectives. For example, the cliff dwellings in Mesa Verde National Park would be most interestingly described if the writer saw them both at a distance and close up and also from different angles. Let the subject of your description determine whether you will be a roving or fixed observer.

Following is a revised student descriptive theme, with brief commentary on it. You can use it as a model in trying to employ the techniques discussed above. But remember that this is not a professional piece of writing, but a good theme that you can really imitate.

SAXMAN VILLAGE

Saxman Village, near Ketchikan, Alaska, is the largest Indian village in the northland, but it is not in actuality large, and, I'm afraid, neither is it attractive. There are just a few cross streets, all dirt and usually muddy because of the almost constant rain. And paint is as scarce as pavement, for all the buildings are a weatherworn dull gray. As you walk down the main street towards Buggy Beach, you see that the few places of business are small and poorly stocked. And as you enter the residential area on the way toward Deer Mountain, you see that the dwellings are ramshackle and about as comfortable-looking as a century-old tobacco barn in the Deep South. But after an initial shock, like finding some distant relatives living in a piggery, you discover some charm.

The few hundred people of the village are mostly purebred Indians of the Tlingit tribe and still adhere to ancient customs. They are suspicious of white doctors, relying instead on their own fancifully dressed and gaudily made-up medicine men. Also they settle disputes by their own hard-to-comprehend code, not by the white man's laws. They dress in American-made cloth, but that does not cover their distinctive appearance. The children are full of Indian play until an outsider appears, and then they are as sobersided as little judges. The young men are handsome and athletic-looking, and the young women, very dark in color, are extremely pretty. But before middle age sets in, the women get fat and ugly and the men rather decrepit. Their life expectancy is two or three decades less than that of the whites.

The opening sentence clearly establishes the subject to be described and also establishes the first unit of impression— the streets and buildings of the town.

The writer poses as a roving observer and shifts perspectives.

Two amusing and vivid figures of speech are created.

The second unit of impression—the appearance of the people—is established.

Another effective figure of speech is used.

With just a few details, the writer creates a full picture.

The Tlingits of Saxman support
themselves mostly by their handiwork
and ancient methods of acquiring
food, not usually by taking the white
man's jobs. They are all expert
basket weavers, making dozens of
different shapes and sizes of sturdy
and useful baskets. These bring
good prices from the tourists, most
of whom come in summer from the
various cruise ships that ply up
and down the coast of Alaska. The
natives also practice scrimshaw, or
the carving of art objects out of
bone and other material. Ivory
scrimshaw sells for a great deal.
Though these natives do have some
money, they still gather food from
the land. They do some gardening,
hunt birds, and, chiefly, fish.
They use an ancient method of
smoking salmon for winter use. The
salmon strips are hung on lines like
wet wash, with smoldering fires
built under them. The resulting
product is delicious.

The greatest tourist attraction
of Saxman is its many totem poles.
A few are scattered throughout the
village, but as you stroll to the
northeast part of the village you
find that most are concentrated in
one small plot. They range from six
feet to forty feet high, and all but
one are gaudily painted carvings
which seem almost to be caricatures
of people's faces and animals. Each
totem supposedly tells a story of
old times. But I wonder about that.
The one not gaudily painted is
simply a tall, smooth pole with a
black figure of Abraham Lincoln
on top. And, to make me more
suspicious of the totems'
storytelling, I learned that they
were all carved in the 1930s as a
WPA project. Nevertheless, it is

A third unit of
impression is established.

Concrete and specific
words are used, forming
images in the reader's
mind.

Another good figure of
speech is created. The
phrasing is concise and
not wordy.

The fourth unit of
impression—the totem
poles—is established.

The writer could have
made his description of
the totems more vivid
and precise.

encouraging to see that the Tlingits
survived the Depression and still
have their own culture.

The concluding sentence
sounds a note of finality.

ASSIGNMENT   Review the techniques discussed above and the model
   theme.
If you have not already done so, you may wish to read the selections
"Sight into Insight: Learning to See" by Annie Dillard (page 215) and
"A Hanging" by George Orwell (page 221). Both have excellent descriptions in them. Then write a descriptive theme of your own. You might
describe a section of your hometown, an interesting geological formation
(such as the Grand Canyon), a political rally, a calamity of some sort
(such as a forest fire), a pet shop scene, a street scene, a particularly ugly
or beautiful building, your car, a deciduous forest in autumn, or any of
countless scenes.

A TIP ON USAGE   Use the possessive form of a noun or pronoun after
   the preposition *of* when the object of the preposition *of* owns the noun
   preceding *of*. For example, *a friend of mine* is correct; *a friend of me*
   is incorrect. Note the difference in meaning between this pair of
   phrases:

1. every word of Richardson (news about him)
2. every word of Richardson's (his words)

So use such phrases as these:

a pal of Joe's
a cat of the Smiths'
an acquaintance of hers
an ailment of my grandmother's

Writing Assignment

3 PERSONAL NARRATIVE

Narrative writing is storytelling—either fictional or factual. Its chief ingredients are characters, plot, setting, theme (or significance), and style. One or more human beings (or occasionally animals or robots) move through a sequence of events in time in a certain environment. Thus narration is a re-creating of experience, either imagined or real. The plot provides suspense, and it is usually suspense that makes most people read stories and novels. Narration is probably the best liked of all kinds of writing.

A **personal narrative** is a little story from one's own life. Without realizing that they are writing narrative, countless people tell countless little stories about themselves in their friendly letters. Thus the personal narrative is the kind of writing assignment that students like best and do best. All those of college age have had many interesting experiences that they can work into a good theme of personal narrative. Following are the basic techniques you should try to employ in writing a little story from your own life.

Organize your story on the basis of a flow of events in time Narration is the easiest kind of writing to organize because a story has a natural flow of events with a beginning, middle, and end. In a short personal narrative it is usually best not to use such sophisticated techniques as flashbacks. But in spite of the ease with which narrative can be organized, you probably should jot down the main events or items of interest in your story before you begin writing; this will help guide your organization of your story. Here is an example from a student's work.

TOPIC: How I escaped a dishonorable discharge from the army
TITLE: The Case of the Innocent Barracks Bags

ORGANIZATION:

1. The approaching end of my stay in an army hospital and in the army

2. My accumulation of stolen articles that I intended to take with me

3. My proceeding with stuffed barracks bags to the point of discharge

4. My witnessing to my horror that the contents of each man's barracks bags were thoroughly inspected

5. My wildly rushing to an upstairs wing and finding an empty room

6. My piling all my stolen goods in the room

7. My passing the barracks-bag inspection with complete innocence

Jotting down the main events of your story in this fashion will help you write with more confidence.

Paragraphing in a personal narrative is simple. You need not plan a separate paragraph for each item in your list of main events. Instead, you should plan to have paragraphs of between 50 and 150 words and should just plan to start a new paragraph where there is a perceptible shift in the flow of events. For example, in the above plan for a personal narrative the student writer merged the first two main points into one paragraph and then started a new paragraph where there was a shift of events to his starting to his point of discharge. (He also included item no. 4 in his second paragraph.) Thus (except for dialogue, in which each new speech is a new paragraph) you should follow only two rules of paragraphing in your personal narrative: (1) do not have very short paragraphs (except for dialogue) and (2) begin a new paragraph only where there is some shift in events.

Make your opening sentence arouse interest and promise a story to come In your opening sentence you need not tell what your whole story will be (as you do tell what your whole subject will be in writing description), but you should catch your readers' interest and promise them a story. For example, here is the opening sentence the student wrote for the theme outlined above:

Stealing is an offense in the army that can lead to a dishonorable discharge, and at the time of my discharge I was very nearly caught stealing a considerable amount of goods.

This is a strong, gripping opening and makes the reader want to know the whole story. Just enough of the story is alluded to to whet the reader's appetite. Such an opening sentence should NOT be a separate paragraph by itself but should be a part of the first paragraph. For example, the second sentence of the theme just described was this: "I had been in an Army hospital for some weeks and had had the opportunity to pick up various valuables." Putting the two sentences in separate paragraphs would have been very poor technique.

A story usually has a natural ending, but you should compose your concluding sentence so that it sounds a note of finality. For example, here is the ending sentence the student wrote for the theme discussed above.

> My relief at being able to present honest barracks bags for inspection must have been similar to that of any sinner that Saint Peter ushers through the pearly gates.

Such a sentence makes the reader *feel* the end of the story. The concluding sentence should NOT be a separate paragraph by itself but just the last sentence of the last paragraph.

Use a first-person style that suits your own personality Because the little story is about you, you should write in the first person (using the pronoun *I*) and should make the style of the story suit your own personality. For example, compare these sentences:

1. The policeman caught me easily, pretended to be taking me to jail, and laughed at my screams of fear.
2. The law officer apprehended me with dispatch, made a pretense of escorting me to the town's institution of incarceration, and expressed mirth at my outcries of consternation.

The first sentence is from a theme that tells a story of the student's childhood, and it sounds completely natural. The second sentence is a rewriting using nothing but "good" words, but it sounds completely unnatural for a first-person narrative. In informative writing (Assignments Five through Nine) you should use the highest level of vocabulary and mature sentence structure at your command, but in a personal narrative make the style sound like "you."

Some techniques discussed in the assignment on writing description—being selective of details, using sensory phrasing, choosing specific and concrete words, and creating a figure of speech or two—also apply to the writing of personal narrative.

Use a bit of dialogue if it will sound natural A short personal narrative need not necessarily have any dialogue, but a patch or two of it can strengthen the reality of storytelling, for people are in the story and people do talk. If you use dialogue, try to make it sound natural.

Tell a story that has some significance There should be a point of purpose to your story; an aimless recounting of a trivial and meaningless experience will interest no one. For example, the personal narrative discussed above has the significance that it is dangerous to try to steal from the army. Or a theme might have, say, the significance that trying to enter a social circle of rich people leads to disappointment. The point of your story does not, of course, have to be moralistic, for an event in one's life can be significant without telling a Sunday school lesson. For example, your story might show that it is advisable to be wary of auto repair shops. You need not tell about a bizarre or highly unusual event in your life, a commonplace occurrence can be interesting and infused with significance. For example, the experience of a young boy trying to sell soap door-to-door could make an excellent personal narrative. Also your story may be humorous and significant at the same time. Many students prefer to write humorous personal narratives.

Following is a revised personal narrative (written by an older student) that you can use as a model. Read it carefully to see how some of the techniques discussed in the first two writing assignments are utilized.

FEAR TRIUMPHS

Privates in the Army use many stratagems to avoid unpleasant duty. Some tricks succeed handily and others backfire. Most soldiers take their failures and consequent punishment philosophically. My failure in an evasive tactic I once took resulted only in damaged pride over my inability to conquer fear.

Note that the opening, though not exciting, promises a story. It whets the reader's appetite to know what happened.

I was not even yet eighteen, though I had survived basic training and gave a fuzzy-chinned imitation of being a soldier. I made my daily toil easier and safer by working as janitor and attendant in the recreation hall, but my nights were miserable and hazardous because our company commander invariably took us on two- or three-hour maneuvers every morning between two and three o'clock. I was a failure on these outings. I crashed into pine trees, tried to force the wrong pieces of

There is a natural order in the flow of events. The paper has really organized itself.

ammunition into my artillery piece, and generally infuriated my platoon sergeant. Night after night I was like a housefly that had wandered into a beehive.

The diction is generally concrete and specific, and there are some figures of speech.

One afternoon I said to my corporal, "I'm not going tonight. I'm going to hide out in the recreation hall." He grunted what I thought was acceptance of my plan. When the call sounded at 2:00 A.M., I dressed hastily and slipped away to the rec hall. I let myself in, lay on a couch in the darkness, and began to feel my heart beat like a trip-hammer. I could hear the activity in the distance and visualized my squad. Had my corporal really agreed to my tactic? Would he report me absent? What kind of sentence would I receive? I lay in dread and misery. Tangible fears raced through my mind. I heard noises at the doors and windows. Once I was certain the door opened and closed. I longed to be in the nearby pine thicket bumping into trees and fouling the mechanism of my antitank artillery fieldpiece. Suddenly the night service seemed a frolic, an opportunity for gaiety and horseplay. Could I get to my unit without detection? I was eager to surrender.

No aimless or trivial details cause the story to lose focus or stray from its point.

The human element is strong. The writer makes himself a created character.

I slipped out the door, forgetting to lock it, and headed for the confusion of the pine thicket, where light rays flickered and died eerily. I was nearing the edge of activity when I bumped into an officer, who grabbed me and peered at me in the pale moonlight.

"What the Hell are you doing way out here?"

Dialogue gives the little story an aura of reality.

My heart stopped, but I babbled, "My corporal sent me on a one-man patrol to check on a suspected enemy entrenchment."

The story has reasonable significance.

```
    "What $G%*$G nonsense," he yelled.
"Get back to your squad. Don't you
know we're preparing to advance?"
    I ran without another word--
escaped. Luck guided me to my squad.
    "I thought you were going to stay
at the rec hall," growled my corporal.
    "Why," I said gravely, "I feel I
must do my duty."
```

The ironic ending is elegant in that it brings a surprising reversal of the narrator's state of mind.

ASSIGNMENT   After reviewing the instructions above and the model theme, you may wish to read, or reread, the reading selections: "A Hanging" by George Orwell (page 221), "Outer Space to Inner Space: An Astronaut's Odyssey" by Edgar D. Mitchell (page 227), or "Verbal Karate, a Marital Art" by Jack Smith (page 233). These selections are all personal narratives, and each uses the form to make a significant statement. Then write a personal narrative of your own. You can recount a sports adventure, an unusual date, a dangerous escape, a family escapade, a classroom experience, a boy- or girl-scout adventure, an unusual and rewarding achievement, a hilarious mix-up of plans, a terror-invoking experience, an event that illustrates the essential kindness and compassion of human beings, an unusual bit of competition you have engaged in, or countless other personal experiences.

Writing Assignment

4 CHARACTER SKETCH

A **character sketch** utilizes both descriptive and narrative writing, and so your last two writing assignments will be repeated and combined. Some new instructions, however, will be added to the old, for characterization is special writing even though both descriptive and narrative. In writing a character sketch of your own, try to use the following techniques.

Organize your character sketch in much the same way you organize both description and personal narrative You may have both descriptive units of impression and narrative main events in your sketch. Try to decide what these are before you begin writing, and jot them down in order, like this example from a student's work:

TOPIC: The sweetness of Charlotte Brown and her kindness to me

TITLE: Puppy Love

ORGANIZATION:

1. How Charlotte and I went to the same small school but were some years apart in age

2. Her physical appearance

3. Her outgoing personality and charm

4. My foolishly trying to become her boyfrind

5. Her compassionate handling of the situation

6. My remembrance of a beautiful and sweet girl

Plan to develop one paragraph for each point you jot down, unless two or more go closely together and are short enough to be merged into one paragraph. In general, try to have paragraphs from 50 to 150 words in length, and start a new paragraph only when you start a new unit of impression or when there is a shift in events. For example, in the above plan the student writer made no. 1 into a short opening paragraph; he developed nos. 2 and 3 each into full paragraphs expressing a unit of impression each; he combined nos. 4 and 5 into one paragraph; and he made no. 6 a short concluding paragraph. Some sort of organization like this should be present in every character sketch.

Though you may have short introductory and concluding paragraphs, do NOT let single sentences stand as opening or closing paragraphs.

Let your opening sentence establish the subject of your character sketch, and make your closing sentence sound a note of finality.

Let description of external appearances tell also something of internal qualities   Much description of external appearances is, of course, only that: color of eyes and hair, height, complexion, and so forth. But many external traits can tell about internal qualities. For example, a person who is not well groomed may be evidencing an inside sense of ill ease and anxiety. Or a person who fidgits and cannot be still may be showing discontent and irritability. Good character description tries to get at the inside of the person through external appearances. Also, of course, you may write directly about the inside qualities of your personage.

Try to create a single dominant impression   Of course, you want to create as full a picture as you can in a short paper, but your reader should form an impression of the person's dominant character trait. *Details should be selected* to develop that impression. After finishing the sketch, the reader may think, "What a (kind, vicious, stimulating, exotic, and so forth) character."

Let the characterization grow and develop; avoid instant characterization   Avoid just stating your single dominant impression at once; let it gradually develop. Try not just to *tell* what the character is like; instead try to *show* what he or she is like. Let the character reveal something of himself or herself in his or her actions, words, or thoughts. Events (narration) can be used to reinforce character description. There can be movement or action in a character sketch. Also dialogue can be used to indicate character traits.

Create sensory images; use specific and concrete words: choose vivid nouns and verbs   All these qualities of good descriptive writing should go into a character sketch. Make the reader *see* your character and understand the character's nature. Review the instructions for descriptive writing before beginning your sketch.

Following is a character sketch written by an older student who returned to college after a career in the navy. You may profitably imitate this sketch.

UNCLE BOB

We all called him Uncle Bob, even though he was not old, and he called each boy "son." He treated the girls with Southern courtliness, addressing each as "Miss ———." The scene was a pre-World War II small private school. Uncle Bob was certainly the best loved and most outstanding member of the faculty and administration. He taught chemistry and physics.

The opening suggests that an engaging personage is to be characterized.

When I was a high school senior, Uncle Bob was about 35, with smooth pink skin, crow-black bushy hair, and oddly contrasting gray eyes. He seldom frowned, but creased his face with smiles indiscriminately. He had a powerful build--a bull-like neck and barrel chest and arms bulging with muscles like a Santa Claus bag full of stuffed toys. But some of the apparent physical power, I'm afraid, may have been fat. When he played baseball with his "sons," he would sometimes hit a ball 500 feet and still manage to get only to second base, puffing heavily. In the chemistry lab he appeared much more professional, with his white coat impressing us greatly.

A unit of impression—his physical appearance—is established.
Vivid details produce sensory images.

An entertaining figure of speech is created.

Uncle Bob was more than kind; he was easygoing to the point of laxness. Many students were not able to learn the material he taught, and thus he often looked the other way when a student got unauthorized help in the lab or even on tests. His attitude seemed to be that these students were required to take a chemistry course they would never use and thus need not be held to strict accountancy. In his advanced courses he was as strict and wary as an honest policeman. These students, he obviously thought, were going to use their

Now his personality is to be the next unit of impression.

Another good figure of speech is created.

courses and thus needed to be held to high standards. Outside the classroom he was affable and always interested in anyone who talked, and he loved to give individual counsel about almost anything. More than once he successfully came to the defense of a malefactor. I never heard a disrespectful word spoken about Uncle Bob.

We get insight into Uncle Bob's character through description and narration.

His amazing understanding of human psychology was demonstrated once in his handling of a case involving me. Though I was a good student, I saw the war coming, decided I would chuck everything and for a few days stopped going to classes. But one day I dropped into Uncle Bob's chemistry class. He announced to the class in general that anyone with six absences would fail the course. I was jolted, for I already had more than six absences. After class I asked him, "How many do I have?"

A bit of narration is used to further the characterization.

Without looking at his roll book he said, "Five."

A little dialogue adds interest and reality.

"I'll be back," I said, and I finished the year in good standing and kept my record clean. Probably no other teacher would have handled my case so well.

Then I entered the Navy, the war came soon, as expected, and I made the Navy a career. Thus I did not see Uncle Bob again for well over thirty years. A friend recently took me to see him. The change in him brought home to me how quickly the ravages of time work. His hair was now thin and white, his once-smooth skin sagged, and he was bent and decidely unpowerful-looking.

Another unit of impression describes his physical characteristics as an old man.

But his rememberance of his students of so long ago was astonishing. As soon as he heard my name, he said, "Aha! I had to straighten you out once." Then he

Specific and concrete words are used. A final segment of the organization is built around another bit of narration. The dominant impression of the

mumbled under his breath: "Walking right past my window when class was going on." His recollection of students from long ago far surpassed mine, and it was obvious that he still thought fondly of them as "son" and "Miss————." And I'm sure that all of Uncle Bob's "nephews" and "nieces" still remember lovingly his patience, compassion, and, when necessary, strictness.

character's inner worth has gradually been developed.

The last sentence sounds a note of finality.

ASSIGNMENT   Review the techniques above and the model theme. You might also wish to look at the character sketch in the reading selection "The Boys' Ambition" by Mark Twain (page 237). Then write a character sketch of your own. You can write about a sweetheart, a teacher, a chance acquaintance, an enemy, a preacher, a relative, or any one of dozens of people you know well.

Writing Assignment

5 EXPOSITORY ESSAY

Expository writing (also called **exposition**) deals objectively with facts, ideas, and opinions. It is writing designed to explain, to make clear, to inform. It deals with information, such as why professional football draws such a huge TV audience, the status of drug use on a campus, the chief causes of divorce, and so on. Opinions are not out of place in exposition, but they should be objectively presented. Neither is a personal tone necessarily out of place in this kind of writing, but it should be a tone of reasonable objectivity. Study the following techniques in order to prepare to write an expository essay.

Either state your topic fully or prepare a thesis sentence for your paper, or both A thesis sentence is a one-sentence expression of the overall content of the paper. It is sometimes called the **controlling idea**. It differs from a fully-stated topic mostly in that it is a complete sentence, but it may also state the content of the paper somewhat more fully. Here are two examples:

1. TOPIC: The superior features of the Mercedes-Benz
   THESIS SENTENCE: The Mercedes-Benz is a superior car because of advanced engineering features in its power train and suspension.
   TITLE: The King of Foreign Cars

2. TOPIC: How our local recreational facilities have deteriorated
   THESIS SENTENCE: Our recreational facilities have deteriorated because the city council will not vote sufficient funds for them.
   TITLE: Our Recreational Slums

Going through the process of expressing your topic fully and composing a thesis sentence will help prepare you to write a good expository composition.

Plan your organization around main points derived from a plural noun stated or implied in your topic Most topics for expository papers

332

will either have a plural noun expressed or one implied that can, in a sense, be divided into **main points** for the paper. Once you spot this noun, you should jot down the three to five main points that it suggests. For example, the first topic above has the plural noun *features*. This is what you are going to write about, so jot down the features you will discuss:

1. The overhead cam engine
2. The fuel-injection system
3. The special type of automatic transmission
4. The air-suspension system

Now you have your paper planned and are ready (if you understand your subject matter well) to begin writing. Here are other examples of topics with expressed plural nouns:

The *disadvantages* of teen-age marriages
The *problems* of being a brilliant student
The *methods* of controlling pollutant emissions from cars

To organize papers for these topics, you just need to think of three to five general *disadvantages, problems*, and *methods*. Main points are **generalizations**, not specifics.

Sometimes no plural noun is expressed in a topic, but in that case one is almost always implied. For example, the second topic on page 332 does not have a plural noun expressed to guide the writer in organization (the noun *facilitates* is not the core of the topic, for you are not going to list facilities). But the word *how* suggests *ways*, and that is the kind of plural noun you are searching for. You would need to think of three to five general *ways* in which local recreational facilities have deteriorated, such as these:

1. Lack of proper maintenance
2. Vandalism directed against facilities
3. No replacement of worn-out equipment
4. No additional equipment purchased as population has increased

Now you have a basic organization to guide you in writing your paper. Here are some other examples of topics that have only implied plural nouns:

The meaning of being human (*characteristics* implied)
How to become self-educated (*steps or ways* implied)
Why we should rebuild our navy (*reasons* implied)

To write on these topics, a student just needs to think of three to five general *characteristics, steps*, and *reasons*. *Reasons* is the most common implied noun in a topic for an expository essay.

Arrange your main points in their most effective order One does not always think of main points in the order in which one wants to take them up. So after you have jotted down your main points, decide the order in which you want to present them.

Plan to have one paragraph for each main point and to express that main point in a topic sentence Do not mix two main points in one paragraph, and do not have more than one paragraph for a main point unless the paragraph runs to more than 150 words; then you may divide it into two paragraphs.

A **topic sentence** expresses a main point clearly and prepares the way for development of that main point. Here are topic sentences for the main points given on page 332.

> Much of our recreational equipment has deteriorated because it is not serviced regularly. For example, . . .
>
> As the city fathers don't themselves seem to care about our facilities, a few vandals cause much destruction. Just the other night . . .
>
> All mechanical equipment eventually wears out, but our city will not spend money to replace worn-out recreational equipment. The swimming pool filters, for example, . . .
>
> Finally, our city has grown greatly in the past decade, but no new recreational facilities have been added. We badly need . . .

Getting main points expressed clearly in topic sentences is very important, but equally important is development of these topic sentences into full paragraphs. You should understand that each main point is a generalization and that details are needed to develop it. The beginnings of sentences after the example topic sentences above show how development of the paragraphs could begin.

Maintain coherence in each paragraph When writing is **coherent**, it is unified, consistent, and intelligible. Coherence (the word literally means "a sticking together") is produced by proper **transition** between sentences. One of the three chief ways to achieve transition is to use transitional words and phrases. Example:

> Most human beings are mostly honest most of the time, and most of us would claim to be honest all of the time. *But* the prevalence of such habits as shoplifting and cheating on income tax returns shows a great deal of frailty in people.

The *but* provides transition and thus coherence; omit it and see how the sentences jar against each other. Other transitional words and phrases are *for example, in addition, also, and, finally, next, second, therefore, however,* and so on.

The second main method of achieving transition is to repeat in one sentence a key word from the previous sentence. Example:

> The horse-drawn traffic in the cities of the 1890s caused as much pollution as cars today. *Horses* produce great quantities of dung, which in the cities bred disease-carrying insects and polluted both the air (in dry weather) and the street surface.

The repetition of the word *horses* provides effective transition. Rewrite the sentence without the word *horses,* and coherence will diminish markedly.

And the third chief method of achieving transition is to use a pronoun in one sentence to refer to a noun (or whole idea) in the preceding sentence. Example:

> Marihuana is gradually being accepted by law officers and elected officials. *Its* harmless effects are being recognized by more and more scientists.

The use of *its* to refer to *marihuana* provides the needed transition and thus produces coherence. You should try to *think* about how each of your sentences is related to the previous one.

Let your opening sentence lead directly into your topic   Do not try to be cute or folksy or startling or teasing in your introduction. Instead, be direct and brief. Here is an example:

TOPIC: A teen-ager's duties to his or her parents
OPENING: Everyone naturally accepts the fact that parents have obliga-
        tions to their children, but it is also true that teen-agers owe
        many duties to their parents. One of these duties is to prepare
        through education to be self-supporting.

The first sentence introduces the whole topic effectively, and the second is the topic sentence (main point) of the first paragraph. Note that a one-sentence introduction should not be a separate paragraph by itself but should be a part of the first paragraph.

Following is a revised student expository essay that you can use as a model. Study it as well as the techniques explained above to prepare yourself to write your own expository essay.

THE DECLINE OF INDIVIDUALISM IN AMERICA

Thesis sentence: There has been a decline of individualism in America since the nineteenth century because of four distinct <u>causes</u>.

The thesis statement and scratch outline are for the writer's use. They need not be handed in.

Scratch outline of main points

1. The frontier has disappeared
2. Mass production has replaced self-sufficiency
3. Our political structure has become more centralized
4. Public and private education has become more uniform

We hear much today about the dangers of conformity and the need for individualism, and it is true, I think, that since the nineteenth century there has been a sharp decline of individualism in America. One clear cause of this decline is that the frontier has disappeared. When the frontier was still in existence, men were taken at face value and because of this felt their individual worth. Also the frontier bred the spirit of individual initiative. Men felt independent, were independent, and scorned conformity because of this independence. With frontier spirit men did not feel the need to keep up with the Joneses and to be like their neighbors. Finally, there was more space available during frontier years and the being spread out contributed to individualism. The crowding in modern cities leads to conformity.

Note that the introduction is only one sentence, but leads into the topic directly and simply.

Each paragraph opens with a topic sentence (second in the first paragraph), and each topic sentence comes from one of the main points of the scratch outline.

Each paragraph is unified, for it deals only with its own main point.

Increasing technology with its mass production and division of labor has also diminished individualism. When men were more self-sufficient, they were more individualistic. In earlier times a man frequently did the whole work, instead of just a

Each main point is developed in a full paragraph. The generality of the topic sentence is illustrated. Details are given. No

part, of whatever he was doing.
There was a time, for example, when
a housewife spun thread, made cloth,
and sewed clothes. Now these tasks
are done by machines and a worker
does only a tiny part. He hardly
feels that he contributes to the
whole and so does not feel his worth
or independence. In addition, mass
production makes all products of a
kind nearly alike, and this likeness
leads to conformity among men. I'm
afraid we must blame the machine for
much of our decline in individualism.

The growth of centralized
government, too, contributes to
conformity. Both on a state and
national level there has in the last
century been a tremendous drive
toward centralization. And as the
government more and more enters our
lives, we are more and more
conformist. Huge numbers of people
now work for the government, the
military, and education, and they
tend to have to think alike and
behave alike. Also government has
so intruded on business that the
same situation exists there. The
organization man is a familiar figure.

Finally, the increased uniformity
of the educational process has caused
a marked decline in individualism.
Curriculum planning has become more
and more centralized. For example,
in my state all grammar school texts
are chosen by the State Board of
Education. So all children are
subjected to the same education.
Furthermore, there are so many
supervisors now that teachers are not
allowed to pursue their own way, and
thus children are further subjected
to conformity. The same trend is very
strong in high schools and even
touches colleges. In the process
private and public schools have

paragraph fragments are
left.

There is a smooth flow
from sentence to
sentence.

Transitional words are
used: *also, for example,
furthermor finally,* and
so on. Also n.any key
words are repeated for
transition.

The conclusion is brief
and simply sounds a note
of finality.

become more and more alike and thus
individualism declines. Perhaps
there will be a reversal in the future,
but now we seem to have much conformity.

ASSIGNMENT Study the above instructions and the model theme. You may also wish to read the essays in the reading selections that are primarily expository essays: "Sharing the Wealth" by S. I. Hayakawa (page 243), "In Defense of Sin" by Phyllis McGinley (page 249), and "The Second Wave of Feminism" by Edward D. Eddy, Jr. (page 255), or "A Last Word from the First Americans" by Vine Deloria, Jr. (page 265). Then write an expository essay of your own. Some topics are mentioned above. Here are some others:

Is television chiefly an instrument of education or escape?

What are the virtues or defects of one imported car you are familiar with?

What special markets and advertising techniques have been developed for the teen-ager consumer?

Explain the care and nurture of a commercially valuable plant, fish, or animal.

What characteristics of Americans make us disliked in some foreign countries?

Discuss discrimination against minority groups other than blacks.

What improvements could be made in American democracy?

What are the characteristics of an ideal children's story?

Discuss reasons why it is or is not desirable for women to be equal to men in the business and political world.

How to avoid a divorce.

Some justifiable uses of lying.

Attack or defend the emphasis on athletics at the college level.

Discuss the values and attitudes expressed in one comic strip, such as "Doonesbury."

A TIP ON USAGE *Avoid* awful *and* awfully *as intensifiers. Instead, use* quite, especially, *or* very.

POOR STYLE: We were **awful** glad to receive extra help in algebra.

GOOD STYLE: The prisoners were **especially** appreciative of the warden's concern for their welfare.

Writing Assignment

6 PROCESS

A **process theme** is one that explains how to do something. It is a kind of expository writing, of course, for it is chiefly factual, being a kind of direction-giving. It is an important type of writing for you to study, for college students are often given test questions or are asked to write reports that call for processes to be explained. For example, in an astronomy course students might be asked to explain how or why eclipses occur. Or in a course in auto mechanics students might be required to write an explanation of how a carburetor works.

Because in a process theme you will usually be writing about something you know well, you might think the assignment easy. But when something is especially clear to writers, they often do not make it clear to the readers, for they either skip steps or assume the readers understand something that they do not understand. Clarity and fullness of explanation are especially important in process themes. Study the following techniques, which will help you write a clear process theme.

Organize your process theme by units of steps   You will be explaining a sequence of steps (or actions), and for good organization and paragraphing you should try to group the steps into units that contain very closely related steps. Each of the units will then form one paragraph. Just as you jot down units of impression to guide you in organizing and paragraphing a theme of description, so you should jot down three to five units of steps to guide you in writing a process theme. For example, your topic might be "How to overhaul a car's engine." Your units of steps might be these:

1. Steps of disassembling the engine
2. Steps of renewing the cylinder sleeves
3. Steps of repairing damaged valves
4. Steps of reassembling the engine

Now you have a framework for your theme, because you have grouped all the steps into four units, each of which will be developed into one paragraph.

Or, for another example, your topic might be "How to bake a cherry pie." Your units of steps might be these:

1. Steps of assembling all needed ingredients, according to the recipe
2. Steps of preparing the filling for the pie
3. Steps of making the crust for the pie
4. Steps of combining filling and crust and baking the pie

Now you have four paragraphs planned. If you just start writing a process theme without trying to isolate a few units of steps, your organization is likely to be poor, and you are likely to leave out steps.

Opening and closing sentences and topic sentences in a process theme should be similar to those discussed in Writing Assignment Five, the expository essay.

Pay careful attention to transitions so that the process will seem smooth Proper organization is not enough. There must be transitional links between the parts. A process theme normally calls for time words, such as *next, then*, and *finally*. It may also call for place words, such as *on the bottom, across the joint*, and *nearby*. It will usually have some result words, such as *consequently, as a result*, and *hence*. And it may even have contrast words, such as *but, however*, and *on the contrary*. Transition for coherence is especially important in process writing.

Give complete details Be full and clear in your explanations. Do not skip steps. Do not assume that your readers know something that they might not know. Be specific; illustrate fully.

If there is a particular or interesting reason for a certain step, mention the reason This will add not only clarity but also interest. You may even, if it seems appropriate, include negative directions—what to be sure not to do.

Analogies may be used for clarification An analogy, you will remember, is a comparison. If you think a particular step may not be very clear to the readers, compare it with something they do understand. The phrase *is like* can be useful in process writing.

Explain or define any technical terms used For example, do not casually mention the pottlecurler without telling what it is.

Normally it is best to avoid the passive voice in process writing Instead of saying "the griffus lever is then raised," say "the operator then raises the griffus lever." Or you can use the pronouns *I* or *you*.

Try to make the subject matter interesting You may use a personal tone. Though this expository writing is factual, you may tell how *you* perform the process, and you may use anecdotes about your personal experiences with the process. In general, remember the lessons you have learned about writing description and narration.

Following is a revised student process theme that you can use as a model. A study of its techniques should greatly improve your ability to write explanations of all sorts.

HOW TO BREAK A WILD MUSTANG

Though the old days of the cowboy are gone, in parts of Arizona wild mustangs are still captured and occasionally broken for use on a ranch. I know from personal experience that breaking a wild horse is one of the toughest jobs a tough rancher can undertake. First, of course, the wild animal must be captured and corralled. The broncobuster then makes his first approach to the mustang, being very careful not to let the animal lash him with either hind or front legs. Mustangs don't charge like grizzly bears but they are very dangerous fighters. The broncobuster will be carrying a whip and on this first day will be content to inflict some pain on the mustang and in general to get acquainted with him.

After a brief and direct introduction, the first unit of steps is established: the details of making the first approach to the horse.

On the second day the broncobuster will try to fit the wild horse with bridle and saddle. First he must subdue the animal. He does this by choking it with a lariat and, after much effort and danger, hobbling and cross-hobbling it. The bridle is composed of the headstall, which is a leather harness for the head, and the bit, which is steel and is put in the mustang's mouth. The reins control the bit. It is the bit that enrages the animal most, for it hurts

Transitional and time words—such as *then* and *on the second day*— provide coherence.

The second unit of steps—fitting the horse with bridle and saddle— is established.

Technical terms are explained.

The use of many details makes the process easy to understand.

him and seems completely unnatural.
But mustangs are broken by the use
of pain, and the broncobuster often
uses the bit savagely, like an ancient
gladiator twisting a sword in a
wound to increase the pain. The
saddle, with a blanket underneath,
is held on by a tightened cinch.
After the bridle and saddle are on,
the hobbles are removed and the
mustang is given a short time to get
used to the new equipment.

An analogy is used.

Next the broncobuster starts his
attempts to ride the horse and to
"gentle" him. The horse bucks
tremendously, and the broncobuster
will be thrown off several times.
This procedure looks quite dangerous,
but the broncobuster is seldom hurt.
The bronco riding that one sees at
rodeos is not very similar to that of
the broncobuster, who is deadly
serious. Few of the professional
rodeo riders would make good
broncobusters--and few would ever
even undertake the task of
breaking a wild horse. But the
broncobuster persists and leaves the
mustang, after the second day,
rather dazed and frightened.

Good transition is used.

The third unit of steps is
an account of the details
of the first riding of the
horse.

The writer avoids the
passive voice and uses
the active voice.

Then in the following days the
broncobuster literally beats the
mustang into submission. He twists
one of the animal's ears as he starts
to mount; the pain distracts the
horse momentarily. And the
broncobuster uses a quirt (or whip)
on the mustang every time it bucks.
The animal must learn that any
disobedience brings instant
retribution. This all sounds harsh
and brutal, but it is the way
mustangs are broken.

The fourth unit of steps
consists of the details of
the actual breaking of
the horse.

The subject matter is
made interesting.

After not too many days the
mustang is completely broken and
almost wholly submissive to man.
He quickly forgets all his wild

The fifth unit of steps
explains what happens
after the horse is broken.

past and begins patiently to play a
domesticated role in ranch life. He
usually gets some reward in return
for the freedom which has been
taken from him. He gets plenty of
good food and is sheltered from bad
weather. Human beings often pet him,
and he seems to enjoy that. There are
at this very time formerly wild
mustangs that are safely ridden on
dude ranches by incredibly ignorant
tenderfeet. The mustang accepts this
almost graciously. The claim that a
tamed animal never forgets his wild
freedom just isn't so.

The theme has good
paragraphing and good
transitions, as in the
repetition of the pronoun
he.

The closing sentence
sounds a note of finality.

ASSIGNMENT Study the techniques above and the model theme. Read
or review the reading selection "How to Read a Book" by Mortimer
J. Adler and Charles Van Doren (page 209), which is a process essay.
Then write a process theme of your own. You can tell how to rebuild
a car motor, how to clean a swimming pool, how to study for an
exam, how to study when you are in love, how to cheat your way
through life, how to perform some factory operation, how to entertain
strange guests, how to make a dress, how to goldbrick in the army,
or how to do any of dozens of operations that you know.

7 EXTENDED DEFINITION

All college students are constantly asked to define terms relating to their studies. Usually, such definitions consist of just one sentence. The pattern for such a one-sentence definition is to put the term to be defined into a class of objects to which it belongs and then to give the characteristics that distinguish it from all others of its class. For example: "Parallelism of structure [term] is a principle of outlining [class] that calls for all headings on any one level and division to be in the same grammatical structure [distinguishing characteristics]." Such a definition just means setting the limits to a term. In fact, that's what the word *definition* means in its original Latin.

Students must sometimes also write **extended definitions.** These are simply definitions that go into some detail about the special characteristics of the term defined. This process of defining is really the same as in a simple definition. Use the following techniques as a guide in writing an extended definition of your own.

Put the term to be defined into its class   Here are some examples: "An axe is a cutting tool that . . ." "Fascism is a kind of government that . . ." "A differential is a kind of gear that . . ." "A poet is a writer who . . ." Identifying the general class to which the term belongs is preparation for giving its distinguishing characteristics.

Identify the special characteristics of your term   This is, of course, the heart of the definition. The length of your definition will depend on how much into detail you go in explaining the distinguishing characteristics of your term. You will want to separate it clearly from similar things with which it might be confused. This calls for giving many details.

Give a brief, limited definition of any special term you use   If, for example, in defining automation you should use the word *cybernetics*, you should certainly define it for your reader in an ordinary one-sentence definition. In this connection, you can also give examples to illustrate special terms or concepts used. You can also give the etymology (word derivation) of a special term.

Comparison and contrast are often useful in an extended definition You can define by showing an object's likeness to or difference from something else. For example: "An axe is somewhat like an adz in that . . ." "Fascism differs from communism in that . . ." "A tragicomedy is not unlike a melodrama because it . . ." Such comparisons and contrasts do a great deal to clarify. And remember that it often helps to mention what a thing is *not* as well as what it is.

You may include a personal note in extended definition Although this kind of writing is highly factual, there is room for writers to mention their own personal experiences with the term in question. For example, if you are defining cubism in art you may certainly mention your own successes or failures in trying such painting. It is not often that the personal pronoun *I* is out of place in writing.

Avoid circular definition Do not define a word in terms of itself. The dictionary habit of defining "opsonification" as "the act of opsonifying" is not useful in college writing. Do not for example, say "parallelism of structure in outlining means that all the headings should be parallel in the way they are constructed." This doesn't tell anybody anything.

Do not use *is when* and *where* sentences This is a very poor kind of sentence to use anytime and is especially weakening to definition. For example, do not say, "Communism is when the central government owns all the means of production."

Organize your theme on the basis of units of characteristics Just as description is organized on the basis of units of impression and the process theme on the basis of units of steps, extended definition is best organized on the basis of units of characteristics (of the term defined). For example, if you were defining the term *duplicate bridge*, you might jot down these units of characteristics.

1. How the same bridge hand is played by many couples
2. How the movements from table to table are arranged
3. How the playing of the hands is different from the playing of bridge hands in party bridge
4. How the hands are scored

Then you would develop one paragraph for each of these units of characteristics.

Following is a revised student extended definition for you to use as a model. Note how it adheres to the instructions above.

THE COMMUNITY JUNIOR COLLEGE

A public community junior college is a kind of institution of higher learning that offers the first two years of college only, in contrast to the four or more years offered by senior colleges and universities. The student body of the community college is mostly local, there often being no dormitories at all at the college. A few such colleges do import athletes, but for the most part they are local institutions for local residents. Because of the community college, many tens of thousands of students in this country are able to attend college when otherwise such attendance would be out of the question for them.

The community college is governed by a local board of trustees who are elected for usually four-year terms. This local control keeps the college in tune with the needs of the community. The financing of the college is mostly by local taxes, which the board of trustees expends cautiously. In some areas, the state government also contributes to the financing, but almost always leaves the control in board hands. Nearly all community colleges offer free tuition, the only cost to the student being a small student-body fee and books. Thus the school is really a community project and truly represents free public higher education.

Admissions standards are generally very liberal at the community college.

The term to be defined is placed in its class and is contrasted with others of its class.

Its special distinguishing characteristics are enumerated in several paragraphs.

The paragraphs are well unified. The writer found small groups of characteristics that fitted together into paragraphs.

There is an implied contrast with senior

The educational philosophy is that all students must be given a chance or even a second chance to prove themselves. Thus most such colleges will admit any high school graduate or any person over twenty-one. This means that the student body is very diverse, ranging from highly superior students to those on a below-high school level. Some students are flunked out, but at least they have had their chance.

The broad-spectrum student body of a community college calls for a widely varied program of studies. Most such schools offer both an academic liberal arts program and a vocational-technical program. Many have a dual-tracking system, called transfer and terminal. A transfer course is a regular university-level course, the credit for which can be transferred to any accredited senior college. A terminal course is one that offers credit for junior college graduation only; the credit for it cannot be transferred. Either track allows junior college graduation with an A.A. (Associate in Arts) degree. In addition to the two tracks, many community colleges also offer remedial work for students who are not yet prepared but want to become prepared for transfer to a senior institution.

Even though it is a commuter school, the community college offers a full line of extracurricular activities. At almost any school one will find the full range of competitive sports, student government, political clubs, social organizations, and special service clubs. A student need not miss out on any college experience.

One area in which the community college is often superior to the senior college is guidance. Most

colleges. The writer should have been more explicit in these contrasts.

Special terms (*transfer* and *terminal*) are given limited definitions. There are no circular definitions.

schools keep a full staff of
counselors who not only help students
plan a two-year college program but
also give them vocational guidance
and often personal guidance.   This
service pays off, for statistics show
that community college transfers to
senior colleges do as well as or
better than the native students of
the senior colleges.   The community   Most of the characteristics
college philosophy of broad services   of good expository writing
to the local students has proved   are in evidence.
itself over many years of operation.
The community college is indeed a
valuable institution of higher   The conclusion gives the
learning.   theme a note of finality.

ASSIGNMENT   Review the instructions above and the model theme.
   You might wish to look at Carl Sagan's complex extended definition
   of *abstraction* in "Can Animals 'Speak'?" (page 271). Then write an
   extended definition of your own. You might define rock music, jazz,
   automation, one of the seven sacraments, a type of literature (such
   as novel, epic, or sonnet), satire, puppy love, Unitarianism (or any
   religious sect), impressionism (or any artistic mode), a ballet, a kind
   of sport, a formation in football, the internal-combustion engine, any
   college major, or any of countless terms with which you are familiar.

Writing Assignment

8 PERSUASION

Persuasive writing attempts to convince the reader of the validity of a cause or proposition. Its purpose is to make ideas, suggestions, and advice acceptable. The world is full of persuasive writing. Think of advertising alone, not to mention political and religious articles. Needless to say, much persuasive writing is fraudulent, for the writer uses underhanded techniques to try to convince the gullible of the truth of a proposition for which there is really no good evidence. That, of course, is not the kind of persuasive writing you are to practice.

In writing a persuasive theme, do not let sheer persuasive techniques replace accuracy and objectivity of detail. You want to try to convince on the basis of sound evidence and judgment. You will, of course, pay attention to the preferences and susceptibilities of your readers, but you should not wheedle, bully, or threaten and should not appeal to sheer prejudices. Assume that your readers are intelligent and not gullible; do not treat them as inferior. Make your persuasion high level. The following instructions will give you guidance in writing a persuasive theme.

Organize your theme on the basis of main points Follow exactly the method of organization discussed at length in Writing Assignment Five on the expository essay. Try to derive three to five main points from a plural noun expressed or implied in your fully stated topic.

Open with a clear and definite statement of what you intend to prove Do not be devious or coy. Do not think that because your proposition might be unpopular, you must trick your reader into paying attention. Assume that you have an honorable cause and that you intend to approach it honorably.

Give a tone of certainty to your argument without being overbearing or conceited A sensible, moderate tone of surety and sincerity goes a long way to persuade. Do not harangue or insist that anyone who opposes you is stupid, but give the impression of being sincerely convinced yourself. Many a girl has married a man just because he seemed sincere and earnest in his profession of love.

Seek clarity, moderation, and objectivity   Do not obscure or obfuscate the proposition you are trying to prove. Do not deal in vague generalities; be specific. Do not just depend on your own subjective inclination; be as objective as you can. Try to convince through clarity and soundness, not murky bombast.

Rest your argument on sound evidence   This piece of advice has already been broached, but it is worth repeating. Intelligent, logical people are more likely to be convinced by sound evidence than by any other means. Do not depend on merely persuasive language; use sound reasoning.

Cite authorities if you wish   But be sure they are sound, reputable, and disinterested. To be disinterested means not to be partisan. Try to cite authorities who know what they are talking about and do not have an axe to grind. You might, for example, cite Hitler as an authority on how to invade an unprepared country, but you would not cite him as an authority on racial matters.

Play down the normal tendency to exaggerate   You do, of course, want to display your material to its best advantage, but you should not deliberately try to deceive. Do not, for example, maintain that all college students think beer should be sold on campus, for of course, all do not. Sheer exaggeration will not convince the intelligent.

Do not slant material too much   Slanting means selecting only the evidence favorable to your cause and suppressing equally valuable evidence. It is using willful imbalance to force conclusions not justified by the evidence. Some letters to the editor, for example, talk about modern schools being "palaces" when actually there are many features of nearly all schools that are not luxurious at all.

Do not overuse loaded words   These are words that are charged with meanings that will prejudice readers. For example, think of the reaction of many people to such words as these: *left-wing pressure group, reactionary, notoriously biased, perverted principles, sterling and wholesome character,* and *dedicated and loyal.* Such words are usually intended to sway beyond evidence. In your writing, do not behave like propagandists who are intent on making their case at any price.

Do not use illogical arguments Logic is the science of reasoning, that is, of drawing conclusions from evidence or opinions one holds. **A logic fallacy** is a misuse of logic—that is, coming to a conclusion without proper evidence or acceptable opinions. Do not assume that one or two instances— of, say, a student flunking out of college after being given a second chance—prove a generalization that will apply to all such cases. Do not use polarized thinking ("either-or" thinking)—such as saying that a person is either a Christian or a crook. Do not judge causation falsely—such as assuming you got a low grade because your teacher did not like you. Do not use a false analogy—such as saying that a country is like a warship and that, therefore, a country must have a captain with absolute authority to do anything. Do not ignore the issue—such as claiming that farm laborers should not have a union because they are ignorant. Do not make an unsound appeal to authority—such as assuming that if a popular entertainment figure is a Republican, then the Republicans must have the best party. And do not jump steps in logic or base a conclusion on a generalization that has nothing to do with the conclusion—such as saying that because people work at different rates of speed, labor unions should be abolished.

Following is a revised student persuasive theme for you to use as a model. Note how it mostly observes the above instructions.

LET'S ABOLISH CAPITAL PUNISHMENT

Capital punishment is much in the news these days, and the legislatures of many states and nations are debating its continued existence. I feel that it should be completely abolished in all states and nations for all offenses. Although it is true that many crimes are unspeakably horrible and might seem to call for the death penalty, sober reflection will, I believe, show that, after all, taking a man's life is not proper punishment for any crime.

Note that the introduction clearly states the writer's cause. It is a direct, simple opening, not startling or bizarre or highly rhetorical.

The main justification advanced for capital punishment is that it deters others from committing the same crimes. But many compilations of statistics show that capital punishment is not a deterrent.

Though the paper is mostly opinion, it does use some sound evidence. In a longer paper the evidence would be documented.

Every state that has abolished capital punishment has actually had a decline rather than an increase in capital crimes. And in England, where there has been a long decline in the use of capital punishment, there has been a similar decline in capital crimes. In the early 1700s in England there were actually 176 crimes which called for hanging and many criminals were hanged. But there was no decline in the crimes. It's a well-known joke that when pickpockets were publicly hanged in England, other pickpockets plied their trade among the crowds watching the hanging. A deterrent indeed! Surely life imprisonment would be at least an equal deterrent.

> The tone is reasonable and moderate. There is no impassioned plea, and no extravagant claims are made. There is objectivity and moderation throughout.

On the other hand, capital punishment is an absolute hindrance to rehabilitation and to the correction of a mistake. All modern criminologists recognize that the purpose of punishment is to bring about rehabilitation, but how can you rehabilitate a dead man? Furthermore, it is being more and more realized that most criminals are sick. It certainly seems more reasonable to treat them than to kill them. Additionally, it happens occasionally that an innocent man is put to death. What restitution can there be for such a horrible mistake? A compassionate society should not legalize murder, but should carry on programs of rehabilitation.

> The writer does not insult readers that might disagree with him. He makes a strong case, but he does not browbeat the opposition.

> He does not exaggerate or try to deceive or use bombastic language. He leaves the impression that he is a person who will sanely discuss issues.

A powerful argument recently advanced by people of my persuasion is that capital punishment is probably unconstitutional, anyway. The Constitution forbids cruel, unusual, and inhumane punishment. Certainly sentencing someone to die is inhumane and cruel. Seldom does the condemned know his execution date

> He does not use any false logic or completely fallacious argument.

> He has main points stated in topic sentences in his paragraphs.

until it is close at hand. Thus he
is in agony about his fate. If he
is to be punished (instead of
rehabilitated), he should be
imprisoned only. He should not be
condemned to die at a specified date.
I feel that eventually the Supreme
Court will abolish capital punishment
because of its cruel nature.

    I think our advanced society
should face the fact that capital
punishment is a relic of a barbarous
age. There has been a continuous
decline in its use for centuries.
Surely the time has come to abolish   His conclusion is quite
it altogether. It may be a one   appropriate for a short
hundred percent deterrent as far as   paper.
the victim is concerned, but it does
no other good, and it does degrade
our society.

ASSIGNMENT   After studying the instructions above and the model
theme, you might wish to read or review one of the essays in the
reading selections that are primarily persuasive: "Civil Disobedience" by Henry David Thoreau (page 279), "Abolishing Grades" by
Dr. William Glasser (page 287), "Self-Reliance" by Ralph Waldo
Emerson (page 295), or "The Driver Education Myth" by Edward A.
Tenney (page 301). Then write a persuasion paper of your own. You
might make a plea for establishing a minimum yearly income for all;
for paying students while they attend school; for electing or defeating
a certain public official or ballot measure (pick a person or issue of
current interest that you feel strongly about); for or against censor-
ship of television, movies, or publications; for the establishment of a
state religion; for or against some current social or political trend; or
for any other cause or issue that you feel strongly about.

A MINI-EXERCISE   Taking word order, word form, and hyphenization
into consideration, rewrite the following sentence so that it is correct.

All compact size sedans are not cramped.

---

9 LETTERS OF APPLICATION AND RÉSUMÉS

A real **letter of application** may be one of the most important pieces of writing you will ever do. It may get you started on a career. As such letters give prospective employers their first impression of you, your letters should be written with great care. If their quality is poor, you may not even get an interview, if their quality is high, you may go into an interview with an already-established favorable impression. You should be especially sure that you have misspelled no words and have made no errors in usage. You should type your letters if possible. Observe the following instructions.

Do not try to butter up your prospective employer   Do not gush. Do not try excessive flattery. Do not boast, but be firm in giving the impression that you will make a good employee.

Do not write too much   Keep the letter fairly short, although you must give full details. Avoid wordiness.

Open your letter by saying what you are applying for and how you heard about the vacancy   Do not hesitate to start the letter with *I* if it seems appropriate.

Give your vital statistics   An employer will want to know your age, size, marital status, state of health, and anything unusual about your person. You may enclose a photo of yourself if you want to.

Give your educational background   Give special emphasis to any educational distinctions you have achieved, such as belonging to an honor group. You may also mention extracurricular activities or achievements.

Give your work experience You should mention all work experience even though it might not pertain to the job in question. Try to relate your previous successes to the success you think you will have on this job.

State your willingness to come for an interview and give references (Note: If you intend to apply to many employers for the same kind of job, much of the above information can be listed on a **personal data sheet**. Then the letter itself will be very brief. But if you are applying to just one organization, you should put all the information into the letter itself.)

    Following is a model letter of application that you may use as a guide.

MODEL LETTER OF APPLICATION

       464 Palindrome Street
       Level, California 91303
       June 6, 1980

Mr. S. Behr
Director of Personnel
State Park System
Agoura, California 91301

Dear Mr. Behr:

    I am replying to your ad in the Agoura Oak offering employment for this summer at Malibu State Park. I wish to apply for the position of trail leader.

Note the direct opening specifying the purpose of the letter.

    I am twenty years old, five feet ten inches tall, and weigh 175 pounds. My general health is excellent, although I wear contact lenses.

Vital statistics.

    I graduated tenth in my class at Level High School and have completed two years at Humboldt State College as a forestry major. I have maintained a 3.3 (B) average so far. I plan to complete my B.S. in land management. I belong to the Ecology

Educational background.

Club and have been moderately active
in student government.

For the past two summers I have
worked as a camp counselor at Camp
Roncom, where I served as counselor
and director for a group of ten boys
aged from eleven to fourteen.

Work experience.

My studies have familiarized me
with the creatures and conditions
at Malibu Park. In addition, I have
taken five walking trips through the
park this year and am familiar with
all of the trails. I believe that
I have many qualifications for the
job you offer. I can come in for an
interview at any time or reached by
phone any evening after five at
(312) 123-4321. For references you
may contact

Firm statement as to
ability.

Samuel Beard
Regional Director
Explorer Scouts, Agoura, CA.

References.

Professor Flora Littlewood
Forestry Department
Humboldt State College

Mr. Alfredo Ramirez
Head Counselor
Camp Roncom, California

Sincerely yours,

Christopher Carson

Christopher Carson

Note that the whole
letter is direct, unwordy,
and to the point.

The Résumé

Many employers request that a **résumé** be sent along with your letter
of application. A résumé is simply a summary of your personal, educational, and employment history. The résumé offers employers a quick and
convenient listing of your qualifications; they do not have to hunt through

a letter for them. The standard résumé—there is a sample form on page 359—contains the following information:

Personal data Include your legal name, address (mailing address if it is different from your home address), telephone number, age, social security number, marital status, and general health. It is no longer necessary to include race, religion, or sex.

Education Usually start with high school. Include any college work, degrees earned, postgraduate work, and special schools or classes you might have attended.

Extracurricular activities Many employers have found that employees who participated in student government, sports, clubs, and other out-of-class activities tend to be more stable and effective than workers who never were involved in such activities.

Work Experience For the first job, it is wise to include part-time jobs that you have held as well as summer work. After you have worked at your profession for a time, most of these part-time jobs are not really important. Your employer wants to know what you have done that will make you effective at the job you are seeking.

Professional activities These include anything you might have published, any special organizations you belong to, any honors you might have won.

References Usually three or four references are requested. These always include former employers or supervisors. A college instructor is always a good reference. Rarely is it wise to use relatives (like your mother) or friends unless the employer asks for them. *Make certain that you have asked the person if it is acceptable for you to use him (or her) as a reference.* Do not surprise anyone.

Additional information If you have any special skills that would make you more valuable to the employer, include them. Such abilities might include knowledge of a foreign language, any special mechanical skills, familiarity with a foreign country from wide traveling, or any other item that would not properly fit under *education* or *work experience*.

The Application

Many employers and all large companies require job seekers to fill out an **employment application**. Usually, they ask for much information to be written in tiny spaces. If you must fill out the application in their office, *take your résumé with you.* Never leave blanks; doing so creates a poor first impression. If possible, a wiser course is to take the application home with you and fill it out completely and neatly. Type it if there is room in the spaces.

Writing Assignments

Select a job that you would like to have. Assume that you have the qualifications necessary, and write a letter of application after studying the directions and the model letter above.

Find a real summer or part-time job from the newspaper or the employment office, if your school has one. Write a letter of application.

Start right now to develop your résumé. You may use the sample form on page 359 as a pattern. It would be a good idea to begin now and to keep your résumé up-to-date by revising it each year. Include even slight honors and jobs. They might be important later when you do not recall the exact details.

Practice filling out a job application by filling out the sample form provided. Remember to be complete, accurate, and honest.

RÉSUMÉ

Name

Home address   Social security number

Mailing Address

Telephone   Marital Status
Age   Dependents
Education   Health

Extracurricular activities (clubs, sports, organizations)

Work experience

Professional activities

References

APPLICATION FOR EMPLOYMENT

PERSONAL INFORMATION

DATE _____   SOCIAL SECURITY NUMBER _____

NAME _____   AGE _____
LAST   FIRST   MIDDLE

PRESENT ADDRESS _____
STREET   CITY   STATE   ZIP

PERMANENT ADDRESS _____
STREET   CITY   STATE   ZIP

PHONE NO _____   OWN HOME _____   RENT _____   BOARD _____

DATE OF BIRTH _____   HEIGHT _____   WEIGHT _____   COLOR OF HAIR _____   COLOR OF EYES _____

MARRIED _____   SINGLE _____   WIDOWED _____   DIVORCED _____   SEPARATED _____

NUMBER OF CHILDREN _____   DEPENDENTS OTHER THAN WIFE OR CHILDREN _____   CITIZEN OF U S A   YES ☐ NO ☐

IF RELATED TO ANYONE IN OUR EMPLOY, STATE NAME AND DEPARTMENT _____   REFERRED BY _____

EMPLOYMENT DESIRED

POSITION _____   DATE YOU CAN START _____   SALARY DESIRED _____

ARE YOU EMPLOYED NOW? _____   IF SO MAY WE INQUIRE OF YOUR PRESENT EMPLOYER _____

EVER APPLIED TO THIS COMPANY BEFORE? _____   WHERE _____   WHEN _____

EDUCATION	NAME AND LOCATION OF SCHOOL	YEARS ATTENDED	DATE GRADUATED	SUBJECTS STUDIED
HIGH SCHOOL				
COLLEGE				
TRADE, BUSINESS OR CORRESPONDENCE SCHOOL				

SUBJECTS OF SPECIAL STUDY OR RESEARCH WORK _____

WHAT FOREIGN LANGUAGES DO YOU SPEAK FLUENTLY? _____   READ _____   WRITE _____

SUBJECTS OF SPECIAL STUDY OR RESEARCH WORK _____

WHAT FOREIGN LANGUAGES DO YOU SPEAK FLUENTLY? _____   READ _____   WRITE _____

U S MILITARY OR NAVAL SERVICE _____

ACTIVITIES OTHER THAN RELIGIOUS (CIVIC ATHLETIC FRATERNAL ETC) _____
EXCLUDE ORGANIZATIONS THE NAME OR CHARACTER OF WHICH INDICATES THE RACE CREED COLOR OR NATIONAL ORIGIN OF ITS MEMBERS

(CONTINUED ON OTHER SIDE)

APPLICATION F. E EMPLOYMENT

FORMER EMPLOYERS (LIST BELOW LAST FOUR EMPLOYERS, STARTING WITH LAST ONE FIRST)

DATE MONTH AND YEAR	NAME AND ADDRESS OF EMPLOYER	SALARY	POSITION	REASON FOR LEAVING
FROM				
TO				
FROM				
TO				
FROM				
TO				
FROM				
TO				

PHYSICAL RECORD:
LIST ANY PHYSICAL DEFECTS

WERE YOU EVER INJURED?   GIVE DETAILS

HAVE YOU ANY DEFECTS IN HEARING?   IN VISION?   IN SPEECH?

IN CASE OF
EMERGENCY NOTIFY
NAME   ADDRESS   PHONE NO

REFERENCES: GIVE BELOW THE NAMES OF THREE PERSONS NOT RELATED TO YOU, WHOM YOU HAVE KNOWN AT LEAST ONE YEAR.

	NAME	ADDRESS	BUSINESS	YEARS ACQUAINTED
1				
2				
3				

I AUTHORIZE INVESTIGATION OF ALL STATEMENTS CONTAINED IN THIS APPLICATION. I UNDERSTAND THAT MISREPRESENTATION OR OMISSION OF FACTS CALLED FOR IS CAUSE FOR DISMISSAL. FURTHER, I UNDERSTAND AND AGREE THAT MY EMPLOYMENT IS FOR NO DEFINITE PERIOD AND MAY, REGARDLESS OF THE DATE OF PAYMENT OF MY WAGES AND SALARY, BE TERMINATED AT ANY TIME WITHOUT ANY PREVIOUS NOTICE.

DATE   SIGNATURE

DO NOT WRITE BELOW THIS LINE

INTERVIEWED BY   DATE

REMARKS:

NEATNESS		CHARACTER	
PERSONALITY		ABILITY	

HIRED   FOR DEPT.   POSITION   WILL REPORT   SALARY WAGES

APPROVED 1.   2.   3.
EMPLOYMENT MANAGER   DEPT HEAD   GENERAL MANAGER

APPENDIX

SPELLING
Our Irregular System

The ability to spell correctly is a valuable asset to writers because no other aspect of writing is so closely observed as spelling. And in the public mind, poor spelling is erroneously equated with poor education and low intelligence. For example, personnel officers of large companies generally think that if applicants cannot spell correctly, they cannot do anything else correctly either. Hence, countless applicants for jobs have not been hired because of misspelled words on their application forms or in their letters of application. And countless people, particularly secretaries, have been fired because of poor spelling. Thus you should be concerned with your spelling, because it might affect your getting or keeping a job.

English spelling, however, is so irregular that really good spellers are the exception rather than the rule. Irregularity in English spelling is mostly due to our using many different ways to spell one sound and to our using one letter to spell different sounds. For example, the long *e* sound is spelled in at least fourteen different ways (the silent *e* after a consonant is part of the spelling of the vowel sound preceding the consonant):

be	heat
athlete (silent *e*)	grease (silent *e*)
lien	feet
believe (silent *e*)	sleeve (silent *e*)
leister	people
receive (silent *e*)	machine (silent *e*)
alley	activity

Conversely the letter *e* by itself (not in combination with another vowel or consonant) may represent these five different sounds:

	English
be	silent
met	sergeant

And so it is with many other sounds and letters. The system is so irregular that it gives most students some trouble during their schooling. If we always used the same letter or combination of letters to spell the same sound, we would have what is called a **phonemic alphabet,** our spelling would be regular, and nearly everybody would spell correctly. But you can be sure there will be no such spelling reform in your lifetime.

We can overcome the irregularities in our spelling system in five ways: (1) to have a good memory; (2) to sound out syllables; (3) in conjunction with sounding out syllables, to use a distorted pronunciation for spelling purposes; (4) to use a number of spelling rules (pages 371 to 383); and (5) to use memory association.

Spelling by Syllables

You can eliminate many of your spelling problems by learning to sound out syllables carefully and individually. Such a practice is particularly useful in spelling long words. For example, instead of thinking of *appropriate* as just a long sequence of letters, think of it as four syllables, and spell each of them separately in sequence: *ap-pro-pri-ate*. Then the word will not seem so imposimg.

In spelling by syllables, one often finds it useful to use a **spelling pronunciation**—that is, a pronunciation suited to the spelling rather than the normal pronunciation. For example, consider the word *approximate*. Its normal pronunciation is something like this: *uh-prox-uh-mit*. Such a pronunciation does not tell you that the word has two *p*'s or that the third syllable is an *i* or that the last syllable ends in *ate*. But you can give the word a spelling pronunciation: *ap-prox-i-mate*. And after you get used to exaggerating the pronunciation in order to spell the word, you will spell it correctly from habit and will not have to think about it.

Here are a few words for you to practice on. Get the habit of sounding out syllables and, when necessary, of exaggerating the pronunciation of a word. Then use this habit with the long words listed with this and succeeding lessons.

ac-ci-dent-al-ly
ac-com-mo-date
ben-e-fit-ed
char-ac-ter-is-tic
com-pe-ti-tion

de-fi-nite-ly
dis-sat-is-fied
en-vi-ron-ment
fas-ci-na-ting
in-tel-li-gence

Sounding out syllables and exaggerating the pronunciation for spelling purposes will not help you with short words such as *dealt, led, lose,* and *course,* but it is an invaluable practice in learning long words.

Prefixes and Suffixes

In conjunction with spelling by syllables, it is valuable to understand that many English words are made up of roots plus prefixes and suffixes For example, most students can spell the word *usual*, but a surprisingly large percentage misspells the word *unusually*. Those who misspell the word fail to understand that it is built from a root, plus affixes (the word *affix* means both prefixes and suffixes). First you have *usual*; out of that you build *un-usual*; and out of that you build *un-usual-ly*. It is really a simple word to spell if you understand how it is built. And so with many other English words.

The following short list shows the way in which many English words are built out of roots and affixes:

press   re-press   re-press-ible   ir-re-press-ible
approve   dis-approve   dis-approv-ing   disapprov-ing-ly
necessary   un-necessary   un-necessari-ly
happy   un-happy   un-happi-ly   un-happi-ness
sufficient   in-sufficient   in-sufficient-ly
grace   grace-ful   un-grace-ful   un-grace-ful-ly
person   person-al   person-al-ly   im-person-al-ly
cease   ceas-ing   un-ceas-ing   un-ceas-ing-ly
advantage   advantage-ous   dis-advantage-ous
    dis-advantage-ous-ly
respect   dis-respect   dis-respect-ful   dis-respect-ful-ly

These examples illustrate the process. The more you become aware of the way words are built in English, the better you will spell. It is valuable not only to sound out the syllables but also to understand when you are adding affixes to root words.

Spelling by Memory Association

All of us use **associational clues** to aid our memories; that is, we associate something hard to remember with something easy to remember and use the association to remember the hard thing. Following is a list of common troublesome words and associational clues to help you remember them. You can also make up clues of your own to help you with other words that happen to give you trouble.

across—Christ died on *a cross* (avoid two *c*'s).
a lot—Think of buying a lot (avoid *alot*).
amateur—Think of *a mate u r*.
attendance—Think of *attend dance* and so use *ance*.

bargain—There is a *gain* in a bargain.
battalion—Think of a *battle* against *a lion* (two *t*'s and one *l*).
breakfast—It is literally to *break* a *fast*.
bulletin—Who put a *bullet* in the bulletin?
calendar—Think of calend*ar art* and so use *ar*.
courtesy—It is a habit with those who *court*.
definite—Give it the spelling pronunciation *de-fi-nite*.
dessert—It has two *s*'s, like strawberry shortcake.
disease—It literally means *dis ease*.
embarrass—It has two *r*'s and two *s*'s.
familiar—Think of a *fami* (whatever that is) *liar*.
forty—*Ninety* retains the *e*, but *forty* does not retain the *u*.
grammar—the *rammar* part is spelled the same both ways.
handkerchief—You use your *hand* to pull out your *kerchief*.
holiday—It comes from *holy* and thus has only one *l*.
ninety—*Forty* does not retain the *u*, but *ninety* retains the *e*.
occurrence—It has *rre* as in *current* evvent.
peculiar—Think of a *pecu* (whatever that is) *liar*.
principal—The principal of a school is a *pal* to you.
principle—It means *rule* and ends in *le* as *rule* does.
rhythm—Remember the *rh-th* sequence.
separate—It is hard to spell; therefore, there is *a rat* in it.
stationery—it means paper and ends in *er* like *paper*.
tragedy—There is a *rage* in a tragedy.

A TIP ON USAGE   *Irregardless* is not a standard word. Use *regardless*.

A TIP ON USAGE   Do not use the erroneous expression *these type of or these sort of*. Use either *this type of* or *these types of*. Examples:

RIGHT: This type of piston ring is long-wearing.
RIGHT: These sorts of books are all interesting.

Exercise for

BUILDING ENGLISH WORDS

DIRECTIONS *Build at least two words from each of the following roots by adding affixes. Tell what part of speech each word is (that is, what kind of word it is).*

1. dispense   _____   _____

2. beauty   _____   _____

3. complete   _____   _____

4. employ   _____   _____

5. frequent   _____   _____

6. manner   _____   _____

7. lone   _____   _____

8. regular   _____   _____

9. commend   _____   _____

10. knowledge   _____   _____

11. appoint   _____   _____

12. appear   _____   _____

13. agree   _____   _____

14. approve   _____   _____

15. natural   _____   _____

A MINI-EXERCISE In the following blanks write words that have the long *o* sound spelled differently. There are at least eleven ways we spell the sound, one using four letters (consonants following a vowel but not pronounced are a part of the spelling of the vowel). See how many ways you can think of to spell the long *o* sound.

_____   _____   _____

_____   _____   _____

_____   _____   _____

_____   _____   _____

The sound represented by *sh* in *shoe* is a single sound. In the following blanks write words that spell this sound in different ways. There are at least twelve ways, some with as many as three letters. See how many ways you can think of.

_____   _____   _____

_____   _____   _____

_____   _____   _____

_____   _____   _____

Also, you may want to discuss the number of ways the sounds *f*, *k*, long *a*, and long *i* are spelled.

The Doubling-of-the-Final-Consonant Rule

The Rule *When (1) adding a suffix beginning with a vowel to a word that is (2) accented on the last syllable and (3) ends in the one consonant preceded by one vowel, double the final consonant.*

This is the most complicated and probably the most important of the spelling rules. It is based on a very important phonetic principle in English spelling, the "long-vowel, short-vowel" principle. The principle is this: *In a vowel-consonant-vowel sequence, the first vowel, IF ACCENTED, is long; in a vowel-consonant-consonant or a vowel-consonant end of word sequence, the vowel is short. (Of course, there are exceptions.)* In the following examples, the vowels in the accented syllables in the first column of words are long, and the vowels in the second column are short:

rate	rat
interfere	refer
bite	bit
rote	rot
cured	occurred

Made-up words will also illustrate the long-vowel, short-vowel principle. For example, you instinctively know that the vowels in the first column following are long and those in the second column, short:

nate	nat
zike	zik
yove	yov

This principle accounts for the doubling-of-the-final-consonant rule.

The rule is complicated. You should master all parts and keep them in mind.

These conditions must be present:

1. You must be adding a suffix beginning with a vowel, such as *ing, ed, er, est*, and so forth.
2. The word must be of one syllable, or it must be accented on the last syllable, as are *reFER, comPEL,* and *ocCUR*.
3. And the word must end in one consonant preceded by one vowel, as in *admit, debar,* and *slap*. If the word ends in two consonants (such as *band*) or if the final consonant is preceded by two vowels (such as *stoop*), the rule does not apply (*equip* and *quit* are exceptions, because the *u* is really a *w*).

occur + ed = occurred	prefer + ed = preferred
refer + ing = referring	quit + ing = quitting
stop + ed = stopped	compel + ed = compelled
omit + ing = omitting	admit + ing = admitting
red + est = reddest	sin + er = sinner
brag + ing = bragging	occur + ence = occurrence

Note what the pronunciation of these words would be if the final consonants were not doubled. For example, if there were only one *r* in *occurred*, it would rhyme with *cured*. Or if there were only one *r* in *referring*, it would rhyme with *interfering*.

If the last syllable of a word is not accented, the consonant is NOT doubled when a suffix beginning with a vowel is added. Examples:

BANter + ing = bantering	proHIBit + ed = prohibited
HAPpen + ed = happened	aBANon + ed = abandoned

When a word ends in a silent *e*, the preceding consonant is never doubled. An entirely different rule governs words ending in a silent *e*. Note particularly the following words. Some people misspell these words by doubling the consonant. Note that in the base word there is no *final* consonant to double.

dine + ing = dining	shine + ing = shining
write + ing = writing	bite + ing = biting
interfere + ed = interfered	come + ing = coming

These are the words most frequently confused with the doubling-of-the-final-consonant rule. Note how their pronunciation would change (except for *coming*) if the consonant were doubled. For example, *dining* would be pronounced *dinning* instead of *dine-ing* (that is, with a short rather than a long *i*).

Exercise for

DOUBLING OF THE FINAL CONSONANT

DIRECTIONS *Build the following words as indicated. In some cases you will double the final consonant. But in some of the words the three conditions calling for doubling of the final consonant are not present; thus you should not double the consonant.*

1. occur + ed = _____

2. interfere + ed = _____

3. refer + ed = _____

4. honor + able =_____

5. omit + ing = _____

6. debar + ed = _____

7. hinder + ed = _____

8. begin + ing = _____

9. come + ing =_____

10. din + ing =_____

11. dine + ing = _____

12. bid + ing =_____

13. bide + ing = _____

14. benefit + ed = _____

15. equip + ing = _____

16. concur + ed = _____

17. note + ing = _____

18. rot + ing =_____

19. confer + ed = _____

20. sin + ful = _____

21. sin + er = _____

22. big + est = _____

23. big + ness = _____

24. drop + ed = _____

25. droop + ed =_____

26. red + en = _____

27. red + ness = _____

28. abandon + ed = _____

29. firm + er =_____

30. war + ing = _____

31. war + fare = _____

32. bite + ing = _____

33. bit + en = _____

34. fog + y = _____

35. submit + ing = _____   42. bat + ing = _____

36. differ + ing = _____   43. stop + ed = _____

37. transfer + ed = _____   44. stoop + ed = _____

38. suffer + ed = _____   45. unforget + able = _____

39. regret + able = _____   46. shine + ing = _____

40. offer + ed = _____   47. recur + ed = _____

41. hate + ing = _____   48. excel + ed = _____

49. confer + ence = _____(note shift in accent)

50. prefer + ence = _____ (note shift in accent)

A MINI-EXERCISE   Write two meaningful sentences, using the following pair of words correctly.

1. a. **robbed:** _____

_____

_____

_____

b. **robed:** _____

_____

_____

_____

Dropping and Retaining Silent E's

The First Rule *When adding a suffix beginning with a vowel to a word ending in a silent e, drop the silent e.*

The long-vowel principle is responsible for this rule too. Remember that in an accented syllable, a vowel-consonant-vowel sequence makes the first vowel long. Thus the silent e in such words as *dine* is doing the work of making the *i* long. But *any* vowel will do the work of the silent *e*, and so when an added suffix begins with a vowel—such as *ed, ence, ing, er, able,* and so on—the silent *e* is no longer needed and is dropped.

Here are a few examples of this simple rule being applied:

dine + ing = dining	mange + y = mangy
shine + ed = shined	like + able = likable
create + ive = creative	use + age = usage
imagine + ative = imaginative	condole + ence = condolence

The silent *e* is NOT dropped when a suffix beginning with a consonant is added:

like + ness = likeness	safe + ty = safety
fate + ful = fateful	hate + ful = hateful
complete + ly = completely	late + ly = lately

Note that if the *e* were dropped, such pronunciations as *lik-ness* and *fat-ful* would result.

However, there are five exceptions to this part of the rule. The *e* is dropped in the following words even though the suffixes begin with consonants:

whole + ly = wholly	argue + ment = argument
true + ly = truly	awe + ful − awful
judge + ment = judgment	

The Sec⟋nd Rule *When a word ends in a silent e preceded by a c or g, reta in the silent e when adding* ous, able, *or* ance.

W⟋en a *c* is pronounced as an *s* (as in *city*), it is known as a soft *c*; when i⟋ is pronounced as a *k* (as in *cable*), it is a hard *c*. Whenever a *c* is foll⟋wed by an *e, i,* or *y,* it is always soft; when it is followed by an *a, o,* or *⟋,* it is almost always hard. Thus when we add *able* (or *ability*) to a wo⟋d ending in a silent *e* preceded by a *c,* we retain the *e* to preserve the ⟋oft *c* sound. If the *e* is dropped, the *c* becomes hard; thus such a mi⟋ spelling as *noticable* would be pronounced *no-TIK-able* instead of *N(⟋TE-iss-able.* Examples:

notice + able = noticeable	replace + able = replaceable
service + able = serviceable	peace + able = peaceable

Also, the *c* is always hard when it ends a word, as in *tic.* Thus when we add a suffix beginning with an *e* or *i* to a word ending in *c,* we add a *k* to preserve the hard *c* sound:

panic + ed = panicked	politic + ing = politicking
picnic + er = picnicker	traffic + ing = trafficking

When a *g* is pronounced as a *j* (as in *gin*), it is a soft *g,* when it is pronounced *guh* (as in *begin*), it is a hard *g.* The soft and hard *g*'s are not completely regular, but a *g* is always hard when followed by an *a, o,* or *u* or when it ends a word. And it is always soft when followed by a silent *e.* Thus when we add *ous, able,* or *ance* to a word ending in a silent *e* preceded by a *g,* we retain the *e* to preserve the soft *g* sound. If the *e* is dropped, the *g* becomes hard; thus such a misspelling as *couragous* would be pronounced *cour-RAG-ous* instead of *cour-RAGE-ous.* Examples:

courage + ous = courageous	arrange + able = arrangeable
advantage + ous = advantageous	change + able = changeable
outrage + ous = outrageous	venge + ance = vengeance

A Tip on Usage Avoid the spelling *alright*; instead, prefer *all right.*

A Tip on Usage One particularly bad spelling and verb-form error is the use in writing of *could of, would of,* and *should of* for *could have, would have,* and *should have.* The error occurs because we frequently use contractions in speech. Examples:

I **could've** come if I had known you were in trouble.
He **should've** phoned you sooner.

The contraction *could've* sounds like *could of,* and so some people ignorantly write the phrase as *could of.* It's about the worst error that can be made in spelling verbs forms.

Name_____Date _____

Exercise for

THE SILENT *E* SPELLING RULES

DIRECTIONS *Build the following words as indicated. I_ some cases you will drop the final e, and in some cases you will ke_ it. Be careful about doubling consonants.*

1. write + ing = _Writing_

2. change + able = _Changeable_

3. service + able = _Serviceable_

4. dine + ing = _dining_

5. come + ing = _coming_

6. shine + ing = _shining_

7. arrange + able = _arrangeable_

8. condole + ence = _condolence_

9. peeve + ish = _peevish_

10. love + able = _loveable_

11. whole + ly = _wholly_

12. argue + ment = _argument_

13. safe + ly = _safely_

14. use + ful = _____

15. care + less = _____

16. pursue + ing = _____

18. use + ing = _____

19. love + ly = _____

20. guide + ance = _____

21. improve + ment = _____

22. sincere + ly = _____

23. sure + ly = _____

24. trace + able = _____

25. outrage + ous = _____

26. venge + ance = _____

27. argue + ing = _____

28. charge + able = _____

29. fame + ous = _____

30. shine + y = _____

31. scare + ed = _____

32. dine + ed = _____

33. late + ly = _____

377

17. complete + ly = _____   34. immediate + ly = _____

35. approximate + ly = _____   38. interfere + ing = _____

36. true + ly = _____   39. fate + ful = _____

37. awe + ful = _____   40. bite + ing = _____

A TIP ON USAGE   Never use *them* instead of *these* or *those* when there is a pointing action. *Them* is used when there is no pointing action. Also *them* is never used directly before a noun, as in *them girls*, for there is always a pointing action when *these* or *those* comes directly before a noun.

> RIGHT: "Do you like **these** beans?" "Yes, I'll take a pound of **them**." (The accent would be on *of*, not *them*; no pointing action with *them*.)
> RIGHT: I prefer **those** (not *them*) books. (pointing action)
> RIGHT: I want **those** (not *them*) over there. (pointing action)

A TIP ON USAGE   For best style, use *plan to do* rather than *plan on doing*, *plan to study* rather than *plan on studying*, and so on.

A MINI-EXERCISE   On the basis of the following bit of dialogue, discuss whether spelling reform in English is desirable. "The Duke of Bedford is dying. He has no heir." "No air? No wonder he's dying."

The Y-to-I Rule;
the IE, EI Rule

The *Y-to-I* Rule *When adding a suffix to a word ending in* y *preceded by a consonant, change the* y *to* i. *If the* y *is preceded by a vowel, do not change the* y *to* i *when adding a suffix.*

When a noun is made plural or a verb is made singular, the *y* (if preceded by a consonant) is changed to *i*, and *es* is added:

baby + s = babies   deny + s = denies
lady + s = ladies   fry + s = fries
harpy + s = harpies   try + s = tries

The rule also operates with many other suffixes. Examples:

lonely + ness = loneliness   necessary + ly = necessarily
cry + er = crier   merry + ment = merriment
dry + est = driest   ally + ance = alliance

The rule does not apply when *ing* or *ist* is added to a word:

study + ing = studying   worry + ing = worrying
deny + ing = denying   copy + ist = copyist

Also there are these common exceptions:

shyly   dryly
shyness   dryness
slyly   dryer (the machine)
slyness   (The adjective is irregular: *drier*)

When the final *y* of a word is preceded by a vowel, the *y* is NOT changed when a suffix is added. Example:

379

annoy + s = annoys
convey + s = conveys
valley + s = valleys

employ + able = employable
donkey + s = donkeys
stay + ed = stayed

There are five common exceptions to this part of the rule:

lay + ed = laid
pay + ed = paid
say + ed = said

day + ly = daily
gay + ly = gaily

The *y-to-i* rule does not apply in spelling the plural of proper names:

Brady + s = Bradys
Crowly + s = Crowlys

Kennedy + s = Kennedys
Munsy + s = Munsys

The *EI, EI* Rule   *Place* i *before* e *when pronounced as* ee *except after* c; *place* e *before* i *when pronounced as a long* a.

This rule tells you whether the combination *ie* or *ei* is to be used in a word that otherwise you already know how to spell. Thus the rule has a limited use, but it is useful for a small number of words that give trouble, such as *niece* and *receive*.

The rule does not cover such words as *science, friend,* and *foreign,* for the *ie* or *ei* in such words does not have a long vowel sound.

Three troublesome exceptions can be learned from this nonsense sentence: *Seize weird leisure.* You should memorize this sentence of exceptions (*Neither, either,* and *species* are also exceptions, but they never give any trouble at all.)

Here are some common words covered by the *ie, ei* rule:

receive	believe	freight
deceive	chief	weight
deceit	achieve	reins
conceive	niece	neighbor
receipt	priest	reign
ceiling	thief	vein

A TIP ON USAGE   The reflexive pronouns are spelled as single words: *myself, yourself, himself; ourselves, yourselves, themselves,* and *itself.* Never use *ourselfs* and so on. Never use *hisself, theirselves,* and *its self.* But *his own self* and *their own selves* are correct.

Name_____date_____

Exercise for

THE *Y-TO-I* SPELLING RULE

DIRECTIONS *Following the y-to-i spelling rule, build the following words as indicated.*

1. deny + al = *denial*
2. mercy + ful = *mercyfull*
3. carry + er = *carrier*
4. carry + ing = *carrying*
5. play + ed = *played*
6. rely + ance = *reliance*
7. copy + ed = *copied*
8. copy + ist = *copyist*
9. try + al = *trial*
10. modify + er = *Modifier*
11. defy + s = *defies*
12. defy + ing = *defying*
13. kindly + ness = *kindliness*
14. enjoy + s = *enjoys*
15. fly + s = *flies*
16. study + ous = *studious*

21. study + ing = *studying*
22. happy + ness = *happiness*
23. greedy + er = *greedier*
24. lovely + ness = *loveliness*
25. pay + s = *pays*
26. pay + ed = *payed*
27. beauty + ful = *beautifull*
28. hurry + ed = *hurried*
29. day + ly = *daily*
30. necessary + ly = *necessarily*
31. dry + ness = *dryness*
32. busy + ness = *business*
33. ready + ness = *readiness*
34. alley + s = *alleys*
35. ally + s = *allies*
38. lay + ed = *layed*

17. delay + ed = _delayed_

18. employ + s = _employes_

19. lonely + ness = _loneliness_

20. busy + est = _busiest_

37. cry + er = _cryer_

38. gay + ly = _gaily_

39. Grady + s = _gradie's_

40. Kennedy + s = _Kennedys_

Exercise for

THE *IE, EI* SPELLING RULE

DIRECTIONS *Following the* ie, ei *spelling rule (as well as the exceptions), fill in the missing letters in the following words.*

1. ach__ei__ ve

2. bel __ie__ ve

3. br __ie__ f

4. c __ei__ ling

5. ch __ei__ f

6. conc __ei__ t

7. conc __ei__ ve

8. dec __ie__ t

9. dec __ei__ ve

10. f __ie__ ld

11. fr __ei__ ght

12. gr __ie__ f

13. surv __ei__ llance

14. sure

15. n __ei__ gh

16. n __ei__ ghbor

17. n __ie__ ce

18. perc __ei__ ve

19. pr __ei__ st

20. rec __ie__ ve

21. rec __ie__ pt

22. r __ei__ ns

23. rel __ei__ f

24. rel __ie__ ve

25. s __ei__ ze

26. sh __ie__ ld

27. s __ei__ ge

28. v __ei__ n

29. th __ie__ f

30. w __ei__ ght

31. w __ie__ ld

32. w __ei__ rd

33. y __ei__ ld

ei = a
ie = ee

A TIP ON USAGE *Many* is better style than *a lot* or *lots of*.

383